Philosophy
of
Social Science

Also by Alexander Rosenberg

Microeconomic Laws: A Philosophical Analysis

Sociobiology and the Preemption of Social Science

The Structure of Biological Science

Hume and the Problem of Causation (with T. L. Beauchamp)

Dimensions of Philosophy Series

Norman Daniels and Keith Lehrer, Editors

Philosophy of Social Science, Alexander Rosenberg

Introduction to Marx and Engels: A Critical Reconstruction, Richard Schmitt

FORTHCOMING

Philosophy of Science, Clark Glymour

Theory of Knowledge, Keith Lehrer

Contemporary Continental Philosophy, Bernd Magnus

Philosophy of Physics, Lawrence Sklar

Philosophy of Religion, Thomas V. Morris

Metaphysics, Peter van Inwagen

Philosophy of Mind, Jaegwon Kim

Philosophy of Biology, Elliott Sober

Philosophy
of
Social Science

Alexander Rosenberg

Westview Press • Boulder

Dimensions of Philosophy Series

Copyright © 1988 by Westview Press, Inc.

Published in 1988 in the United States of America by Westview Press, Inc., 5500 Central Avenue, Boulder, Colorado 80301

Library of Congress Cataloging-in-Publication Data
Rosenberg, Alexander, 1946–
  Philosophy of social science.
  (Dimensions of philosophy series)
  Bibliography: p.
  Includes index.
  1. Social sciences—Philosophy. I. Title.
II. Series.
H61.R668 1988   300'.1   88-5573
ISBN 0-8133-0616-7
ISBN 0-8133-0617-5 (pbk.)

Printed and bound in the United States of America

⊗ The paper used in this publication meets the requirements of the American National
   Standard for Permanence of Paper for Printed Library Materials Z39.48-1984.

10   9   8   7   6   5   4   3

For

STUART THAU and DAVID SMITH,

who have always followed Hume's best advice:
"Be a philosopher: but amidst all your philosophy,
be still a man."

Contents

Preface

THE PHILOSOPHY of social science is an unavoidable topic for any social or behavioral scientist. Or so this work argues. This is because the choices social scientists make in answering their questions inevitably force them to take sides on issues in philosophy. The subject is equally inevitable for philosophy, as I also hope to show. For the social sciences raise the most fundamental questions about knowledge, human action, and moral philosophy. This book aims to explain and illustrate these connections between social science and philosophy, connections that reveal themselves in reflection on the methods of economics, sociology, political science, psychology, and the disciplines on the intersections of these subjects.

I begin with an explanation of exactly why philosophy is relevant to the social and behavioral sciences, and then I explore the problems for alternative explanatory strategies in these disciplines that are raised by our conception of human action. These problems have spawned theoretical and methodological movements like behaviorism, hermeneutics, and critical theory, and they have led to significant shifts in the aims and methods advocated for social science, like those of Durkheim, among sociologists, and Friedman, among economists. Each of these shifts and the problems that produced them are explored in the chapters to follow. The last part of each of the first seven chapters is an introduction to the literature. These sections identify and relate the canonical books, monographs, and articles that are the foundation for further work in these areas. Full citations for these works are to be found in the bibliography.

My interest in this subject was first sparked when I was an undergraduate at City College by Willard Hutcheon and by discussion with a friend and fellow student, Bruce Bueno de Mesquita. It was nurtured at Johns Hopkins University by the late Maurice Mandelbaum, by Steven Barker and Peter Achinstein, and by a fellow graduate student, Tom

Beauchamp. Since that time, colleagues have continued both to encourage me and to shape my views about the philosophy of social science. Among the most influential of them is David Braybrooke, with whom I first taught and pursued research in this subject. Though parts of the present work may not find favor with him, I am enormously in his debt. It was, however, conversations with John Wallace that made me realize that the philosophy of social science must come to grips with the central problems of philosophy: metaphysics, epistemology, and the philosophy of language and of psychology. This realization, for which he is responsible, is manifest in the present work.

Social and behavioral scientists have influenced me mightily as well. Among them I must especially thank W. K. Honig, Donald Campbell, Bruce Mesquita (now as a colleague instead of a fellow student), Marshall Segal, Peter Marsh, Barry Bozeman, Amartya Sen, Hal Varian, Wade Hands, E. Roy Weintraub, and E. O. Wilson (who counts for present purposes as a social scientist as well as a biologist).

This work has been shaped by discussion with Jonathan Bennett, Peter van Inwagen, Daniel Dennett, Phillip Kitcher, Elliott Sober, Alisdair McIntyre, Alan Donagan, Jules Coleman, Alan Gibbard, Martin Hollis, Christina Bicchieri, Jon Elster, Philippe Mongin, Gilles-Gaston Granger, Larry Laudan, Adolf Grunbaum, Harold Kincaid, and especially Daniel Hausman and Alan Nelson.

To Hausman and Nelson I am indebted not only for their own important contributions to the philosophy of social science but also for reading, commenting, and making important corrections throughout the entire manuscript. I regret that I was not able to produce a result that does complete justice to all their help and advice. Because I was unable to do so, neither they nor the others who have earned my gratitude can be supposed to share any of the views here expounded or defended. Nevertheless, I hope the result will be of some use in advancing the study of the subject that they have done so much to stimulate.

I am also indebted to Kenneth Dickey for comments on the entire work and to Shari Starrett for lending her expert advice to the improvement of Chapter 4. I am also grateful to Marian Safran for helping to smooth the reader's way through a tangle of pronouns. For the greatest improvements in this manuscript I am indebted to my editor, Spencer Carr. Only a philosopher would have noticed the defects he uncovered.

I must also thank Loki for helping me explore infrahuman intentionality, my son for what I have learned about Gene-culture interaction, my daughter for helping conduct an experiment shedding light on the nature/nurture controversy, and Merle for being a coprincipal investigator in these three projects.

Alexander Rosenberg

1

Why a Philosophy of Social Science?

IT'S SAFE TO ASSUME that you know what the social and behavioral sciences are—psychology, sociology, political science, economics, anthropology, and you might include also disciplines that intersect and overlap these fields, such as geography, demography, social psychology, history, and archaeology. It's not safe to assume you know what philosophy is, even if you have studied a good deal of it already. The reason is that there is nothing like consensus among philosophers about exactly what their subject is. But in order to understand what the philosophy of social science is, and to see why it is important, it is crucial to have some agreement on the nature of philosophy.

Philosophy: A Working Definition

The discipline of philosophy attempts to address two sorts of questions.

1. Questions that the sciences—physical, biological, social, and behavioral—cannot answer
2. Questions about why the sciences cannot answer the former questions

Now of course, there might not be any questions that the sciences cannot answer eventually, in the long run, when all the facts are in, but there certainly are questions that the sciences cannot answer *yet*. These include new questions science hasn't had a chance to answer

1

because it has only just noticed them and doesn't yet have either the experimental equipment or the right theories to deal with them. For example, every year high-energy physics faces new questions about matter that it could not have solved or even entertained before the latest particle accelerators came on-line. There are also questions that scientists have faced for millennia but only at present think themselves able to answer. For example, most biologists now believe they can answer questions about human nature, the origins of man, and the nature of life that have perplexed science and philosophy since their beginnings. And there are other questions that are equally old and still remain unanswered. For example, questions about consciousness, thought, sensation, and emotion remain unsolved.

Of course, modern psychology claims to be making substantial progress in answering these questions. But this claim is controversial. So is biology's contention that questions about human nature, for instance, can now be answered scientifically; for example, some theologians, social scientists, humanists, and even some biologists reject this claim. The debate about whether these questions can be answered by any one science, or even all of them, is a characteristically philosophical one. Those who deny it in effect tell us there are limits to what scientific inquiry can discover. The debate about whether there are limits on the sorts of questions science can answer hinges on two things: First, we need to identify the methods of science, and second, we need to identify the limits on what questions these methods can address. Delineating these methods and deciding on these questions are matters that no one science can by itself address. This is in part what makes them philosophical questions.

Another sort of question that scientists often forswear involves evaluative and normative matters—what ought to be the case, as opposed to what is the case. Science, it is often said, describes and explains the way the world is, but it cannot answer questions about what is right or good or ought to be the case. These fundamental questions are ones for which people do not need scientific qualifications to give informed and well-grounded answers. Or so it is often claimed. But like the question about the powers of biology to explain all the facts about life and human nature, this issue is highly controversial, and the controversy is pure philosophy.

If there are limits to the questions science can answer, then we will want to know why these limits exist: What is it about science that prevents it from addressing these questions? We will also want to know how, if at all, they can be answered. If, however, there are no such limits, as some would claim, we will want to know why some questions have remained unanswered since the birth of science with the Greeks.

The core areas of philosophy each address different aspects of one or both of these two types of questions. Their focus on these two types of questions is what connects the core areas and makes philosophy a single discipline. Thus, *logic* examines the nature of sound and valid reasoning, as it figures in mathematics, in the sciences as well as in other areas of intellectual life that proceed by argument and inference. Is there just one body of valid principles of inference or do different sciences and subject matters require different logics? *Epistemology* considers the nature, extent, and justification of knowledge: Are all claims to knowledge justified in the same way, by appeal to broadly the same kind of evidence, or are some theories—say, those of mathematics, the social sciences, or the humanities—warranted by considerations different from those natural scientists demand? *Metaphysics* pursues questions about the nature of things: Are there just the material things with which natural science deals? Is the mind a distinct sort of nonphysical substance? Is human action free from physical constraints that determine the behavior of purely mechanical systems? Are there numbers, as opposed to the numerals we employ to express them? *Ethics* and *political philosophy* address those questions that scientific progress raises but cannot answer: Once we know how to build a nuclear weapon, how to implant embryos, how to redistribute wealth, or how to manipulate behavior, *should* we do any of these things? What binds these disparate areas of inquiry together is that they all address aspects of the two questions that provide our working definition of philosophy.

As previously noted, at various times in the history of science, questions at first deemed unanswerable by science, and addressed by philosophy, have been expropriated by science. In fact the history of science is the story of how each of the sciences emancipated itself from philosophy: mathematics in the time of the ancient Greeks, physics in the seventeenth century, chemistry one hundred years later, biology in 1859 with the publication of Charles Darwin's *Origin of Species*, psychology in the early part of the twentieth century, and linguistics and computer science in our own lifetimes. Each of these disciplines has left parting gifts to philosophy, questions that it could not answer, for example: What are numbers? What is time? What is the relation of psychological processes to neural ones?

Sometimes in the course of this history, a question philosophy has preserved is expropriated by science because it is ready to answer that question. Occasionally, a question is expropriated by science from philosophy, only to be returned. Opinion about the ability of science, especially social science, to answer ethical and moral questions has shifted, sometimes frequently, over the distant and the recent past.

Philosophy and the Social Sciences

Even if there are questions the sciences cannot answer, and further questions about why the sciences cannot answer them, why should a scientist, and in particular a behavioral or social scientist take any interest in them? The reason is simple. Though the individual sciences cannot answer these questions, individual scientists have to take sides on them, and the sides they take will affect and sometimes even determine the questions they address as answerable in their disciplines, and the methods they employ to do so. Sometimes scientists act consciously, sometimes by default, in their choice of questions to address and methods to employ. Because addressing these questions is important for the scientist, it is certainly better if the scientist makes an informed and conscious choice.

The unavoidability and importance of philosophical questions is even more significant for the social scientist than for the natural scientist. For the natural sciences have a much more established body of successful answers to questions than social science. And they have many more well established methods for answering them. Thus, many of the basic philosophical questions about the limits and the methods of the natural sciences have been shouldered aside by more immediate questions clearly within the limits of natural science.

The social and behavioral sciences have not been so fortunate. Among these disciplines there is no consensus on what the questions are that each of them has the power to address, nor agreement about the methods to be employed, nor about why some questions are beyond their purviews. This is true both between disciplines and even within some of them. Though schools and groups, movements and camps, claim to have developed appropriate methods, identified significant questions, and provided convincing answers to these questions, there is certainly nothing like the agreement on such claims that we find in any of the natural sciences. In the absence of agreement and benchmark accomplishments among social scientists, every choice with regard to research questions and methods of tackling them is implicitly or explicitly a *gamble* that the question chosen is answerable, that questions not chosen are either less important or unanswerable, that the means used to attack the question are appropriate to it, and that other methods are not. When social scientists choose to employ methods as close to those of natural science as possible, they commit themselves to the position that there are laws of human behavior we can discover and employ in predicting and controlling it. When they spurn such methods, it is because they hold that such methods can't answer the really important questions about human activity. Either view arises in response to the first of the two sorts of questions that define philosophy: questions that science cannot answer.

Whether these gambles really pay off can usually not be known within the lifetimes of the social scientists who make them. And yet the choices must be justified, either by an explanation of why the methods of natural science can answer the question the social scientist addresses, or why they cannot. The adequacy of such explanations is our only reasonable basis for choosing methods of inquiry. But such explanations address the second of the two sorts of questions that define philosophy: questions about why the sciences cannot answer the first sort of questions. They are therefore philosophical arguments, regardless of whether the person who offers them is a philosopher or not. Indeed, social scientists are in at least as good a position to answer the two kinds of questions that define philosophy as philosophers themselves are. And this is what makes the subject so important for the social scientist.

The traditional questions for the philosophy of social science reflect the importance of the choices of research questions and of methods of tackling them. And in this book we shall examine almost all of these questions at length. First, there is the question of whether human action can be explained in the way that natural science explains phenomena in its domain. Alternative answers to this question raise further questions: If the answer is yes, why are our explanations of human action so much less precise and less improvable than scientific explanations? If the answer is no, that the methods of natural science are inappropriate, then what is the right way to explain action scientifically? And if there is no way to explain human action scientifically, as some philosophers and social scientists claim, why does human action require an approach different from that of natural science, and what approach is required? These will be the topics of the next three chapters.

Our discussion of these issues will involve a study of the nature of explanation and causation, the testing of generalizations and laws; and it will reflect on the nature of thought and its relation to behavior and to language. It will reveal the tension between the (future) purposes that explain our actions and the (prior) causes that determine our behavior. The future purposes give our actions meaning and make them intelligible. The prior causes act without revealing the significance of our behavior. We shall consider how social scientists, behaviorists for example, have attempted to substitute new questions about human action for old ones, because of the social scientists' inability to answer the old ones. And we shall have to decide whether this change is an intellectually defensible one. For it is in effect the claim that some questions that science cannot answer are not after all coherent, legitimate questions that require an answer.

In Chapters 5 and 6 we will turn to questions about whether the primary explanatory factors in social science should be large groups of people and their institutional interactions instead of the choices of individual human agents. Differing social sciences, especially economics and sociology, have profound differences on this point, differences along many dimensions, differences so abstract and general that they have long concerned philosophers. The social scientist who holds that large-scale social facts explain individual conduct, instead of the reverse, makes strong metaphysical assumptions about the reality of groups independent of the individuals who compose them. Such a theory—called holism—also requires a form of explanation, functionalism, that raises other profound questions about differences between the explanatory strategy of social and of natural science. This theory, which gives pride of explanatory place to social wholes, might seem quite unappealing if the only alternative to it, "individualism," as advanced by economists and sociobiologists, for instance, were not faced with equally profound philosophical questions.

In Chapter 7 we turn to the relation between the social sciences and moral philosophy, examining whether we can expect answers to questions about what is right, or fair, or just, or good from the social sciences themselves. Even if, as some hold, no conclusions about what ought to be the case can be inferred even from true theories about what is the case, it will still turn out that alternative approaches to social science and competing moral theories have natural affinities to each other and make strong demands on one another as well. We must also examine the question of whether there are morally imposed limits to legitimate inquiry in the social sciences.

In the final chapter I try to show why the immediate choices that social scientists make in the conduct of their inquiry commit them to taking sides on the most profound and perennial questions of philosophy. If I am right, then no social scientist can afford to ignore the philosophy of social science or any other compartment of philosophy.

As a start in establishing this conclusion, let us consider one of the most serious questions facing the philosophy of the social sciences. In a way, this question organizes many of the problems mentioned above to be addressed in later chapters, and it provides a framework that shows how serious the problems are, despite their apparently abstract and general character.

The question arises in the comparisons made between the natural and the social sciences. The natural sciences are often *alleged*, especially by natural scientists, to have made far greater *progress* than the social sciences. Those who hold this view have frequently drawn substantial conclusions from it about the social sciences and about human behavior.

Those who reject this view have also drawn striking conclusions about both of these subjects. Therefore, the distinctive controversies in the philosophy of social science may be said to begin with this question. Indeed, these debates begin with the word "alleged" in the claim about differences in progress between the disciplines, and they include disputes about what constitutes "progress," whether the natural sciences evince it, and whether the social sciences do, can, or should aim at similar "progress."

The philosophical issues this controversy raises can be ignored by only the most insular of social scientists, for on the sides we take in the debate about these issues hinge many very practical questions about the aims, conduct, and application of and public support for research in the social sciences. If, on the one hand, you agree that progress in the social sciences leaves much to be desired, by comparison with natural science, then you will be inclined to seek an explanation for this fact in the failure of social science to fully or correctly implement the methods of natural science in the study of human behavior. If, on the other hand, you consider that the social sciences cannot and/or should not implement the methods of natural science in the study of human behavior, you will reject as misconceived the invidious comparison between the natural and the social sciences. You will conclude that the study of human action proceeds in a different way and is appraised along different standards than the natural sciences.

I shall outline below the arguments for and against the claims that the social sciences have failed to progress and that this failure needs explanation. The arguments on both sides make it clear how a question about the history of social science is really a question about its philosophy. These arguments share one common view: A neat compromise is impossible. Such a compromise would suggest that the social sciences have not made so much progress as has natural science but that they have made some. It suggests that very broadly the methods of the social sciences are the same as those of natural science, though their specific concepts are distinctive, and the human interests they serve are different. Though this is a possible view, much of the effort of philosophers and social scientists who have dealt with the philosophy of social science suggests that this nice compromise is a difficult one to maintain.

The problems of whether the natural sciences have made more progress than the social sciences and whether it even makes *sense* to say this are especially important in light of the needs of humans to understand and *improve* our social lives, individually and in the aggregate. For such understanding and improvement require increased knowledge of human behavior. And how such knowledge is to be sought depends on how we answer these philosophical questions.

Some philosophers and social scientists will reject this question as less central to the philosophy of social science. On their view the social sciences raise distinctive philosophical problems that need to be addressed independent of this problem, and the chief goal of the philosophy of social science is to understand these disciplines, without casting an eye to questions that are at best premature and at worst a distraction. One way to decide who is right about the importance of the question of progress in social science is to see how well the question helps us organize and fit together all these other distinctive problems of the particular social sciences.

Progress and Prediction

First I shall set forth the argument for the unfavorable comparison: Natural science has provided increasingly reliable knowledge about the physical world since at least the seventeenth century. From precise predictions of the positions of the planets, the natural sciences have gone on to unified explanations of the properties of chemical substances and detailed characterization of molecular biology of life. In addition to systematic explanation and precise prediction, the natural sciences have provided an accelerating application of technologies to control features of the natural world. This sustained and apparently *cumulating* growth of knowledge and application seems absent from the sciences of human behavior.

In varying social disciplines there seem to be moments at which a breakthrough to cumulating knowledge has been achieved: Adam Smith's *Wealth of Nations,* or Emile Durkheim's work in *Suicide,* or perhaps John Maynard Keynes's *General Theory of Employment, Interest and Money,* or B. F. Skinner's *Behavior of Organisms,* for instance. But subsequent developments have never confirmed such assessments. Though the social sciences have aimed at predicting and explaining human behavior and its consequences at least since Thucydides in the fifth century B.C., some say we are really no better at it than the Greeks.

So, the argument concludes, something is the matter with the social sciences; probably, they are not "scientific" enough in their methods. They need to adopt methods that more successfully uncover laws, or at any rate generalizations, that can be improved in the direction of laws, which can be brought together in theories that explain them and their exceptions.

Why laws? It's pretty clear that technological control and predictive success come only through the discovery of general regularities, ones that enable us to bend the future to our desires by manipulating present conditions and, perhaps more important, to prevent future misfortunes by rearranging present circumstances. The only way this is possible is through reliable knowledge of the future, knowledge of the sort that only laws can provide.

There is a less practical and more philosophical argument for the importance science attaches to laws, though in the end this argument shares the practical concerns of our interests in controlling nature. The kinds of explanation science seeks are *causal,* and the certification of scientific claims as knowledge, or at least justified belief, comes from observation, experiment, and the collection of data. Both of these features of science demand the discovery and improvement of generalizations and laws.

Consider how we distinguish a causal sequence from an accidental one. Suppose I walk under a ladder on which a carpenter is standing, and I am hit immediately by a falling hammer. Why do we say that it was the carpenter's dropping the hammer, as opposed to my walking under his ladder, that caused the hammer to fall and injure me? One might be tempted to say that we can tell, just by looking, what caused the accident. But a little reflection shows that this is wrong. For all we know, there might have been a complicated device at the base of the ladder, tripped by my leg, that wrenched the hammer from the carpenter's hand.

The fact is that there is no regularity in our experience connecting walking under ladders and accidents (that's why we call such a connection a superstition), and there is one connecting the release of heavy objects and their falling. It is our experience of the regular succession of pairs of events in the past that leads us to describe the sequences like them as causal, and those unlike them as accidental.

As David Hume argued in the eighteenth century, there is certainly nothing we can directly *observe* in any single sequence, independent of our past experiences, no glue attaching causes to their effects, that enables us to make the distinction between causal sequences and accidental ones. And when we trace observed causal sequences back to fundamental physical regularities, like the law that bodies exert gravitational attraction on one another (and that's why the released hammer fell), there is nothing more to them than universality of connection. When we reach the most fundamental laws of nature, they will themselves be nothing more than statements of constant conjunction of distinct events; they will not illuminate less fundamental sequences by showing them to be necessary, or "intelligible," or the inevitable result of the operation of hidden causal powers. Causal explanation must inevitably appeal to laws connecting the cause and its effect. And there is no stopping place in the search for more and more fundamental laws. The role accorded to laws, and to generalizations that can be improved into laws, has been a continuing feature of empiricist philosophy and empirical methodology in science ever since the work of Hume. Because our knowledge of causation in individual cases is based on the identification of laws, which themselves are discovered through the observation of repeated sequences, it is no surprise that such observation is what tests our explanatory and predictive hypotheses and certifies them as justified knowledge.

Why have the social sciences not progressed in the provision of cumulating scientific knowledge with technological payoff? The social sciences have failed, despite long attempts, to uncover laws or even empirical generalizations that could be improved in the direction of real laws about human behavior and its consequences. This diagnosis calls for both an explanation of why no laws have been discovered and if possible a proposal about how we can go about discovering them.

One compelling explanation is that social science is just much *harder* than natural science: The research object is we human beings, and we are fiercely complicated systems. It is therefore no surprise that less progress might be made in these disciplines than in ones that deal with such simple objects as quarks, chemical bonds, and chromosomes. After all, the human being is subject to all the regularities of the natural sciences, as well as to those of psychology, sociology, economics, et cetera. Teasing out the separate effects of all the forces determining our behavior is more formidable a task than that which faces any other discipline.

Add to this the restrictions of time, money, and morality in the construction of controlled experiments needed to uncover causal regularities, and the relatively underdeveloped character of social science should be no surprise. On this explanation, the social sciences are just "young sciences." By and large they are or can be scientific enough in their methods; they just require more time and resources in order to produce the social knowledge we seek.

The trouble with this explanation is its counsel of patience and its historical perspective. Are the social sciences really young, by comparison to the natural sciences? From when should we date these disciplines? From the post–World War II effusion of research money, statistical methods, cheap computation, and improved scientific education of social scientists? From the self-conscious attempts, like Durkheim's in the late nineteenth century, to establish a quantitative science of society? From the Marquis de Condorcet's or Thomas Hobbes's attempts to lay out a rational choice theory of human behavior in the eighteenth or seventeenth centuries, or from Thucydides' *Peloponnesian War* in the fifth century B.C.? Certainly, the desire to understand and predict human behavior is at least as old as the desire to understand natural phenomena, and the search for laws of human behavior goes back at least past Machiavelli.

For some philosophers and for even more social scientists, the claim that the social sciences are young rings hollow. Behaviorists in all the social sciences provide good illustrations of this attitude. For them patience has worn out, and they provide a different explanation for the failure to discover laws. To begin with they don't accept the argument that the complexity of human beings leads to the difficulty of discovering laws about them. Behaviorists note that as natural science developed, its subject matter became more complex and more difficult to work with; for example, we need to erect vast particle accelerators to learn about objects on which it is extremely difficult to make even the most indirect observations, in order to advance our knowledge in physics nowadays. But the increasing complexity of research in the natural sciences has not resulted in any slowdown in scientific advance. Quite to the contrary, the rate of "progress" has if anything increased over time. Thus, complexity by itself can hardly be an excuse for the social sciences' lack of progress.

Moreover, the argument continues, the social sciences have had a great advantage over the natural sciences, one that makes their comparative lack of progress hard to explain as merely the result of complexity and the difficulties of experiment. In the natural sciences, the greatest obstacle to advance has been conceptual, not factual; that is, advances have often been the result of the realization that our descriptive categories needed to be changed because they were a barrier to discovering generalizations. Thus, the Newtonian revolution was the result of realizing that Aristotle's distinction between *rest* and *motion* needed to be replaced by one between *uniform motion* (motion in a straight line at constant velocity) and *acceleration.* Our commonsense supposition that if something is moving, there must be a cause, is wrong and must be given up, in favor of a counterintuitive assumption, if we are to discover the laws of motion. Similarly, the pre-Darwinian conception of unchangeable, immutable species must be surrendered if we are to entertain a biological theory that explains diversity by appeal to blind variation and natural selection that change species into new ones.

But in the social sciences, there has been almost universal agreement that the descriptive categories that common sense has used since the dawn of history are the right ones. Traditionally, what we have wanted to know in social science is the causes and consequences of our *actions,* and we hold that these actions are determined by our *desires* and our *beliefs.* Accordingly, social scientists have long searched for laws connecting actions, beliefs, and desires, on the venerable conviction that these are the natural categories into which human behavior and its causes fall. If these are the right categories with which to describe human behavior, and if we have had them available from time immemorial, then the social sciences have been *free* from the greatest obstacle to advance in the natural sciences: the need to carve out entirely new ways of looking at the world. Thus, we might have expected progress in the social sciences to have been possible or, perhaps, even more rapid in the social than the natural sciences. The absence of it makes the excuse that these are young disciplines, facing subjects of great complexity, unconvincing to many social scientists and some philosophers.

In fact, these people argue that the basic categories of social science are wrong. The reason no laws have been uncovered is that the categories of action, desire, belief, and their cognates have prevented us from discovering such laws. And they seek to supplant these categories with new ones, like those of operant behaviorism, sociological functionalism, sociobiology, and others. It is easy to see how a category scheme can prevent us from uncovering laws or regularities, even when they would otherwise be easy to find.

Suppose we define "fish" as "aquatic animal" and then attempt to frame a generalization about how fish breathe. We do so by catching fish and examining their anatomy. Our observation leads to the hypothesis that fish breath through gills. Casting our nets more widely, we begin to trap whales and dolphins, which leads us to modify our generalization to "all fish breath through gills, *save for* whales and dolphins." But then we start to drag along the ocean floor and discover lobsters, starfish, crab, not to mention jellyfish floating at the surface, all breathing in different ways. There's no point adding more and more exceptions to our generalization. There just isn't one generalization about how all fish breathe, not as we have defined fish. The trouble is obvious: It's our definition of fish as "aquatic animal." A narrower definition, like "scaly aquatic vertebrate" will not only, as Aristotle said, "carve nature closer to the joints"—that is, reflect its real divisions more accurately, it will also enable us to frame simple generalizations that stand up to testing against new data. Indeed, the difference between a "kind-term" like "gold," which reflects real divisions in nature, and one like "fake gold," which does not, is the fact that there are laws about the former, and not the latter. That is what makes the kind-terms that figure in laws "natural kinds," as opposed to artificial ones.

Now there is doubtless a good explanation of why we have become attached to the kind-terms *action, desire,* and *belief* as the explanatory variables for human behavior. They have emerged as tools for guiding our expectations about how others will act, but we have uncovered no laws about the behavior they explain. Perhaps the failure to find laws about this behavior is the result of the fact that these kind-terms are not "natural," they just don't carve things up at the joints. Like our example "fish," every generalization that employs them is so riddled with exceptions that there are no laws we can discover to be stated in these terms. The prescription is obviously to substitute new explanatory variables for these unnatural ones, terms like "reinforcer" from behaviorism, or "repression" from psychoanalysis, "alienation" from Marxian theory, or "anomie" from Durkheim's sociological tradition. Advocates of each of these theories promise that the application of their preferred descriptive vocabulary will enable the social sciences to begin to progress and cumulate in ways that the natural sciences have. If these social scientists are correct, their disciplines will indeed turn out to be young sciences. For in the absence of their preferred system of kinds and categories, the social sciences are rather like chemistry before Lavoisier: trying to describe combustion in terms of "phlogiston," instead of "oxygen," and failing because there is no such thing.

Every step in this chain of reasoning is philosophically controversial: the claim that the natural sciences show cumulating progress, whereas the social sciences do not; the assumptions about what progress in the growth of knowledge consists of; the role of laws in providing the growth of knowledge; the purported explanations of why the social sciences have not yet uncovered any laws; and the prescriptions about how social scientists should proceed if they hope to. It will be easiest to see how philosophically controversial is every one of these steps if we outline the challenges to this chain of reasoning made by those who reject it.

Understanding and Intelligibility

Those who reject the argument that natural science has progressed, whereas social science has languished, begin their counterargument at the very foundations of the philosophy of natural science. To begin with, they hold that the natural sciences have not in fact made the kind of cumulating progress ordinarily attributed to them. In doing so they exploit the account of science advanced in Thomas Kuhn's *Structure of Scientific Revolutions*, which, since its publication in 1962, has been the work most frequently cited in social scientists' writings on method. Many of these social scientists interpret Kuhn as claiming that instead of by progress, scientific history from Aristotle to Einstein is characterized by change, by the succession of theories, or what Kuhn called "paradigms," which replace one another without improving on their predecessors.

According to these opponents of cumulative "progress" in science, the reason that scientific theories do not build on their predecessors is very roughly that they constitute irreconcilably different conceptual schemes, and accurate translation between them is impossible. There is no neutral basis for translation, no theory-free language to describe observations that would enable us to compare theories for predictive success. One theory's confirming data will be another theory's experimental error. Thus, the claim that science shows persistent improvements in predictive success is moot, for any such alleged demonstration begs the question against theories that have been superseded. The appearance to the contrary, Kuhn held, is the result of scientists in each generation rewriting the history of their subjects in order to give the appearance of cumulation, so that the latest view can carry the mantle of success borne by the scientific achievements it replaces.

In fact, Kuhn seemed to claim that the whole idea that predictive success should constitute a transdisciplinary criterion for scientific knowledge is part of a conceptual scheme: the positivism or empiricism associated with Newtonian science. But the positivist or empiricist paradigm has now been replaced in physical science by relativistic and quantum theoretical conceptual schemes that deprive Newtonian demands of their authority. Because it was a deterministic theory of causal mechanisms, Newtonian science made prediction a requirement of scientific achievement. According to quantum mechanics, the world is indeterministic; thus definitive prediction can no longer be a necessary condition of scientific success. Nor does it make sense to search for causal mechanisms described in strict and exceptionless laws.

For the same reasons that scientific standards change within each of the natural sciences, they differ extensively between them and differ even more widely from the aims and methods of the social sciences. Thus, the charge that the social sciences have made less progress than the natural sciences is often said to rest on a myopic absolutism that improperly generalizes from the methodological recipes of an obsolete paradigm.

Of course, within a given discipline prediction and practical application are important ways of "articulating the paradigm." But once we identify the paradigm that governs a social science, we will be able to identify what kinds of predictions and applications are appropriate. Moreover, we will be able to see that in the light of these standards, the social sciences are as cumulating as we could demand. In the social sciences there is as much progress as in the natural sciences. It's just a different kind of progress.

Whereas the natural sciences aim primarily at providing causal theories about underlying mechanisms, the social sciences are held to seek an understanding of behavior by rendering it *intelligible*. They uncover its meaning or significance. Meaning or significance, the interpretation of human behavior that enables us to understand it, is not fundamentally causal, nor is it provided by the discovery of laws or generalizations of any interesting sorts. Unlike the natural sciences, the social disciplines have an identifiable stopping place: intelligibility. The social sciences concern themselves with that part of human behavior ordinarily described as *action* and not with mere movements of or at the surface of the body. Speech, not snoring, jumping, not falling, suicide, not just death—these are the subject matter of certain social sciences, and the social sciences that do not deal with individual action deal with its consequences and its aggregation into large-scale events and institutions.

Though understanding the meaning of actions is not in the end a species of causal inquiry, opponents of prediction as the chief goal of social science insist that this understanding certainly satisfies *appropriate* standards of predictive success: the standard required to navigate successfully in a society of other human beings. When we step back and consider how reliable our predictions of the behavior of others are, we cannot fail to be impressed with the implicit theory that growing up in society has provided us. This theory, known among philosophers as "folk psychology," tells us that people do the things they do roughly because they want certain ends and believe these acts will help attain them. It includes an implicit theory about how people's environments shape their beliefs (if the traffic light turns red, and I'm looking, I will acquire the belief that it's red) and desires (if there are two indistinguishable goods available at different prices, I will want the cheaper one). It is a theory in which we place great confidence. (Consider, every time you cross the street in the presence of cars stopped at a stop sign, you stake your life on this theory's predictions about the actions of car drivers.) Of course when we try to express the central principles of this theory, we seem to produce only banal and obvious principles, like the one expressed above: People act in ways that they believe will attain their desires. However, this is no defect in the theory. It just means that though the theory is very complicated, we know parts of it very well. Moreover, as we shall see, folk psychology is claimed to have important and highly unbanal extensions (see Chapter 4).

The regularities we dredge up when we seek to identify these principles seem too weak to do justice to our very considerable predictive powers about other people's actions. But this shows that the very complex theory we use is somehow unconsciously represented, like the grammatical theory that governs our speech and prevents us from making silly syntactical errors, though we could never express very much of it consciously. And our folk psychology had already reached a high degree of predictive power well before the beginning of recorded history, long before we acquired a comparably powerful theory in natural science.

Therefore, even on the questionable standard of predictive success, folk psychology does very well. And it does so by identifying the meaning of behavior—by showing that it is action undertaken in the light of beliefs and desires.

Social science, it is argued, is and should be the extension and development of this theory. It inherits the great predictive strength of folk psychology, but the main aim of social science is not to improve on this predictive power. Its aim, rather, is to extend this theory from the understanding of everyday interactions of individuals, to interactions among large numbers of individuals in social institutions, and to interactions among individuals whose cultures and forms of life are very different from our own.

Opponents of a "scientific" approach to social science claim that much of the apparent sterility and lack of progress in these disciplines is the result of slavish attempts to force folk psychology into the mold of a causal theory of the determinants of action. If social science has not progressed, it is because many social scientists have misunderstood this theory and misconstrued it as a causal one, to be improved by somehow sharpening its predictive power. The result, as in microeconomic theory, has been to produce general statements that are not laws because they are either vacuous definitions or else flatly false. In other disciplines, like psychology or parts of sociology, the misunderstanding of folk psychology has produced jargon-ridden pseudoscience.

The trouble is that folk psychology has reached its maximal level of predictive power. This is because folk psychology is not a causal theory, to be improved by the means that scientists employ to improve theory in natural science. Opponents of a "scientific" approach hold that the predictive power of folk psychology is a sort of by-product of its real objective: providing understanding through interpretation. When we accept this objective as the proper study of social science, we will recognize the important advances social science has attained. Doubts about progress will be shown to be not only groundless but also fundamentally misconceived.

Proponents of this view invite us to consider how much more we now know about other cultures, their mores, morals, institutions, social rules and conventions, values, religions, myths, art, music, medicine, than we knew a century ago. Consider how much more we know about our own society as a result of what we have learned about other societies. Our understanding of these initially strange people is not the product of "scientific investigation" but of the cultural anthropologist's "going native," attempting to learn about a foreign culture from the inside, coming to understand the meaning of his subjects' actions in the terms his subjects employ. It also reflects important discoveries about the hidden, deeper meanings behind behavior that social scientists have uncovered.

This hard-won knowledge represents progress in two different ways. We can understand people of differing cultures, indeed acquire as much predictive confidence about them as our own folk psychology provides us about ourselves, for what we are learning is in effect their folk psychology. Moreover, learning about other cultures teaches much about our own: Specifically, it leads us to see that what we might identify in our beliefs, values, and institutions as universal or true or optimal is really parochial, local, and merely relative to our transitory condition. Coming to understand another and very different society, by learning the meaning of its features, is a cure for moral absolutism, xenophobia, racism, and other ills. This is how social science progresses, not by providing us with the means to control the behavior of others, but by providing us interpretations that will enable us to place our own society in perspective.

A scientific approach to human behavior is also held to miss, when it fails to come to grips with the centrality of meaning and significance to social knowledge, the moral dimension of social science. The natural sciences aim, in part, at technological progress: That's what makes predictive power so important for them. The social sciences aim at ameliorating the human condition. This involves choices that natural science does not seem called upon to make, moral choices about what will count as improvements and what will not. It involves identifying the real, as opposed to the apparent, meanings of social institutions and emancipating human beings from their mistaken beliefs about these meanings.

If the conceptual apparatus we need in order to uncover the meaning of human events, individual or aggregate, is irreconcilable with the search for causal laws, as some social scientists hold, then so much the worse for this vain attempt to discover such laws. The idea that we should replace our explanatory system with one that "carves nature at the joints" is based on a fundamental misunderstanding of the nature and aims of social science. The philosophical problem it raises is not that of whether the search for meaning can be given a causal interpretation, but of what sort of conceptual confusion should have led so many philosophers and social scientists down the blind alley of attempts to construct and advance a discipline that apes inappropriately the methods of natural science. So goes the rebuttal to the claim that the social sciences have not progressed and need to be reorganized on the model of a natural science.

Are There Right Answers in the
Philosophy of Social Science?

The two arguments that we have canvassed cover a lot of ground and touch on both very practical questions of social scientific method and the most fundamental problems of philosophy. These two arguments reflect what may be polar positions on a continuum along which most social scientists should be able to place themselves. But though they are extreme views, they have real proponents. More important, whether they want to or not, all social scientists take sides on the problems these arguments reflect. That is what makes the philosophy of social science relevant to social science itself.

The extreme views are probably beyond serious adjudication. No one is going to convince a proponent of either extreme that the view all the way across on the other side of the continuum is right. The reason is that the differences between them rest on very fundamental issues of philosophy, claims about epistemology, metaphysics, ethics, issues that have not been settled in philosophy since they were first raised by Plato twenty-four hundred years ago.

But then why should the rest of us bother about these issues? They cannot be settled, and we don't occupy these extreme positions in the philosophy of social science. Indeed, many social scientists aren't interested in the subject at all. They claim to have good reason not to be: Its problems are insoluble and therefore irrelevant to their concerns. Insoluble perhaps, but irrelevant, no.

Between the two polar positions I have described, there may not be intermediate theories that are in coherent, stable equilibrium. In philosophical matters the policy of finding a happy medium that splits the difference between rival theories is often impossible, for the positions are logically incompatible, and many attempts to embrace parts of each result not in compromise but in incoherence. Picking and choosing components of these two philosophies, with a view to developing a "third way," may result in a coherent position, but one vulnerable to being shifted by unanswerable arguments all the way to one extreme or the other.

For example, economists or political scientists committed to citing individual expectations and preferences as the causes of human behavior need to explain why we have secured no predictively reliable laws about individual action framed in these terms. Or they must show why no such laws are necessary. Without such an explanation, the economists leave themselves open to the claim that the knowledge they provide is not causal, but at best information that helps us *interpret* the actions of consumers or voters in late capitalist society. Or if they don't give an account of how causal claims can be made and justified without the support of laws, these social scientists are vulnerable to the charge that their explanatory variables are not natural kinds and need to be surrendered in any serious causal theory of human behavior. In effect, for such a social scientist to find an intermediate position involves facing several classical philosophical problems about causation.

The sociologist or cultural anthropologist who brings back an account of the meanings of other cultures, and who defends its accuracy by comparing its predictive success with that of folk psychology in our own culture, must answer the challenge that for all its alleged successes, folk psychology is notoriously vague, often fails us at crucial times, and has manifested no improvement throughout recorded history. If these social scientists reply by repudiating improving predictive success as a mark of knowledge, they have willy-nilly taken sides in the most profound dispute of epistemology: The notion that beyond a certain point confirmation by observation no longer controls what we identify as knowledge or improvements in it is certainly incompatible with empiricism. It can be underwritten only by a rationalist's epistemology: a theory of knowledge that explains how truths can be justified a priori, that is, without appeal to empirical evidence.

Social scientists who wish to embrace both the natural scientific approach to human behavior and the moral agenda of learning from this approach what *ought* to be done to improve the human condition must face several of the thorniest problems of moral philosophy. They must derive what *ought* to be the case from what *is* the case, a derivation widely held to be impossible (as we shall see in Chapter 7). They need an explanation of how we can acquire moral knowledge "scientifically" and a good account of why such moral knowledge does not justify paternalistic imposition of its particular claims on a potentially unwilling society.

Many social scientists adopt what they believe to be a method of advancing their discipline as a body of scientific theory that is predictively relevant for policy applications. Let us call such social scientists *naturalists* to indicate their commitment to methods adapted from the natural sciences. Other less apt labels for naturalism are empiricism, behaviorism, and positivism—the latter often a term of derision among opponents of naturalism. Most naturalists believe they can endorse these methods while doing justice to the meaningfulness and significance of human action. And they do not think anything can force them to choose between these two commitments. But this combination has been subject to repeated objection over the course of the past hundred years, and current controversies about social science are but reiterations of this objection and replies to it.

Those who hold that we cannot do justice to actions as meaningful while we seek a naturalistic or scientific analysis of them and that the aim of social science must be intelligibility, whereas its means should be interpretation, have adopted a succession of labels since the late nineteenth century: idealists, phenomenologists, structuralists, ethnomethodologists, students of semiotics or hermeneutics, post modernists, and deconstructionists. For convenience, I shall sometimes refer to their view as *antinaturalism*, and sometimes as *interpretational* social science.

The history of science presents both naturalists and antinaturalists with a common problem. On the one hand, the study of man that does not treat his behavior as *action*, guided by intentions and meanings, is simply not a *social* science. On the other hand, the history of natural science is held to be that of continually increasing its explanatory scope by augmenting its predictive power. And it has done this by successively removing meaning and significance from nature.

After Galileo the stars and planets were deprived of the goals that Aristotelian science had attributed to them; then Darwin showed that the adaptation of flora and fauna to their environments was to be explained without attributing meaning to it or intentions to their creator. Now the only arena of intention and meaning left is their "home base," human action. In each of the previous cases, the greatest obstacle to scientific advance was the conviction that any adequate explanation of the phenomena required appeal to meanings. The record of the history of science requires every social scientist to face the question of why human behavior should be any exception to this alleged pattern. Every potential answer to this question is general enough, metatheoretical enough, and abstract enough to count as an exercise in the philosophy of social science, and in philosophy as a whole, broadly considered. For every answer will bear directly on the two questions with which we have defined philosophy.

Introduction to the Literature

The two classical introductions to the philosophy of science are Carl Hempel, *Philosophy of Natural Science*, and Ernest Nagel, *The Structure of Science*. The latter work is both somewhat more difficult and far more comprehensive than Hempel's. It includes an extended defense of naturalistic philosophy of social science. Clark Glymour, *The Philosophy of Science*, forthcoming in this series, will provide an introduction to contemporary problems and philosophical issues surrounding statistical testing and hypothesis confirmation, a subject that goes untreated in this book. Readers interested in the philosophical foundations of the probability, a subject of great importance in social science, should consult R. Giere, *Understanding Scientific Reasoning*, as well as B. Skyrms, *Choice and Chance*.

The locus classicus of the naturalistic view of method in social science is David Hume, *Treatise of Human Nature*, and *Enquiry Concerning Human Understanding*. In these works one will also find the account of causation as law governed, which motivates much empiricist philosophy of science. Hume's approach is in many ways developed in John Stuart Mill, *A System of Logic*, especially Book 6, "On The Logic of the Moral Sciences." Among sociologists the most famous defense of a naturalistic position is Emile Durkheim's *The Rules of the Sociological Method*. A position similar in some respects is also defended in Richard Rudner, *Philosophy of Social Science*, which was meant to be an introduction to the subject but is difficult for nonspecialists to follow. David Papineau, *For Science in the Social Sciences*, is a recent argument for naturalism. Robert Brown, *The Nature of Social Laws*, provides a concise account of the history, from Machiavelli to Mill, of the claim that there are such social laws. B. F. Skinner's *Science and Human Behavior* carries the argument for this approach to social science further than any other social scientist has. Among philosophers a different argument with similar conclusions is provided in Paul Churchland, *Scientific Realism and the Plasticity of Mind*.

The antinaturalistic view has closely embraced T. Kuhn's *Structure of Scientific Revolutions* as a counterweight to postpositivist philosophy of science. An anthology tracing the antinaturalistic view's influence in social science is G. Gutting (ed.), *Paradigms and Revolutions*. Interpretive social science is a tradition that goes back to the nineteenth century. Its history is traced and defended in R. G. Collingwood, *The Idea of History*. Among social scientists its locus classicus is Alfred Schutz. Papers by Schutz defending this view are anthologized in M. Natanson (ed.), *Philosophy of Social Science*, and David Braybrooke (ed.), *Philosophical Problems of the Social Sciences*. An influential work elaborating on this view is P. Winch, *The Idea of a Social Science*. A. Giddens, *Sociology: A Brief but Critical Introduction*, sketches a position that brings this approach together with critical theory (see Chapter 4 below).

Among introductions to the philosophy of social science, the best is Alan Ryan, *The Philosophy of Social Science*. Ryan has also edited an anthology on the subject, *The Philosophy of Social Explanation*. Two other anthologies include many papers discussing topics treated in this book: L. I. Krimerman (ed.), *The Nature and Scope of Social Science*, and M. Brodbeck (ed.), *Readings in the Philosophy of Social Sciences*. D. Braybrooke, *Philosophy of Social Science*, attempts to reconcile the two traditions, naturalism and antinaturalism.

2

The Explanation of Human Action

WE CAN DIVIDE human activities roughly into two classes: those we count as "mere" behavior and those we view as actions. Mere behavior includes what happens inside our bodies, like the beating of our hearts and the opening and closing of the eye's iris. Action is behavior that does not just happen to us, but that somehow we "control." The difference between action and behavior is difficult to state, for some things we do seem to fall on the borderline between these two categories— yawns, for example. But nevertheless there is a difference. It is the difference between a blink and a wink, and it is crucial for the social sciences, for social science begins with the aim of explaining *human action*, not "mere" behavior. When and why the eye blinks is a matter of physiology, not social science. But when and why people wink at one another—that's a question that does concern the social scientist.

Although social science begins with the aim of explaining action, it does not end there. Much social science is concerned with explaining large-scale events and institutions made up of organized aggregations of actions as well as with explaining significant statistical findings about large groups. And some social scientists, especially psychologists, are interested in explaining human action by incorporating it into "mere" behavior. The attractiveness of either of these objectives, as alternatives or additions to the traditional objective of explaining individual human action, hinges on the success in achieving this central aim of social science.

How then do we go about explaining human actions? Long before the self-conscious attempts of the social scientist, common sense had provided us all with a theory about the behavior of our fellow human beings. It is a theory that we use every day to form our expectations about the behavior of one another and to explain our own behavior to one another. This implicit theory, often given the label "folk psychology" by philosophers, has always been the natural starting place for explanations social scientists have given. In fact to the extent that social scientists, like historians, expound no explicit explanatory theory at all for the human actions they explain, they refrain from doing so because they have taken over folk psychology without even noticing. Of course, many social scientists have been well aware of the theory they were endorsing from common sense and have made great efforts to improve it. Microeconomic theory is perhaps the best example of this approach, and we shall consider its improvements in Chapter 3. But first we need to identify this theory and consider how it works, what kind of a theory it is, and what sorts of explanations it provides.

We will discover that there are serious obstacles facing any effort to treat folk psychology as a theory of the sort familiar in natural science or even as a primitive precursor to such a theory. The consequences of this difficulty for the view we have called naturalism are serious and troubling.

Folk Psychology

Human actions are explained by identifying the beliefs and desires that lead to them. Often, such explanations are elliptical, or abbreviated, or proceed by making tacit assumptions that most people can be expected to share. If we explain why someone moved his king in a chess game, simply by saying he did it to avoid a check, the explanation works because it assumes that the player wanted to avoid check and believed that moving his king was a way of doing so. If we don't mention his desire, but simply attribute a purpose (to avoid check), and don't make it explicit that he believed that moving the king would attain this purpose, that is because these features of commonsense explanations "go without saying."

We can find the same form of explanation in many a classic of social scientific explanation. For example, in *The Protestant Ethic and the Spirit of Capitalism,* Max Weber explained the collapse of the European pre-capitalist order by appeal to just such forces of desire and belief. Weber of course had to be more specific, for his twentieth-century readers could hardly be expected to have tacit knowledge of the specific beliefs and desires of seventeenth-century Calvinists. But once Weber has made clear to us Calvinists' intense desire to know their predestined fate as saved or damned and their belief that worldly success may be a sign of salvation, their commitment to capitalism in the face of traditional obstacles to it becomes clear to us. Even a social theorist like Freud who sought to substitute a deeper psychoanalytical explanation of our actions for the one common sense provides nevertheless adopted its commitment to desires and beliefs as the determinants of behavior. Only in Freud's theory the determinants of behavior are unconscious, repressed desires and neurotic beliefs.

Therefore, when we explain an action we do so by identifying the desires and beliefs that give rise to it. It is typical of philosophers to go beyond this point on which all agree, to ask *why*, that is, why is citing the desires and the beliefs *explanatory*? What connection obtains between the desires and the beliefs and the action they explain that makes them *relevant* to the behavior, that enables them to satisfy our curiosity about the behavior? It is hard to have patience with this question. It seems so obvious that citing the desires and beliefs explains the actions, that nothing further need be said, and it is hard to think of what further could be said.

Naturalistic philosophers will justify the question of their connection by pointing out that only if we can identify the link between beliefs and desires on the one hand and action on the other will we be able to *improve* upon folk psychology's explanations of human action. Otherwise perhaps we should seek the explanation of action elsewhere. Interpretationalists will argue that only by identifying this link can we convince misguided social scientists that understanding human action is not a species of causal inquiry. Both sides to the dispute about the progress of the social sciences agree that we cannot ignore the question of what enables beliefs and desires to explain actions.

What we need in order to show how particular desires and beliefs work together to explain actions is some general theory about desires, beliefs, and actions. The situation is no different from explanations in physical science or mathematics, and both raise difficult philosophical questions. If we say that 148 is an even number because it is divisible by 2, then this explanation works only because it is a general truth of mathematics, indeed, a definition, that any number divisible by 2 is an even number. Anyone who still doesn't understand after this definition is provided would need to know what a *definition* is, and how it can explain things. But this is no longer a matter for mathematical explanation—it's a matter for philosophy.

Likewise, we can explain why a penny is a good conductor by saying that it is made of copper, and in general, copper is a good conductor. This generalization is not a definition but a general law. And anyone who still does not understand the explanation needs to understand why general laws are explanatory. But this is no longer a scientific question—it is a philosophical one.

Similarly, we need some sort of general connection between desires, beliefs, and actions, and once we have identified this generalization, we will want to know how it enables the two former to explain the latter. Will the connection be more like a mathematical definition or a general law? Or will it be different from either in its explanatory power? On our answer will hinge the proper research strategy for social science: Should it be more like natural science, focused on observation and experiment in order to discover laws, or more like mathematics, focused on logical connections and the meanings of its concepts; or should it be different from either?

Something like the following oversimplified general statement seems to lie behind our ordinary explanations of human action, our predictions about how people will behave in the future, and explanations in social science that trade on folk psychology:

[L] Given any person x, if x wants d and x believes that a is a means to attain d, under the circumstances, then x does a.

This then is the leading explanatory principle folk psychology offers us. It isn't the only one. There are others, ones that connect our desires and beliefs to our environments and our past experiences. For example, there's the "generalization" that if an agent is standing before a medium-sized object in normal environmental conditions, then if the agent's eyes are open and working properly he sees the object and, furthermore, believes it is before him. Or again, if someone has been deprived of water for several days, then other things being equal, he desires to drink. There are of course many more such generalizations about our perceptual abilities, beliefs, desires, memories, fears, hopes, regrets, and so forth, embedded in folk psychology. But as we shall see, the most central of them to our explanatory needs in social science is [L]. Like the others, [L] must be understood either as embodying a pretty strong "other things being equal," or "ceteris paribus" clause, or else as an approximation for some more precise general law that can be expected to replace it. Why is this? Because as it stands, [L] is false.

Consider how easy it is to construct exceptions to it. Suppose that x wants d, but x wants something else (d') even more strongly than he wants d. If the actions required to secure d and to secure d' are incompatible, x will not undertake action a, but some other action (a') required to attain d'. Or suppose x believes that a is a means of attaining d, but not the best, or most efficient, or enjoyable, or cheapest means of attaining it. Then x won't do a, even if he wants d, has no overriding incompatible wants, and believes a is a means of attaining d. Things can get even worse for [L]. Even if x believes that a is the best means

of securing *d*, *x* may not know how to do *a*, or knowing how, may be
unable to do it.

We can of course "improve" [L] by adding clauses to it covering each
of these problems. The result will be a much more complex statement
like this

For any agent *x*, if
 1. *x* wants *d*
 2. *x* believes that doing *a* is a means to bring about *d*, under the
    circumstances
 3. there is no action believed by *x* to be a way of bringing about *d*
    that under the circumstances is more preferred by *x*
 4. *x* has no wants that override *d*
 5. *x* knows how to do *a*
 6. *x* is able to do *a*,
then
 7. *x* does *a*.

Of course, the four clauses we have added to [L] may not be enough.
An acute philosopher could doubtless construct a counterexample, a
case that shows that the first six conditions are not sufficient for someone's
doing *a*, so that we need to add a seventh, and perhaps an eighth, and
so on. But instead of adding clauses to [L], we could simply argue that
these exceptions are rare and treat [L] as bearing an "other things being
equal" clause that implicitly excludes each of the exceptions excluded
by (1) through (6) and any further clauses [L] needs. Such clauses are
called ceteris paribus conditions. They are implicit in most of the
generalizations we believe. Thus we say that dry matches light when
struck, implicitly excluding the objection that they don't do so in a
vacuum, on the ground that this condition is excluded by an "other
things being equal" clause. Most of the rough empirical generalizations
of a science include such clauses. Reading such a clause into [L], at least
initially, is preferable, for we can't be sure that the fuller version we
have just constructed is not itself still subject to further counterexamples
and may not need still more clauses. However, an unremovable ceteris
paribus clause, requiring that other things be equal when the desire for
d and the belief about *a* lead to doing *a*, opens up [L] to a potentially
serious charge of vagueness. The scope of a ceteris paribus clause must
in the long run be reduced, if not eliminated.

It's worth noting that when economists avail themselves of [L], their
version of it often includes all the provisions mentioned in the expanded
version. Microeconomic explanations of, say, consumer choice attribute
to economic agents perfect information about available alternative choices

and their consequences, complete information about the constraints within which the consumer operates, and a consistent preference order—a ranking of wants—that lead the consumer to a unique choice. Though the theory is expressed in terms like "expectations" and "preferences," these are just cognates for the beliefs and desires that figure in [L].

Reasons and Causes

Now that we have identified a general statement (with or without a ceteris paribus clause) that connects beliefs and desires to actions and thus can serve to underwrite our explanations, both ordinary and social scientific, we need to ask what kind of a general claim this is. [L] certainly looks like one that identifies the *causes* of actions and thus bids fair to be a law, or at least to be an important precursor to a law, in the natural scientists' sense of the term, of human action. After all, the terms ordinarily employed to connect beliefs and desires to actions are mostly cognates for causation: Beliefs and desires "bring about action," "result in it," "produce it," "determine it." Insofar as scientific explanation is causal, any scientific approach to explanation in social science should attempt to establish a causal connection to underwrite the explanatory one common sense accepts. And that must be the function of [L]. It is a causal law or a precursor to one.

This naturalistic approach to the relation between folk psychology and a science of human action has long been associated with the views of Max Weber. Weber recognized the role of desires and beliefs in the explanation of action but also went on to insist that the sort of explanation they provide must be like those provided in the explanations characteristic of natural science. Weber viewed a general statement like [L] as an "ideal type"—an unrealistic model, like those of natural science—which needs to be filled in and refined in its application to individual actions. (The role of ideal types and models generally is discussed in Chapter 3, "Instrumentalism in Economics," and extensively in Chapter 6.) The demand of Weber's followers for a *law* of human action has rested on the argument that causation is a matter of laws. But the requirement of laws, connecting desires, beliefs and actions, can be separated from this argument. We could, for instance, admit that causation does not always consist of law-governed sequences and still insist that our goal of predictively improvable knowledge requires laws or approximations to them. For simplicity hereafter, we will use the word "causal" to mean law governed. What is crucial is the insistence that scientific explanation requires laws, whether causation is really always law governed or not.

However, as Weber recognized, unlike (other) causes, beliefs and desires are also *reasons* for action: They justify it, show it to be rational, appropriate, efficient, reasonable, correct. They render it intelligible. So, perhaps explanations in ordinary life and social science work by showing that actions are reasonable, efficient, appropriate, or rational in the light of the agent's beliefs and desires. In this case, [L] will certainly not work like a law or the precursor to one. For causal laws don't provide intelligibility. Rather, [L] will reflect the fact that beliefs and desires justify or sanction some action as reasonable. If this is how [L] works, then the fundamental explanatory strategy in social science is not that of revealing brute causation. The aim is instead one of making the action *rationally intelligible*. If [L] also mentions causes, then this is a secondary by-product that it will provide derivatively.

In fact, [L] has often been identified as a *principle of rationality*. That is how it is described by some of the economists who employ it. An agent is rational to the extent that he undertakes those actions that are most justified, given his ends—his desires or wants. Thus, far from being a contingent law describing the causes of actions, [L] turns out to be a definition, implicit or explicit, of what it means to be rational. And the social sciences that exploit [L] are not inquiries into the causation of various actions. Rather, they are investigations into the rationality of these actions.

This is a crucial contrast that every account of the explanation of human action must face. This difference between reasons and causes is sometimes difficult to keep clear, especially if, as most social scientists hold, beliefs and desires are *both* reasons for actions *and* their causes.

But if they are both, then why distinguish between reasons and causes? We do it because we need to identify where the explanatory power of action explanations lies. Even if beliefs and desires are both reasons and causes, their explanatory power with respect to actions may rest on only one of these two features. And on which of them it rests will determine much about the methodology of social science. If reasons for actions explain because they bring about actions, then the naturalism described in Chapter 1 is vindicated: The social sciences must search for causal laws. If the causes of an action explain it because they are resons for it, then the aim of science is interpretation and intelligibility, and the antinaturalist approach to social science turns out to be correct.

So, what *is* the difference between reasons and causes? It's easier illustrated than expressed: Suppose we ask a jogger why she jogs 10 kilometers a day. She replies, "because it's good for me." There is a fair amount left unsaid in this typical explanation: First, it's not just that jogging is good for her, it's that she *believes* it is; second, she *wants* to do things that are good for her; third, she believes that jogging won't prevent her from doing other things equally good for her. Doubtless there are other things she wants and believes that are "understood" in this explanation. All these things *justify* her jogging 10 kilometers a day. They make it seem intelligible, reasonable, rational: If we were in her shoes, that is, had her beliefs and desires, we'd jog that much too.

But suppose the "real reason" she jogs every day is that physiological changes in her body have over the years addicted her to it, so that if she doesn't jog, she feels lousy all day. Though she never notices this correlation, it keeps her jogging by physiologically punishing her for skipping a day and rewarding her with a "runner's high" when she does jog. This is a typical behaviorist's explanation, and the scare quotes around "real reason" are there because if this is what explains her jogging, then clearly it does so not by *justifying* it but by causing it in virtue of some *contingent causal law*. In this case, reasons do not explain behavior—causes do.

Of course, most social science proceeds on the supposition that the desires and beliefs that explain behavior are both reasons for it and its causes. A scientist tells us that cigarettes are harmful to our health; there are reasons for the claim, in the form of scientific data that the scientist believes. His beliefs about the scientific evidence thus may *justify* as reasonable, or rational, his claim that cigarettes are harmful. Anyone in possession of this evidence would be justified in holding this view because the evidence and conclusion are connected by some *logically necessary* but *trivially true principle of reasoning*, like "claims supported by good scientific evidence are generally reasonable to make."

Furthermore, presumably, the scientist's claim about cigarettes is caused (in part) by these beliefs: They produced it as well as justified it. But if they produced his belief, then they did not do so simply because of the logically necessary principle of reasoning. People often make logical mistakes, they violate rules of logic, they fail to make claims that their beliefs logically justify, because they don't make the inferences these principles and their beliefs permit. And people also draw conclusions from their beliefs that are illogical, that the principles of logic forbid as fallacious. So, if the scientist's beliefs about the evidence brought about his claim that cigarettes are harmful, these beliefs would have to do so in virtue of some causal law or laws connecting beliefs to actions and not in virtue of a sound principle of logical reasoning alone.

Consider a third case, more interesting to the social scientist. Imagine a woman who hates the smell of cigarette smoke and claims that cigarettes are harmful. Suppose that this person is acquainted with the scientific evidence that leads the scientist to make the same claim. If asked to explain why she says cigarettes are harmful, the woman cites her beliefs about the evidence. However, what if her "real reasons" for saying that cigarettes are harmful is her hatred of cigarette smoke's *smell*, which she has no reason to think harmful. How do these "real reasons" explain her claim? Certainly not via a logical principle of inference justifying reasoning from something's smelling bad to some people, to its being harmful to all. For there is no such principle. If there is a logical principle involved, it will be [L] or something like it, a principle to the effect that it is *reasonable* to do those things that one believes will lead to the attainment of one's desires, in this case to say that cigarette smoking is harmful because saying this may reduce the smoking of others and thus reduce one's exposure to the smell one hates.

However, perhaps the woman's hatred of the smell of cigarettes explains her claim because her hatred (along with her beliefs) *causes* her claim, in virtue of some contingent general law. [L] will serve for this as well, if interpreted, not as logical principle underwriting the reasonableness of her action, but as a contingent law identifying its causes.

Now, explaining human actions requires us to identify their "real reasons." And the crucial question for social science is whether the "real reasons" are connected to actions in virtue of some logically necessary principle of reasoning or in virtue of some contingent causal law. As we can see, this is a question about [L]. For [L] is what connects someone's real reasons, his beliefs and desires, with his actions. Does [L] underwrite our explanations of actions because it describes causal relations—that is, lawlike connections—in virtue of which actions are determined by beliefs and desires? Or does [L] underwrite these explanations because it helps us identify the reasons that make a particular action justified, intelligible, rational, meaningful, or somehow significant to us?

Of course, it is just possible that [L] does both: helps us identify the causes for actions and the reasons for them. This is the view that Weber and his successors among the naturalists have embraced. But as we shall now see, this happy reconciliation is not on the cards.

The Conspiracy of Desires, Beliefs, and Actions

Chapter 1 identified the distinctive problem of the philosophy of social science as that of explaining or explaining away its alleged lack of progress by comparison to natural science. This problem has haunted the social sciences largely because it has vexed folk psychology's theory of human action, and social science has adopted this theory through much of its history. The problem of progress is (1) the difficulty facing attempts to improve [L] into a general theory of human behavior with increasing explanatory unity and predictive precision; and (2) the question of why no replacement for [L] has so far been found. To see this, let us try to apply [L] to the *causal* explanation of a particular action.

There is a standard "recipe" given in the philosophy of science for causally explaining an individual event, the so-called deductive-nomological or "covering law" account: The occurrence of the event should be derivable from one or more general laws and a statement of "initial" conditions—roughly the set of circumstances or conditions that constitute the cause of the event to be explained. For example, we can explain why the gas in a certain container maintains a given pressure by deriving that pressure from the ideal gas law, $PV = rT$, and a statement about the temperature of the gas and the volume of the container. This model is called deductive nomological because it is a deductive argument that contains a law that "covers" the event to be explained. It is important to note that with the information in a deductive-nomological model, we can predict the pressure as well as explain it.

Of course, natural science isn't generally interested in the explanation of particular events, and this is true to a lesser extent of many of the social sciences. Only history is explicitly devoted to the explanation of particular events. But such explanation is important because it provides us with a means of testing and improving the laws and theories employed in the explanation.

So, scientifically explaining a particular human action presumably involves deriving a statement describing the action from [L] and a set of statements about the agent's desires and beliefs. Let's take a prosaic example: Smith is carrying an umbrella as he goes to work. Why? Here is an explanation:

Initial conditions:
1. Smith wants d, to stay dry today.
2. Smith believes that a, carrying an umbrella, is the best way for him to d, stay dry today.

Law:
3. For any agent x, if x wants d, and x believes that doing a is the best way for him to secure d, then x does a.

Therefore:
4. Smith does a, carries an umbrella today.

This explanation may be a little stilted and unnecessarily cluttered. But it is what stands behind the briefer explanation "Smith thinks it's gonna rain." Now, how good a scientific explanation is this?

What if someone challenged it, demanding evidence to show that the initial conditions actually obtained? For all we know, Smith might be a British merchant banker, who always carries an umbrella because it's part of the required uniform, rain or shine. For all we know, Smith thinks he needs a cane to walk but doesn't want to look like an invalid, so he uses an umbrella. For all we know, Smith wants to get wet today and superstitiously supposes that if he carries an umbrella it will rain. We can go on and on dreaming up farfetched combinations of beliefs and desires to attribute to Smith that will work with [L] equally well to explain why Smith is carrying an umbrella today. To confirm our explanation we need evidence that Smith has the wants and desires that it attributes to him, instead of these farfetched alternatives.

Or suppose we want to be able to predict whether Smith will carry an umbrella tomorrow. To do this we also need to be able to establish exactly what Smith will want and believe tomorrow morning before he passes the umbrella stand in his front hall. Without this information we cannot employ [L] to predict what Smith will do. For we can't determine the initial conditions to which we can apply [L] so as to generate a prediction about what Smith will do.

How do we find out exactly what people believe and desire? The most convenient way is of course to ask them. Failing that, we can experiment: We try to arrange their circumstances so that their behavior will reveal their beliefs and desires. But usually the only way to discern the desires and beliefs of others is to observe their behavior. One thing we cannot do is read their minds. Now all three methods, asking, experimenting, observing, are really aspects of the same strategy: All three involve inferring back from action to desire and belief. Sometimes in the case of asking this fact escapes our notice. We are tempted to think that asking a question is a direct approach to what someone believes or wants.

But a little reflection reveals that asking is just a version of arranging subjects' circumstances and then watching their actions. After all, speech is itself intentional action. Suppose we ask Smith whether he wanted to stay dry today, or will want to tomorrow. Suppose he emits the noise "yes." Is this an assent to our inquiry? That is, is it an action Smith undertook in order to attain his desire to answer our question in the affirmative, with the belief that producing the noise "yes" would do it?

Treating the noise that Smith produced as an answer to our question, instead of, say, a funny-sounding sneeze, involves attributing to Smith at least the following: the belief that the noise we produced expresses a question in English, the belief that we understand English, and the belief that we want an answer to the question, the belief that in English one way to signal assent is to produce the noise "yes," and the desire to signal assent to our question. But even this catalogue of beliefs and desires is still not enough. Treating the noise he makes as a sign of his desire to stay dry today requires us to add to our assumptions about Smith's desires: the desire to tell us what exactly he believes, the desire to be sincere and not to lie to us.

But this means that the *easiest* way to establish what someone believes and wants is fearfully complex. And what is more, establishing what a person wants and believes requires that we make further assumptions about other beliefs and desires of theirs, and it requires us to employ [L] itself. But this raises a brace of serious methodological problems.

The first is a regress problem in identifying initial conditions: In order to explain an action we need to identify the beliefs and desires that produced it in accordance with [L]. In order to identify these beliefs and desires, we need to make assumptions about other beliefs and desires. But our original problem was that of determining exactly what people believe and want. If to do this, we already need to know many of their other desires and beliefs, then our original problem faces us all over again. We have made little progress in answering the challenge to our original explanation. In ordinary circumstances we don't face this problem because our explanations are not challenged, and there is little interest in improving on their vagueness and imprecision. But science requires both challenge and improvement.

Second, there is the problem in testing [L]. In order to employ [L] in the explanation of an action, we need to use [L] to establish that the action's causes—the initial conditions—obtain. But this means that as long as what is to be explained is an action, nothing could even conceivably lead us to surrender [L] itself, and this casts doubt on its claims to be a causal law, as opposed to a definition. Recall that in order to use Smith's answers to questions as a guide to what he believes and desires, instead of as an irrelevant sneeze, we had to assume that he wanted to answer our question sincerely and correctly and believed that the way to do so was to use the noise "yes." We had to make these assumptions because we employ [L] as a guide to when behavior constitutes *action*—speech instead of noise, as opposed to "mere" movement of the body.

The employment of [L] as a guide to what people believe and desire is even clearer when we have to rely on nonverbal behavior to guess people's beliefs and desires. How can we tell that people believe a ten-dollar-bill is worth more than a five, or prefer the former to the latter? Offer a choice of one or the other to passersby. They all pick the larger bill. But this is a mark of their belief that the ten-spot is worth more than the fiver only if their behavior reflects their beliefs and desires in accordance with a principle like [L].

In fact, the situation is rather more complicated. For in order to employ behavior as a guide to belief, we have to hold the agent's desires constant. And in order to use behavior as a guide to his desires, we have to hold beliefs constant. Any action can be the result of almost any belief, provided the agent has the appropriate desire, and vice versa.

Thus, someone might light a cigarette because, say, he believed that the theory of relativity is false. How is this possible? Well, suppose he believed that someone was asking him whether the theory of relativity was true and also believed that the way to signal dissent in the language of the questioner was to light up and that he wanted to so signal. Bizarre? Well, of course. But that's the point. By itself an action never identifies a single belief or desire. It only does so against the background of a large number of other beliefs and desires.

It's worth emphasizing this point: If we know what someone's beliefs and desires are, then [L] will tell us what actions he will undertake. If we know what actions a person performs and we know his beliefs, then [L] will tell us what his wants are. And if we know his wants and what actions he performs, then [L] will tell us what he believes. But without at least two of the three, belief, desire, and action, the third is not determinable. This is the nature of the conspiracy among them. It is the basis of the view that in explaining action, our aim is to render it intelligible by identifying its meaning or significance, in a "hermeneutical circle" where coherence among the three variables is the criterion of explanatory adequacy.

Of course it is clear why commonsense explanations of human action are so disputable and fallible and why folk psychology's predictive powers are so weak. The number of specific beliefs and desires that lead to actions is so large, and the difficulty of identifying them exactly is so great, that our explanations of action cannot help but be seriously incomplete. Additionally, they will be subject to considerable doubt because it is so difficult to nail down much of what a person actually believed and wanted on a given occasion. And our predictions must be equally weak, for they rest on nothing but guesswork about the vast number of specific beliefs and desires that are needed for a precise prediction using [L].

Of course [L] has some predictive content: We can predict with considerable confidence that our professors will not strip off their clothes in the middle of the next lecture, that the driver of the oncoming car will hit the brake as he approaches the stop sign, that a hundred-dollar bill left on the pavement will be picked up, that someone will have dinner ready when we get home. The reason for this sort of predictive success is clear: We can with confidence attribute a certain number of widely held beliefs and desires to everyone, including strangers, and even some more specialized ones to family and friends. Now, the number of such predictions is indefinitely large. Professors won't strip in class tomorrow, or the next day, or the day after that. Therefore, someone might be tempted to say that [L] has great predictive power.

But predictive power isn't just a matter of numbers of successful predictions. It's a matter of at least two things: proportion of confirmed to disconfirmed predictions and success in providing highly precise and surprising ones. On both these counts [L] fares poorly. Beyond the "safe" predictions, the application of [L] falls down very badly. Strangely enough, most people have been well satisfied with [L] despite this problem, for most of recorded history. Only twentieth-century social and behavioral scientists have been troubled by [L]'s predictive weakness. But that's because its weakness undermines its claims to be a causal law and thus undermines a scientific approach to human action.

It's clear that in order to improve our predictions of human action we need to do either or both of two things: We need to be able to "measure" people's beliefs and desires with greater precision. And we need to improve [L] itself, fill in its ceteris paribus—other things being equal—clause, for example. That is how all causal explanations and causal laws are improved.

To see this, consider again the ideal gas law: $PV = rT$. Suppose we want to explain why the pressure gauge on the gas container reads 15.2885 atmospheres. To do so, we measure the temperature with a thermometer, discovering it to be 99.5° C, and measure the volume of the container, discovering it to be 2.001 liters. When we plug the temperature and volume into the equation, the result is that the pressure is 15.3101. Now this is probably close enough for most purposes. Indeed, all measuring instruments, such as thermometers, manometers, and metersticks, have margins for error. For all we know, the theoretically derived value for pressure may be closer to the real value than the pressure gauge reading. How can we decide which is more accurate—the predicted or the observed value? By improving our measuring instruments. A thermometer that reads out digitally to more decimal places, a micrometer instead of a meterstick to measure length, breadth, depth for volume, and a digital pressure gauge instead of an analog dial will help give more accurate measurements of the initial conditions. If the more accurate numbers are plugged into the equation, the resulting calculation may be much closer to the observed values. In other words, the precision of our explanation will have been improved; and the accuracy of our predictions using the ideal gas law will also have been increased by these new instruments.

Even more important is what happens when improvements in measurement of initial conditions do not result in calculated values closer to observed ones. Such an outcome disconfirms the law. In such a case, we try to improve the law instead of the measurements. In fact the history of improvements and complications in the kinetic theory of gases involves successive refinements of the equation we have been working with. The theory with new variables and constants added can explain and predict the behavior of a gas to a greater degree of accuracy, over a wider range of values of pressure, temperature, and volume. These improvements rest on our ability to measure initial conditions with increasing accuracy over wider and wider ranges.

But neither of these sorts of improvements is possible for [L] or the explanations and predictions in which it figures. $PV = rT$ can be applied to explain and predict, in part because there are thermometers to measure initial conditions. What functions as the "thermometer" for [L], the means for measuring its initial conditions? As we have seen, the answer is [L] must serve as its own "thermometer": To measure people's beliefs and desires we have to use [L]. What is more, although we use different instruments to measure temperature, pressure, and volume, we need the same instrument—[L]—to measure *all* three of our explanatory and predictive variables.

This means, however, that we start out with a "law," [L], with only relatively little predictive power, given the difficulty of establishing precisely its initial conditions of application. And then there's little chance to improve it. For to improve it, we need first to find cases where it has gone wrong in its prediction, then "measure" the values of the initial conditions and the actual behavior that it failed correctly to predict, and finally revise [L] in order to accommodate the observed action. But in order to "measure" beliefs and desires, we must use [L] itself, plus the observed action we failed to predict, and then work back to a more accurate determination of the beliefs and desires. Once we've done this and plugged the more accurate initial conditions into the predictive argument, [L] gives us the observed action after all. So there's never any opportunity to add to or subtract from [L] in order to improve it.

One popular way of describing this problem for [L] is to say that it is unfalsifiable: There is no conceivable evidence about human action that could lead us to surrender it. And if it is unfalsifiable, then it cannot provide empirical, scientific knowledge. Therefore, if it does provide knowledge essential to social science, then the explanations of human action that social science uses [L] for are not ultimately empirical ones. Rather, they are interpretative and provide meaning. Moreover, social science's failure to provide predictions beyond those of folk psychology reflect no discredit upon social science, merely its differences in aim from that of the natural sciences. This of course is the interpretative or antinaturalist's view of [L].

The Logical-Connection Argument

In the two decades before 1970 roughly, arguments like this one provided the main challenge to the notion that social science is a form of causal inquiry. The arguments were simpler than the one just given and were unsound, but they reflected a partial realization of the complex problems facing a causal approach to the explanation of action. In fact, the more complex argument just given is the result of reflections on the simpler ones. The simpler arguments began with the claim that causal claims had to be contingent, not necessary, truths or definitions, and that causal explanations required contingent generalization. Thus, for example, no one could causally explain why Smith was a bachelor by pointing out that he was an unmarried man and all unmarried men are bachelors. Being a bachelor and being an unmarried male are logically connected. It is inconceivable that a bachelor not be an unmarried male. An instance of the first is identical to some instance of the second. The generalization here is a definition, and the initial conditions in effect redescribe the fact to be explained. But just as nothing can be its own cause, nothing can causally explain itself. Thus, whatever enlightenment this information provides, it cannot be a causal explanation of why Smith is a bachelor.

Now, the argument goes, every explanation of a human action is in fact tantamount to a redescription of the event to be explained. It does not identify other distinct and logically independent events, states, or conditions that determine the action. If a statement like [L] is essential in the explanation of human action, it is because [L] is part of what we need to effect these redescriptions. [L] *defines* what it is to be an action or interdefines the notions of desire, belief, and action. [L]'s functions are to show us what counts as having a reason for doing something and to show us when a movement of the body is an action. Thus, desires, beliefs, and actions are logically connected, not contingently connected, by [L] and therefore not causally connected by [L] or by any causal law.

The role [L] plays in identifying beliefs and desires seems to testify to this claim, as does the fact that no failures to predict human action would lead us to improve [L]. It is pretty evident that [L] is not the result of any self-conscious experimentation, observation, or data collection, undertaken with a view to framing a general law about human behavior. It is, as we have noted, a piece of folk psychology, embedded in our consciousness as far back as recorded history, which reflects our conception of ourselves as responsible agents, as persons who act on reasons. If nothing could lead us to give it up, then the connection [L] expresses between desires, beliefs, and actions cannot be the sort of causal link reported in our scientific laws.

Recall the brief account of causation in Chapter 1, "Progress and Prediction." Its claim was that causal links must be *contingent*. That is, when one event *a* causes another event *b*, it must be conceivable for either to have occurred without the other's having done so. If this were not the case, then knowledge of the occurrence of the effect would be enough to establish the occurrence of the cause, and vice versa. But it never is.

In order to determine something's effects or causes, we need to do empirical research, undertake experiments, conduct observations, collect data. This empirical evidence is expressed in contingent laws and generalizations, propositions that could conceivably be false, unlike definitions. These laws sustain our singular causal claims even when they are unmentioned in these claims. Thus, the statement that striking the iceberg caused the *Titanic* to sink is grounded on a large number of physical laws. Of course none of these laws mention the *Titanic*, or even ships of any kind. They are laws of buoyancy, tensile strength of materials like cast iron and ice, and so forth. And most people who correctly claim that striking the iceberg caused the *Titanic*'s sinking don't know any of them. Nevertheless, making the claim commits such people at least to the existence of such laws, even if they don't know what these laws state.

Now, the argument continues, return to the explanation of actions by appeal to beliefs and desires. It's clear that our description of Smith's belief that carrying an umbrella today will help keep him dry is logically connected to its alleged effect, Smith's carrying the umbrella. For the description of the belief makes reference to the action itself. We could not characterize or describe this belief except in a way that refers to one or another of its alleged effects. And we cannot describe an action without thereby committing ourselves to the existence of desires and beliefs that contain descriptions of that action. But this precludes the existence of contingent connections between desires, beliefs, and actions. For they can only be described in terms that refer to one another. Accordingly, such connections will not be causal. And any generalizations that link them will not be general laws either. Rather they will be a priori truths, which we can know without experience and which provide some form of noncausal explanation. That is why [L] is not open to rejection or improvement as a result of empirical findings about contingent matters of fact. Philosophical analysis of [L] thus reveals it to be a definition, one useful for interpreting action and rendering it intelligible. It is a philosophical confusion to view it as a contingent generalization, a mistake that leads to the sterility and frustration characteristic of naturalistic social science. So goes the logical-connection argument.

However, this argument is too strong and doesn't really prove that beliefs and desires can't be causes of action, nor does it establish that statements like [L] can't be treated as causal generalizations. But it does reflect a real difficulty for the attempt to treat [L] and its explanatory applications this way.

To see what is wrong with the argument, we have to distinguish events and processes from the descriptions we give of them. An event, a thing, or a person can be described in many different ways: George Washington is also described as the Father of His Country, the first president of the United States, the owner of Mount Vernon in 1799, Martha Washington's husband, and so on. Sometimes the description of one thing includes reference to another. Thus, describing George Washington as "Martha's husband" makes reference to Martha as well as George. Sometimes a description may make reference to a future time and place, as when we say, "The man who owned Mount Vernon in 1799 was born in 1732."

This means that we can describe a cause and its effect in different ways. Thus, we may say that the *Titanic*'s striking the iceberg caused it to sink, or we may say that the striking of an iceberg by the fastest ship on the Atlantic in 1912 caused the sinking of the largest vessel in the White Star Line. Someone ignorant of the fact that the fastest ship on the Atlantic in 1912 was also the largest ship in the White Star Line might find the second causal claim less informative than the first or perhaps even misleading. But both are true, and both report the same causal sequence.

Let's consider the following claim: The sinking of the *Titanic* was caused by the event that caused the *Titanic* to sink. Well, this looks like the degenerate case of an uninformative causal claim, but is it still a causal statement, one asserting a *contingent* connection between two distinct events? Or is it true by the definition of cause and effect? Once we bear in mind that the same event may be described in many different ways, our answer to this question must be yes; the statement still reports a contingent causal claim. For the *Titanic*'s striking of the iceberg is identical to what we describe as "the event that caused the *Titanic* to sink." If we substitute the former description into the statement above, we get the right answer: The sinking was caused by the striking.

But in our degenerate case the events are "logically connected" in that the description of the cause refers to the effect. Yet the connection it claims to obtain is still contingent. True, the description is no longer *explanatory*; it is, as we said, uninformative, useless in any significant inquiry; it tells us almost nothing more than we already knew: Namely, the effect, the *Titanic*'s sinking, occurred, and it had a cause.

Suppose, however, that we didn't know any more about why the *Titanic* sank than that it did so and that it was the effect of some event or other. This is the situation we would be in if we did not know any other description true of the event that caused the sinking besides the uninformative one that it caused the sinking. We would be in the position of the insurance investigator or detective who, confronted with an event, must find an explanation for it. He searches for another true and informative description of the event uninformatively described as the cause of the accident or crime. Causal inquiry always starts with this sort of ignorance, reflected in an uninformative description of the cause logically connected to the effect. Thus, just because true descriptions link events logically, it does not follow that they are not also linked causally.

The moral of the story for beliefs, desires, and actions may seem clear. Beliefs and desires are usually described in terms that make reference to the actions they produce. So there is a logical link between the descriptions we use to identify beliefs and desires on the one hand and actions on the other, but from this it does not follow that beliefs and desires are not causes of actions, nor that [L] or some improvement on it cannot be a law of human action.

Thus the logical-connection argument turns out to be too weak to show that beliefs and desires cannot be causes. But it does reveal why the explanation of actions by beliefs and desires often seems so empty. If I say, "Smith carried an umbrella because he wanted to," this may be a causal claim, but it is as close to an empty description of the cause of Smith's action as one can come. Saying "Smith carried an umbrella because he believed doing so would help attain his desires" is only slightly less uninformative. And accepting either provides no means to predict what Smith will do tomorrow.

Moreover, what if it turns out that there are no descriptions of beliefs, desires, or actions that we can actually *discover*, no matter how much we search, that link them contingently instead of logically? Or what if it turns out that we found such descriptions of beliefs and desires, but that they only enable us to explain what people do as "mere" behavior instead of action? Then we would be in the position of a detective who knows in principle that his crime won't be solved because he can't uncover any informative description of the crime's cause.

But this conclusion, that there are no descriptions of beliefs, desires, or actions that can even conceivably be independent of one another, is one widely accepted in the philosophy of psychology. Its ramifications for the philosophy of social science are very great. For if this conclusion is right, even though desire/belief explanations of actions do link causes to their effects, their explanatory power does not consist in this fact. This suggests to some naturalists that we surrender such explanations and search for more satisfactory causal explanations of human behavior. Among interpretationalists the conclusion is an argument for surrendering the aim of causal explanations of action. Instead we should attempt to determine in what the evident and unarguable explanatory power of folk psychology consists. The first of these strategies is adopted by behaviorism. The second is that of hermeneutics. The next two chapters take up these strategies in turn.

Before we consider either of these two extreme views, however, we need to be convinced of the thesis that motivates them: Beliefs and desires may be causes, but we can never find descriptions of them independent enough from one another to enable us to frame laws about them that have much informative content or improvable predictive power. Finding evidence for this claim takes us into the heart of contemporary philosophy of psychology.

Intentionality

All three of the variables of folk psychology, desire, belief, action, are "intentional." This term has a special meaning in philosophy, though one that is related to its ordinary meaning of purposefulness. To say that a state of mind, like belief, for example, is intentional in the philosopher's sense (and this is the only sense in which the term will be used throughout this work) is to say that it has "propositional content"—that beliefs "contain"—in some sense—statements. Thus, there cannot be a belief without a statement believed. Belief, it is often said, is a relation between a sentient creature and a statement: x believes that p. When we describe a belief of ours or claim another has a belief, the linguistic expression following the "that" in our statement is a grammatically complete sentence, one that expresses some proposition, which is true or false. Thus, "Stalin believed that Hitler would not attack Russia" is a sentence that contains another sentence within it: "Hitler would not attack Russia." The mental state that the whole sentence attributes to Stalin presumably must itself "contain" this statement.

The quotation marks around the word "contain" remind us that no one understands exactly how the physical matter in our brains can "contain" (store and retrieve) statements and that the use of the term "contain" is at best metaphorical. The puzzle about how the gray matter of the brain can represent the way the world is or, in the case of a desire, the way someone wants it to be has been a central problem for philosophy since its beginnings. It is not an easy problem to recognize. But many of those who do recognize it base their opposition to a naturalistic approach to man, whether in psychology or in the other social sciences, on the alleged insolubility of this problem.

When we say that mental states contain statements about, or representations of, the world, the term "contains" is metaphorical because there is no suggestion that the statement is "written" in any language on or in the synapses of the brain. Why not? Because to take take this claim literally seems to involve an absurdity. Consider a library card catalogue. The ink marks on each card in the catalogue represent a book. But they do so because there are library users who *interpret* the ink marks. These ink marks and the cards they are on don't *intrinsically* and *directly* represent anything; they are just pigment on pieces of wood pulp. It is perfectly conceivable for such ink marks to have been formed on pieces of wood pulp by accident, in the way that a cloud might resemble a face or a tree might naturally take on the shape of the letter Y, without the intervention of any agent who wanted it to represent the letter Y. Only the existence of sentient creatures who treat the ink marks as having a meaning can give the cards and the ink marks their representational character.

Now consider the gray matter. When a statement about the world, like "the sun is setting," is represented in one part of the brain, b', who is the interpreter who treats the configuration of synapses at b' as expressing this statement? Can we say that the mind reads the meaning off the configuration at b'? Yes, but then we have admitted that the mind is distinct from the brain, and we must face all the puzzles about how a nonphysical mind can represent and how it could possibly influence physical matter like the brain.

Is it more attractive to suppose that there is some other part of the brain, b'', "reading" the statement off the gray matter at b'? If we are tempted to say yes, we must face the same question all over again for b'', the part of the brain that does the reading. For it to read, it must represent, somewhere within it, the meaning of what it reads in the synapses at b'. Let's call this part of b'', which represents the statement b'' reads off b', the subsystem b'''. But the same question arises for b'''. We are off on an infinite regress, and we have explained nothing about how physical matter can represent the world to itself.

Those who hold that the representational powers of human thought will never be explained in terms of the activities of the brain, or any other purely physical system, have a powerful argument that social science cannot be a naturalistic enterprise. For it deals in just those vehicles of representation that cannot be explained in a scientific way: belief and desire.

Therefore, viewing ourselves as purely physical systems, how we represent the world to ourselves is a mystery. Beliefs and desires "contain" statements only in a sense that we cannot take too seriously. What is not metaphor is the idea that beliefs have some sort of *propositional content*. Indeed, this is how we distinguish one belief from another. Thus, the difference between your belief that $124 + 37 = 161$ and your belief that $125 + 34 = 159$ is given by these two different sentences that your beliefs "contain." And presumably your belief that Paris is the capital of France is an instance of the same type as my belief that

Paris is the capital of France because the two statements they contain are identical.

Wants and desires are also identified by the statements they "contain": My desire to go to the movies is the desire *that* I go to the movies. Here the content of my desire is again a whole grammatical sentence that expresses a complete proposition. The grammar of the usual way English expresses a desire obscures this fact by dropping the "that" and changing the indicative form "I go" to the infinitive "to go": "I want to go to the movies."

It is also important to bear in mind that just as we can have false beliefs, we can desire nonexistent objects. The Spanish explorer Ponce de León wanted to find the Fountain of Youth. The fact that there is no such thing did not deprive his desire of content, only of satisfaction.

One mark that desires and beliefs "contain" statements is grammatical: The sentences that describe them literally contain sentences, introduced by "that-clauses." But being described by sentences containing that-clauses is not what *makes* beliefs and desires intentional. There are many sentences in which that-clauses figure but that are not intentional: "The *Titanic*'s striking the iceberg caused it to be the case *that* the *Titanic* sank." This is a nonintentional sentence containing a that-clause introducing another whole sentence. What shows that a belief or a desire is intentional is, not the grammar of the sentence describing it, but what happens when you make certain apparently *innocent* changes in the sentences that describe it.

This is easier to explain by illustration: Take the sentence "My eleven-year-old son believes that the *Titanic* sank." Now, he knows little more about the *Titanic* than this. Among the things he doesn't know is that the *Titanic* was the largest ship in the White Star Line. But it was. Now suppose we substitute "the largest ship in the White Star Line" for "the *Titanic*" in our statement of his belief. This will turn our statement about my son's belief from a *truth* to a *falsity*, for he doesn't know that the *Titanic* was identical to the largest ship in the White Star Line, and he does not believe that the largest ship in the White Star Line sank. By contrast, make the substitution in our statement about the cause of the *Titanic*'s sinking and the result will still be a true statement, not a false one. My son, of course, has a belief about the largest ship in the White Star Line, but not "under that description." This is the sense in which the terms used to express a belief are crucial in a way that they are not crucial to express nonintentional facts.

This sensitivity of intentional states to the descriptions and terms we use to identify them is even clearer in the case of desires. Thus, "Lady Astor wanted to sail on the *Titanic*" is a true statement about that wealthy socialite's desires. But the *Titanic* is identical to the only trans-

Atlantic liner to sink on its maiden voyage. And under that description of the *Titanic*, Lady Astor certainly had no desire to sail on the *Titanic*. If we substitute "equals for equals" in the true statement that she wanted to sail on the *Titanic*, we get the false one that "Lady Astor wanted to sail on the only trans-Atlantic liner to sink on its maiden voyage." Lady Astor wanted to sail on the *Titanic* "under one description," but under another description she didn't want to.

Therefore, intentional states are ones in which we cannot freely substitute synonymous descriptions without risking the chance of changing a truth to a falsity. If we think about it, this should not really be surprising. Beliefs and desires are "subjective": They are mental or psychological states. They reflect the ways we look at the world: our points of view, which differ from each other and change as we acquire different information about the world. They represent some facts about things in the world or some state of affairs we desire. But never all the facts, the complete picture. A representation of how things are or could be must always be drawn from a perspective, one that is partial and incomplete. Now, there are many objective facts about the world that we don't represent to ourselves because we don't know them or are wrong about them. The subjectivity or incompleteness in our beliefs about the world reflects itself in this curious feature that substitutions that make no difference to truths about objective states of the world make a great deal of difference in descriptions of subjective states.

Philosophers have a special name for this feature of intentional statements. They call them "intensional"—with an *s* instead of a *t*. This is regrettable, because it breeds confusion between intentionality—a property of psychological states, and intensionality—a logical property of statements that report them. One reason philosophers use this new term "intensionality" is that there are other statements besides those reporting intentional—that is, psychological—states that are intensional, that is, are sensitive to "equals-for-equals" substitutions in their terms. We shall not concern ourselves with these other statements. But we need the notion in order to show that actions are intensional, just like their intentional causes, beliefs, and desires.

The intensionality of desires and beliefs makes the explanation of actions intensional as well and thus makes actions derivatively intentional. Consider the Spanish explorer Ponce de León: In the case of his search for the Fountain of Youth, searching cannot have been a relation between Ponce de León and any particular object hidden in the uncharted jungles of southern Florida. For there is no such object. Yet the description "searching for the Fountain of Youth" must be related to Ponce de León's behavior, for this is what he was doing. What makes his behavior the action of searching for the Fountain of Youth is that it was produced by beliefs and desires that *contain* statements about the Fountain of Youth. So the explanation of action is intentional because it results from intentional states like desire and belief.

What makes "mere" behavior into action is intentionality. Action is intentional, at least derivatively, for behavior is only action if there are intentional states—desire and belief that lead to it. Because desires and beliefs "contain propositions," action reflects them as well; and thus all of the apparatus that common sense and social science employ to describe what people do (as opposed to what merely happens to them) has an intimate connection with *language.* For it is sentences of a language that give the content of desires, beliefs, and actions, that express the propositions about the world that belief and desire relate us to. It's not just that these states "contain" statements; the statements they contain are of their *essence.* What distinguishes one belief or desire from another is the difference in the sentences they contain. When two different people have the same desire or belief the sameness is due to the identity of the statement they believe or want to be true. Change the terms in which a statement someone believes is expressed, and you may well change the belief itself. Thus, to explain an action with *full* precision, one must identify the very sentence in which the agent would describe his action and *therefore* the very sentences in which the agent would describe his beliefs and desires. The fact that we can rarely if ever do this certainly puts limits on the precision with which we explain action after the fact and restricts even more our powers to predict actions yet not taken.

It will come as no surprise to many social scientists that language is intimately connected with action and its explanation. In fact, we have in this account of intentionality perhaps the strongest argument for this claim. Many social scientists and philosophers have long held that the aim of social science is to reveal the meaning of behavior or its significance. And they have usually contrasted meaning and significance with causation as incompatible alternative aims. The analysis of the description and explanation of action as intentional doesn't just give new force to this idea. It gives it a hardheaded argument. For to give the meaning of an action is now taken out of the realm of the metaphorical and made an essential step in explaining it. We cannot explain an action till we know what action it is. We cannot know this unless we know how the agent views it, that is, under which linguistic description the agent brings it. Once we know this, we can explain it by showing its significance, its role in meeting the agent's desires, given his beliefs. Because both desires and beliefs are meaningful states of an agent, the explanation they provide action gives its meaning in a very literal sense.

Some philosophers, and many cultural anthropologists, have likened social science to language learning. Others have held the stronger view that social inquiry *is* nothing but language learning. Thus, once the anthropologist has gone native and learned the language of a hitherto strange culture, he has acquired all the resources there are for explaining the actions of his subjects; he has uncovered as much theory as there is to uncover, for now he knows the terms in which his subjects describe their behavior and express to themselves the beliefs and desires that produce it. This view of social science is pretty clearly an interpretationalist one, and we shall return to it in Chapter 4. For the moment it is enough to see how much this view is fostered by the intentionality of human action and to see what problems it makes for naturalism. This last is the subject of the next section.

Intensionality and Extensionality

But the main upshot of the intensionality of action and its determinants is that it seems to make the causal approach to human action ultimately impossible. For it shows that there is no way even in principle to provide a description of the beliefs and desires that cause action independent of one another and independent of the actions they are said to cause.

Recall the admission that [L] is employed in everyday life and in social science in order to establish the initial conditions, which are then harnessed together with [L] again, in order to explain an action. Indeed, [L] is also employed in order to determine whether a bit of behavior is action or not and therefore within the purview of social science instead of, say, the physiology of reflexes. For [L] not only links desires and beliefs to the action they explain, it is our tool for identifying what beliefs and desires the agent has.

In and of itself this multiple use of [L] in order to carve out its own domain of explanation, as well as to establish its own initial conditions, is not *logically* illegitimate. It is methodologically suspect, for it makes it impossible to surrender [L] in the light of any empirical evidence. Among social scientists who demand that their theories have substantial testable content, [L] will not fare well. [L] certainly does not seem to be falsifiable by any conceivable observable evidence: Whenever a person does something that looks utterly irrational, given the beliefs and desires we have attributed to him, the reasonable thing to do is to change our estimate of his beliefs and desires; in the light of really crazy beliefs and/or desires, any action will look rational. We could, of course, decide that the behavior really is irrational, but then we wouldn't explain it as action, but rather as a form of pathological behavior. What we cannot do is give up [L] to preserve the original estimates of agents' beliefs and desires. For [L] is what we use in order to estimate the beliefs and desires we would be giving up [L] to preserve. If our explanatory generalizations must be falsifiable, then [L] must be surrendered as a causal law.

But the demand that our explanatory hypotheses must be falsifiable is generally viewed as too strong a demand on scientific theorizing. It neglects the fact that theoretical hypotheses often make no claims about observation directly and thus cannot be tested except when brought together with other hypotheses. The actual or merely conceivable falsification would cast doubt on the whole set of hypotheses needed to derive the tested observational result. Under these circumstances, a favored hypothesis can be retained, no matter what observations are made, by making suitable adjustments in the other hypotheses needed to test it. For example, $PV = rT$ cannot be tested by observing the temperature, pressure, and volume of a gas unless we add hypotheses to it about how heat affects the length of a column of mercury—the hypothesis that guides thermometer construction. Any divergence between observed and predicted values for pressure, given temperature and volume, can always be blamed on faulty measuring devices or on the falsity of the hypothesis about thermal expansion of mercury columns. We can revise our measuring hypotheses instead of the ideal gas law.

If no general law is strictly falsifiable, then [L] can hardly be held to this standard. The real problem for [L] isn't testability, it's that in applying and improving [L], we need to formulate the right sort of auxiliary hypotheses about desires, beliefs, and actions that will enable us to test and improve it. Even in their absence, [L] might still be said to convey some minimum causal force, as, for example, illustrated in its powers to guide our most basic everyday expectations about how others will and will not behave. If we could but provide an alternative means to establish [L]'s domain and its initial conditions, then we could in fact proceed to test [L] and begin to improve it.

Now, what the intensionality of our descriptions of beliefs, desires, and actions shows is that no such alternative means will ever be found. There are only two sources for a determination of what someone believes or desires: his behavior or his brain. What we need is something that will "measure" what a person believes by some distinct effect of the belief, in the way that a thermometer measures heat by its quite distinct effect, the *height* of a column of mercury or alcohol. We need an equation with a belief (or a desire) on one side of the equal sign and a brain state or description of behavior on the other. But this is impossible because something will always be missing from the brain or behavior side of the equation: intensionality. The description of behavior or brain states is never intensional. It is, in the philosopher's lingo, *extensional*. In fact, it is widely held that all of the rest of science, biological, chemical, physical, and mathematical, can be expressed in extensional terms. That is, any true description of a bit of mere behavior or of a brain state, whether in the language of anatomical displacement, physiology, cytology, molecular biology, chemistry, or electromagnetic theory, will remain true whenever we substitute equivalent descriptions into it, no matter how farfetched.

Providing an equation that identifies the extensional facts about brain or behavior in which a representation consists in fact constitutes a solution to the mind-body problem. Of course, we can just assert that every intentional state is identical to some brain state or other. But this is no solution to our problem. For it does not enable us to identify the belief or desire that any particular brain state constitutes. But if what I believe is a function of all or most of my other beliefs and desires, then my belief state is identical with the state of a big chunk of my whole cerebrum. But no description of that much of my brain could be used to provide a useful "thermometer."

If the intensionality of mental-state descriptions is missing from the description of the brain states that we attempt to use as indicators, then the equation must be wrong. And, in contrast, if the description of brain states or behavior is intensional, we have not solved our problem, but simply shifted it to a new level. For now we will need a test for the intensional content of a piece of behavior or a brain state. (Recall the discussion of the mystery of how physical matter can represent the way the world is: "The Logical-Connection Argument," earlier in this chapter.)

Philosophers of psychology have expressed this point by saying that mental states are not *reducible* to behavior or brain states. The problem they face is the ancient one of the mind and the body: How is the former related to the latter, and what kind of a thing is the mind anyway? Philosophers of the other social sciences may think they can ignore such arcane questions. But in the end they cannot. For the modern version of the mind-body problem is that of how physical matter can represent, or have content, in light of the fact that a complete description of it will be extensional and never intensional. This becomes a problem for philosophers of social science when they realize that the only way to justify its explanatory strategy as scientific, or to improve on its unity and precision, is by showing the "measurability" of naturalistic social sciences' causes by means that the rest of science recognizes. Only if such linkage is possible will there be, even in principle, alternative means for identifying [L]'s domain of application, and determining the occurrence of its initial conditions, that are independent of [L]. Because such linkage is impossible, it looks as though the conclusion of the logical-connection argument is right after all, even though the argument is unsound. For there is no description, known or unknown, of the intentional causes of action, which is itself *extensional*, and thus none that is independent of a description of their effects. [L] thus turns out not even to be of limited employment as a causal regularity, for the elements it connects cannot even in principle be shown to bear contingent relations to one another.

This is a pessimistic conclusion for the naturalist who hopes to meet scientific standards in the explanation of human *action*. Whether it is too pessimistic hinges on the resolution of fundamental metaphysical problems about the nature of mind and its relation to the body. Equally the answer rests on deep epistemological issues about the possibility of empirical testing and its relation to scientific knowledge. In the next chapter we explore the effects of this sort of pessimism on some naturalistic social scientists. In Chapter 4 we turn to the ramifications of this pessimism about naturalistic theories of human action for the opposing view. We shall see how antinaturalists draw optimistic conclusions from it about the character of a nonscientific approach to human behavior.

It is worth keeping in mind that some social scientists will turn their backs on both of these alternatives and indeed on the whole project of explaining individual behavior. On their view, the subject matter of the social sciences or at least one particular social science—sociology—is large groups of people and the institutions in which their interaction consists. These social scientists and the philosophers who agree with them are called "holists": They not only insist that such "social wholes" are the proper subject of one or more of the social sciences, but they go on to claim that such wholes are not themselves explainable by appeal to theories of individual action. They will be indifferent to the present problems. But they face equally serious ones of their own. Holism's prospects and problems are dealt with in Chapter 5.

Introduction to the Literature

This chapter connects problems in the philosophy of psychology to traditional questions in philosophy of the social sciences about the nature of explanation. The centrality of action explanations to social science is emphasized in both the methodological and substantive work of Max Weber, one of the founding fathers of sociology. The debate about what Weber called *Verstehen*—empathetic understanding and "ideal types"—that is, unrealistic assumptions in explanatory models, began before his work, but its twentieth-century form is due largely to his formulation of the issues. See M. Weber, *The Methodology of the Social*

Sciences. The role and nature of idealizations in social science is treated in Chapters 3 and 6 below.

An excellent introduction to the contemporary philosophy of psychology and the problems of intentionality is Paul Churchland, *Matter and Consciousness.*

The demand that there be a law connecting desires, beliefs, and actions reflects the thesis that scientific explanation must involve laws. For a long time this question was the most widely discussed topic in the philosophy of social science. Several of the most influential arguments in favor of the cover-law model's applicability to human action were written by Carl Hempel and have been collected in an anthology of his papers, *Aspects of Scientific Explanation.* See, especially, "The Function of General Laws in History." See also his essay, "Rational Action," in *Proceedings of the APA,* 1962. These views are challenged in William Dray, *Law and Explanation in History.* Dray's introduction to the philosophy of history discusses this issue lucidly. Section 4 of Krimerman's anthology and Section 5 of Brodbeck's include important contributions to this debate. Churchland's paper "The Logical Character of Action Explanations," in *Philosophical Review,* defends [L] as a law cogently.

The claim that [L] and propositions like it are necessary truths is defended in several works, P. Winch's *Idea of a Social Science,* R. S. Peters's *Concept of Motivation,* A. Melden's *Free Action,* and most ably in Charles Taylor's *Explanation of Human Behavior.* These works are the source of what has come to be called the logical-connection argument. The most powerful rejoinder to these arguments is found in D. Davidson, "Actions, Reasons, and Causes," *Journal of Philosophy,* 1968, reprinted in Davidson, *Essays on Actions and Events.*

Problems of intentionality and intensionality are among the most vexed in philosophy. The best introduction to the subject is D. C. Dennett, *Content and Consciousness.* S. Stich's *From Folk Psychology to Cognitive Science* pursues the matter further and expounds as well as criticizes alternative accounts of intentionality, including the view that there is a language of thought, written into our brains. This view is defended by J. Fodor, especially in *The Language of Thought* and *Representations.* By contrast, John Searle, *Intentionality,* draws very different conclusions from those of these philosophers about belief and desire. So does Thomas Nagel, in *The View from Nowhere.*

3

Behaviorism

BEHAVIORISM is a pretty accurate name for a variety of responses social scientists have made to the problems of intentional explanation described in Chapter 2. Some of these responses are the direct result of reflection on the sorts of problems laid out in that chapter. But behaviorism reflects a general frustration with intentional explanations of action, together with a diagnosis of why intentional strategies don't work and a suggestion about what should replace them.

What behaviorists seem to agree on is that the test of good social science should be predictively successful explanatory unification of observable phenomena, that is, of *behavior,* whether of individuals or groups. Or at least social science should aim at consistent improvement in that direction. Behaviorists also agree that intentional explanations have not met this challenge. Some behaviorists have given explanations of this fact rather like that offered in Chapter 2. But most behaviorists simply express skepticism about "theory" in general and especially about hypotheses that involve attributing undetectable mechanisms—particularly, mental ones—to people. For there seems no way to test such claims directly and independently. Intentional states are especially objectionable to sophisticated behaviorists, for not only are they unobservable, it is difficult to see how they could even be physically embodied causes of behavior. Yet it is such causes that we should seek.

Not all behaviorists use that term to describe themselves, and some will not even recognize themselves as behaviorists. But we can identify movements in each of the social sciences that have endorsed the position described here as behaviorist.

In experimental psychology behaviorism is a well-known label and in fact encompasses sharply divergent views on some issues. As a methodology, behaviorism dates back to the early twentieth century, but its most visible recent exponent has been B. F. Skinner. Taking their lead from Skinner, psychological behaviorists hold that the aim of their science is not to understand the mind, but to systematize observable behavior. Systematizing behavior means providing general statements that enable us to correlate observable environmental conditions with the behavior they trigger. For reasons we shall explore in this chapter, behaviorists hold that this systematization cannot be accomplished by an intentional theory. Social psychologists and behavioral sociologists, like George Homans, have adopted this view and adapted the theory that psychological behaviorists formulated to deal with social phenomena.

In political science, the label is slightly changed: Behavior*al*ism is widely held to be a revolutionary development with much the same goals and effects in the study of politics as it had in psychology. Behavioralists advocate substituting the study of observed political behavior for the study of political institutions through the documents that codify them. In general, they have been concerned with explaining what people do, rather than what they say they do. Their aim is generalization with predictive power. Of course, many behavioralist political scientists have no animus against intentional theories to account for the data their research generated. But this is because, as we shall see, behavioralism in political science and economics often employs an intentional theory without taking it literally.

In economics and the part of political science that takes its methodological inspiration and its theory from economics, behaviorism has two forms: Sometimes it embodies a certain interpretation of the intentional theory of rational choice that purports to circumvent the difficulties intentionality raises; and sometimes it excludes from the intended domain of economic theory the actions of individual economic agents altogether, so that the problem of explaining their actions is not one economics need deal with at all.

Behaviorism's Attack on Teleology

Behaviorism begins with despair about the limits of folk psychology and other intentional theories that attempt to improve upon it. Such theories all too often substitute jargon terms, like "drive" for the ordinary notion of "desire" or "want," although it turns out these terms mean exactly the same as the words they replace or make no improvement in the explanatory powers of the theory. And often the intentional theories rely on introspection—looking into our own minds— for hypotheses that explain our actions and for evidence testing such hypotheses. But the behaviorist argues that introspective testing makes the "mind" judge, jury, and executioner of its own theories about itself, when in fact we know almost nothing about our own minds and nothing directly about other people's minds.

Behaviorism takes seriously the philosophical problem of "other minds": the question of how we can know the apparently private mental states of others, if all we have access to is their behavior. The philosophical skeptic challenges us to prove that others even have minds: "For all I know, everyone else might be a robot." Behaviorism resolves this issue by arguing that for purposes of psychology we don't need to solve the problem. We don't need the hypothesis that people have minds—mental states like belief and desire, sensations like pain or colors.

The reason we have no need of such hypotheses is that psychology is not the study of the mind, but the science of behavior. One argument for this view is known as "philosophical behaviorism": a thesis about the meaning of psychological terms and not a thesis about the facts those terms are used to describe. According to philosophical behaviorism, psychology is about behavior, and only behavior, because even statements that look as if they are about the mind are really disguised claims about behavior or translatable into statements about behavior. Thus, when we say someone believes it will rain, this is not a report of some inaccessible inner state; rather, it means that that person will be disposed to carry an umbrella, or a raincoat, or stay indoors, et cetera.

Now, even if we allow an "et cetera" in a definition, this one will not do. For the belief will only be expressed by such behavior if the agent *wants* to stay dry. So the definition must include, along with descriptions of behavior, a statement about the person's *wants*. But what a person wants turns on other *beliefs*. So, the clause about a person's beliefs required to make the definition correct deprives the definition of its behavioral character.

The idea that we can translate away statements about the mind, and thus show that there is no mind (as distinct from behavior), did not last long either among philosophers or psychologists. It's worth mentioning only to distinguish it sharply from "psychological behaviorism," a far more substantial doctrine. Its claim that psychology is the study of behavior does not involve denying that there is a mind. Rather it declares that questions about the mind are irrelevant on the following grounds: First, human behavior can be explained without appeal to the mind; second, it cannot be explained by such appeals; and third, questions about the mind are themselves unanswerable in any case. Therefore, for purposes of science, we might as well just ignore the mind.

The upshot is that intentional hypotheses like [L] cannot explain human actions because [L] is mentalistic, that is, refers to mental states of belief and desire. Behaviorists, like Skinner, are generally in agreement with Chapter 2's reasons for [L]'s failure as a causal hypothesis. But they locate the problem even deeper than the obstacles to any real testing or predictive improvement of folk psychology. Behaviorists view intentional explanations as the last refuge of a form of scientific theory that started out, with Aristotle, as the ruling explanatory strategy for everything and has been shown by five hundred years of scientific advance to be incapable of really explaining anything.

In Aristotle's physics, biology, and explanation of behavior, the crucial notion is that of *purpose*, or goal. All natural and human phenomena were explained in terms of the purposes served by behavior. Thus, objects fall to earth because they seek their "natural place," birds migrate in order to survive the winter, and people do those things that serve their ends. Such explanations are called *teleological*—from the Greek "telos," meaning end.

We can see the difficulty of such explanations: They involve later, future states of a thing explaining its earlier, past states. But such an explanation cannot be *causal*. For the future cannot cause the past. So, how future states explain is a mystery. One traditional solution to this mystery among "prescientific" peoples is to adapt the desire/belief model of human action to the explanation of natural processes. Explaining human behavior in terms of prior states of belief and desire *seems* to avoid this problem because the goals are represented in the causes of behavior—the mental states that bring it about. So before Isaac Newton, the most popular way to underwrite teleological explanations of why rocks fall to earth or birds fly south was to appeal to an intelligent creator of the universe and to explain what happens in the world in terms of his purposes, his desires.

Thus, birds fly south because God designed them that way, and he did it so that they would survive the winter. The purpose that flying south serves isn't the birds'—it's God's. It is relatively easy to explain anything that happens by this strategy, "it's God's will," though correctly identifying the purposes served by phenomena is no trivial undertaking. For example, William Harvey's discovery that the function—the purpose— of the heart's beating is to circulate the blood required great observational and experimental accomplishment. The teleological form of explanation thus leaves much real work for the scientist. But the explanation worked by harnessing together God, or some intelligent designer of the universe, with particular hypotheses that render his will intelligible to us.

The history of natural science is the history of the shrinking of the domain of this explanatory strategy. It's not just that atheists, who do not believe in an intelligent designer, can't avail themselves of this sort of explanation. Rather, those who do believe in God discovered that they could provide more accurate and more powerful explanations of phenomena, explanations that were not teleological, that didn't involve attributing purposes to anyone. These discoveries started with Galileo, Kepler, and most of all with Newton, who showed that the motion of objects could be explained and predicted to extraordinary degrees of accuracy by appeal to the position and momentum alone of the objects, without any reference to what purposes their motions might have served. This kind of causal theory, which had no need for teleology, has been the dominant explanatory strategy in physical science to the present day.

This kind of theory has been preferred to teleological explanations, not just because it needs no hypothesis about God or about inanimate objects having purposes, but also because it is so much better at predicting phenomena than any teleological theory. After all, even if we can be sure what God's purposes are, we still can't tell how he will attain them—that is, what behavior aimed at this purpose will be produced. For example, if God wants birds to survive the winter, there are many ways he could have arranged it besides having them fly south in September. Once we see what the birds do, we can explain it after the fact. But before we see what they do, knowing his purposes doesn't narrow down the alternatives enough to enable us to make a prediction.

But, of course, since Newton few scientists of any kind have been willing to appeal to God to explain phenomena, and for a long time this has made teleological explanations even more problematic, especially in biology, where teleological description and explanation are impossible to eliminate. For in the absence of someone's intentional states, there seemed no basis for identifying the purposes and functions served by an organism's behavior. And yet it seems undeniable that biological behavior serves *purposes*. What biologists needed was either an alternative explanatory strategy that made no appeal to teleology or a theory that provides a purely causal underlying mechanism for biological teleology. Charles Darwin's theory of natural selection is sometimes said to have done the first of these, and sometimes said to have done the second. In either case it solved the biological problem of teleology.

Darwin's theory taught that the purposive *appearance* of biological phenomena is the result of a large amount of blind, unpurposeful heritable variation—the production in an entirely random way of many different traits, including behavior, and the natural selection of the fittest of them. By fittest, Darwin meant likeliest to survive and enhance the organism's chances of reproduction. Thus, flying south came about because those birds that just happened to be genetically programmed to move away from cold weather survived and reproduced, whereas those not so programmed didn't. And how did the genetic programming arise? It arose, along with many other less adaptive behavioral traits, through the random recombination of genes, or mutation, or some other entirely causal, nonteleological process.

Some biologists and philosophers argue that Darwin's theory showed that teleology is just as unneeded, indeed just as unscientific, in biology as it is in physics. When we talk about biological functions or goals, we are just using a shorthand for Darwinian adaptation—variation and natural selection. We are not talking about real purposes in nature. Biology is thus every bit as causal as physics.

Other biologists hold a less radical thesis. They claim that Darwin's theory didn't explain away the appearance of teleology; rather, it justified teleological explanation in biology by showing that underlying such explanations was a purely causal mechanism. We don't need to settle this dispute. For our purposes the moral of the story is that the appeal to *intentions* has been as ruthlessly read out of biology as it was cast out of physics. Both the life sciences and the physical ones are thoroughly causal disciplines, committed to the search for laws that will provide causal explanation.

This leaves only the social sciences as the last refuge of an explanatory strategy that started, over two thousand years ago, as the ruling paradigm in all of science. And the behaviorist wants to rid social science of it as well, to substitute causal theory for teleological theory on its home territory. Why? Not because of some atheistical denial that there are intentional states, but because of an agnostic conviction that appeal to such states won't provide the kind of causal theory of human behavior the rest of science aims at. The reason is that despite the appearance of being causal, the explanations of folk psychology really are teleological after all. First of all, behaviorists argue, they cannot be underwritten by appeal to an underlying causal mechanism like the one Darwin provided for biological explanations. Recall the problem of Chapter 2: We cannot identify beliefs and desires in terms of brain states or other signs independent of their effects, actions. Desires and beliefs look like distinct prior causes of action, but they are not distinct enough from their future effects to explain them really informatively. But, behaviorists argue, if such explanations are not informative, they cannot be causal, for behaviorists hold that providing factual information is the hallmark of a causal explanation.

If intentional explanations can't be causal, then, the behaviorist claims, they must be disguised teleological explanations. To see this, suppose I explain someone's going to a food store by pointing to his desire to get food and his beliefs that food is available in the store he's heading for. If the only way I can identify his desire for food is by citing the food he eventually gets, then the cause of his behavior, the desire to get food, is identified only by reference to an event that occurs later than the action his desire explains—heading to the store. This reveals that the apparently causal explanation, in terms of prior desires, must make covert reference to a future event, the satisfaction of his desire, in order to explain an earlier event, his going to the store. The apparently causal explanation is really a disguised teleological one. And the teleology is ineliminable because the only way to identify his desire is in terms of the event that ultimately satisfies it. Of course sometimes desires are unfulfilled. For instance, our hungry person may be run over on the way to the store and never fulfill his desire. But this makes matters worse. For now if his going to the store is explained by the desire to get food, it is ultimately explained by an event that never happens at all, his getting the food.

Therefore, intentional explanations are at least covertly teleological, the behaviorists argue. And in their objections to teleology, history is on their side. The replacement of teleological forms of explanation by causal ones has been a consistent trend over the past four hundred years. Moreover, it has been a trend with big payoffs for increasing explanatory unification and predictive precision that teleology cannot obtain. And it should make sense to effect this same replacement in the social sciences as well.

Some philosophers and social scientists will add philosophical arguments to this historical one. They read the historical record as vindicating a metaphysical world view known as materialism. This is the idea that the world is composed of nothing but matter in motion— from quarks to stars, matter behaving in accordance with mechanistic laws, which together with initial conditions determine the world's future— completely or, if quantum mechanics is right, to precisely determined levels of probability. This is a world with no room for teleology and with no room for irreducible intentional states. Our belief that there are such states is an illusion, perhaps even a temporarily adaptive one, fostered by a misleading reliance on introspection. Behaviorists do not openly acknowledge such a view, for they claim to be agnostic about matters of metaphysical philosophy, without a direct payoff for observation. But to the extent that a scientific method and the arguments for it do reflect metaphysical commitments, materialism is a view behaviorists should be comfortable with. Psychology is thus the science of behavior, because in the end, that's all there is for any science to study: matter in motion—behavior.

The Experimental Analysis of Behavior

What theory of human behavior do behaviorists offer in place of folk psychology and its reliance on [L]? One alternative ruled out by most behaviorists is a theory that explains human behavior in terms of neurological events and processes in the brain. The reasons for this elimination are, however, purely tactical. We could, to be sure, eventually provide the neurological causes for any particular action of any particular person at a particular place and time. But for the purposes of social science, this explanation would be useless, even if we were prepared to wait for the time when neuroscience would be well enough established to provide this sort of information.

Neurological fine structure differs so much between people that the details of our explanation in one case would probably not be applicable to anyone else doing exactly the same thing—for instance saying, "please hold the door." And yet the details are just what is crucial to neurology's claims to improve on the predictive weakness of folk psychology. As scientists, psychologists want to explain *kinds* of behavior, not individual instances of it. Explaining individual instances is crucial to testing our theories, but predicting future events requires laws and theories about the *kinds* of events these future events will exemplify. The kind-vocabulary of neuroscience will include synapse firings, and acetylcholine production, but it won't include "interrupting a speaker," "choosing coffee ice cream over vanilla," or "setting the table."

The behaviorist aims to develop a theory of behavior that can be systematically linked up with neuroscience. In fact, in the ideal case, the laws and theories of behavior will themselves be explainable by neuroscientific ones, in the way that the behavior of chemical substances is explained by the laws governing the atoms that compose them. But this "reduction" of psychology to neuroscience is a long way off, and it will never be accomplished anyway unless behavioral psychology first finds some laws and theories that will supersede and improve on folk psychology. Otherwise, there is nothing to link to neuroscience.

Behaviorists themselves hold that there is another reason we can neglect neuroscience in the short run, for behavior, both human and animal, is in fact largely a function of environmental factors alone. Or at least there are predictively powerful explanatory generalizations about behavior that link it directly with observable environmental variables. In fact, behaviorists like Skinner and his followers lay claim to having formulated a generalization of this sort to replace our intentional law [L]. This is the "law of effect," the leading principle of "operant" behaviorism. Examining that law will be a convenient way to assess the claims and prospects for behaviorism as a more scientific alternative to folk psychology.

Recall the distinction that specifies the domain of social science. It is the difference between "mere" behavior and action—the product of beliefs and desires. According to behaviorists, this distinction needs to be replaced if folk psychology is to be superseded, just as Aristotle's distinction between rest and motion was superseded by Newton's distinction between rest (including rectilinear motion) and acceleration. Skinner's distinction is between "mere" behavior—roughly, reflexes like blinking—and what he calls "operant" behavior. Reflex behavior can generate relatively complicated results, provided that it is properly linked to environmental conditions: Recall the famous experiments of the Russian psychologist Pavlov. By associating the sound of a bell with the presentation of food, he was able to get dogs to salivate when the bell rang alone, in the absence of food. However, it's clear that little of what we call human action can be the result of conditioned reflex.

But, claim behaviorists, human action can be the result of conditioning operant behavior. Operant behavior is behavior emitted by the organism as a result of neural causes that are too varied and irregular to be of interest, unlike reflex behavior, which is produced at least originally as the routine result of a single, easy-to-identify neurological reaction to a single, easy-to-identify stimulus. Operant behavior is the sort of thing we might describe in ordinary terms as voluntary. But once emitted, these more complicated bits of behavior become subject to environmental conditioning, in accordance with the law of effect:

[LE] If emitted behavior is reinforced, it will be repeated with greater frequency (or intensity or duration). If it is punished, it will be repeated with lower frequency (or intensity or duration).

Roughly, the law of effect claims that once emitted, for whatever cause, behavior that as a matter of contingent fact provides some sort of benefit—the reinforcement—to the organism is likely to recur. Behavior whose frequency, or intensity, or duration can be increased by such reward or reinforcement is operant behavior. And so is behavior that once emitted will be reduced in frequency if it results in some sort of loss or cost to the organism. All human action, on this view, is operant behavior, and its occurrence is explained by the frequency with which it has been reinforced or punished in the past.

Skinner first exploited the law of effect in the explanation of the relatively complex behavior of rats and pigeons. By providing them with food pellets after the emission of some behavior like bar pressing or key pecking, he was able to get them to emit this behavior in a predictable fashion. By varying the schedules of reinforcement, he was able to vary the frequency per unit time of the behavior and to control other aspects of it. By reinforcing successive refinements of emitted behavior—"shaping" through "response differentiation"—he was able to get these animals to undertake complex and highly unnatural movements and to produce remarkable feats of discrimination. A pigeon can be trained in this way to discriminate dozens of different geometrical shapes. By associating an environmental feature with a reinforcing stimulus—"secondary stimulation"—operant behavior can ultimately be controlled by factors without any connection to the direct reinforcement of the organism. For example, monkeys can be trained through the right sort of reinforcement to respond to tokens or chips—money—that they can exchange for direct reinforcers like food.

Skinner was able to replicate his experiments in a way that convincingly confirmed the theory with regard to the behavior of these animals. What is more, by identifying and employing appropriate reinforcers, by shaping and secondary stimulation, psychologists have wrought remarkable changes in the behavior of people, for example, psychiatric patients otherwise impervious to treatment.

Skinner has certainly not been timid about claiming that all human behavior we identify as action is scientifically to be explained as operant behavior, caused by the complex and varied arrangement of reinforcements in our environments. Subtle and sophisticated behavior, like speech, for example, is the result of shaping and secondary reinforcement. Of course, as adults teach babies to talk, the adults do not realize that they are engaging in operant conditioning, that by their behavior they are setting up schedules of reinforcement, shaping, and associating secondary reinforcers in such a way that a child successively refines emitted noises into speech. And once a child has learned to speak, its verbal behavior continues right through adulthood to be subject to reinforcement and punishment, as is the rest of human behavior, by nature and by other people.

One thing should stand out about this theory: It seems a thoroughly teleological one. It explains a bit of behavior in terms of apparently *subsequent* reinforcement. For example, people speak grammatically because they are reinforced *after* doing so and punished *after* failing to do so—by grimaces and corrections. Here we have a claim just like the biological assertion that the heart beats in order to circulate the blood. But the behaviorist claims that this is entirely innocent teleology or perhaps only apparent teleology. For it is either shorthand for, or backed up by, an entirely causal theory, indeed exactly the same type of theory that backs up the functional analysis of the heartbeat: Operant behavior is another form of natural selection. Just as successive hereditary variations are shaped by selection for their consequences, so successive bits of behavior are selected for their consequences. In evolution, the consequences are the survival and demographic expansion of the species. In individual behavior, the consequences are the survival and flourishing of the individual. "My heart beats in order to circulate the blood" means roughly that my heart beats because hearts have been selected in the past for their efficiency in circulating the blood. "I speak grammatically because this behavior is reinforced" means that speaking grammatically has been reinforced in the past, and therefore it recurs now.

In both evolutionary selection and operant selection there is a question about mechanisms. How does the selection of hearts for circulation in the distant past get connected to my heart's present behavior? Natural selection is silent on this question, but the answer is provided by genetics and physiology. The genes bear the program of the heart's structure. Nature didn't select the most efficient hearts directly; rather, it selected the genes that encoded successively more efficient heart structures. These genes are passed down by reproduction, thus providing the mechanism connecting the evolutionary past to the present.

Operant behaviorism requires a similar mechanism. Presumably, this mechanism is ultimately to be given by neuroscience: Somehow the reinforcement of earlier behavior must rearrange the neurology of the individual in such a way as to increase the frequency of the behavior's occurrence later; and punishment of behavior must neurologically extinguish it. Indeed a start has already been made on this process in neuroscience. But just as evolutionary biology can do some things independent of and without the required genetic theory of underlying mechanisms, so too, it is argued, experimental psychology can do much without the mechanism that neuroscience must ultimately provide for it.

Operant behaviorism has been an outstanding success in the laboratory: Though it has serious limitations, its power to predict and control behavior in the stereotyped conditions of the experimental analysis of animal behavior are undeniable. However, its application to human behavior, to the domain of folk psychology, has been far less successful. Indeed, it seems no more powerful in its ability to explain and predict human action, under the description operant behavior, than intentional theories have. This may simply be because operant psychology is a young science that requires far more research to parlay its undoubted successes with laboratory animals into an equally successful approach to people. As a young science it needs to be given a chance. At any rate, claim behaviorists, it does not have the obvious methodological defects of folk psychology and its intentional successors.

But in fact, what plausibility it has is said by some to derive from its being old wine in new bottles, nothing more than folk psychology translated into new jargon. Critics of behaviorism argue, first, that theories of behavior are just as teleological as the intentional theories that they are meant to supplant, and second, that they turn out to be intentional theories themselves, so that behaviorists are really just fooling themselves about their "alternative" to folk psychology.

This is a charge behaviorists will resolutely reject. They make no suggestion that organisms, rats or people, emit certain sorts of behavior because they want to be reinforced for it and believe that they will be. However, it is easy to see how an operant explanation of a bit of behavior can dovetail with an intentional one. But this is a strength and a weakness: a strength because it makes clear how any behavior explained by [L] can be explained by [LE], a weakness because it reveals that [LE] may face the same problems that [L] does unless we can identify reinforcers and stimuli independent of the behavior they control. Otherwise, reinforcers and stimuli will be in the same boat as wants and beliefs.

Indeed, [L] and [LE] dovetail so nicely that it is tempting to explain one in terms of the other. Advocates of intentional psychology will explain why reinforced behavior is emitted by pointing out that people (and maybe animals too) like reinforcements and will do what they believe necessary to secure them. Behaviorists can run the explanation in the opposite direction: People want certain things and do what they believe will secure them because these things are reinforcing. But behaviorists are not inclined to offer this explanation of folk psychology because they consider [L] to be without explanatory merit, and they consider the intentional concepts in which it is expressed to be unscientific. They don't want their explanatory notions to be closely related to those of folk psychology because this would tar them with the brush of its failures.

Yet it is very difficult to show that operant theory is really different from folk psychology or that in fact operant theory escapes from the intentional approach of folk psychology. And if operant theory doesn't, then the excuse for its present predictive weakness, that unlike folk psychology, behaviorism really is a young science, will turn out to be a hollow one.

As we shall see, the problem for behaviorism is that [LE] turns out to have all the methodological infirmities of [L]. And the best explanation for this fact is sometimes said to be that the law of effect, [LE], is just [L] dressed up in new and more scientific-sounding terms.

To distinguish itself from folk psychology, operant behaviorism must do two related things: It must provide a means for identifying environmental stimuli, reinforcers, and operant behavior independent of each other, and it must demonstrate that none of these three factors is directly or indirectly intentional. That is, it must show that they don't involve "content" or representation of the way the world is or could be.

Let's start with behavior. Behavior under the contol of operants is "learned" behavior. Behaviorists define learning as simply a change in the response rate to a certain stimulus. But what is learned? Take the case of a rat in a maze. When a rat learns the maze's configuration, so that it learns to take a direct route to the food, what is the behavior it has learned? A series of steps, twelve steps of 2 cm each straight ahead, 4 cm to the right, 2 cm to the left, and so on? No, for the rat does not always take the same number of steps of the same stride to get to the food, and sometimes it stops to scratch, sometimes it runs, and other times it walks in a leisurely way. It never takes exactly the same route at the same speed twice. Yet all these responses are examples of the learned behavior as long as it gets there fast enough. What do they all have in common? What makes them all instances of the behavior it has learned? It cannot be that they are the same because they all result in eating, for sometimes the experimenter removes the food, and yet the same behavior is produced.

It seems unavoidable to say that the behavior the rat has learned is food-finding behavior. The behavior learned thus is defined by reference to its goal. But first of all, this is improperly teleological, and second, the food is sometimes not there to be found, yet the behavior is the same. The obvious solution to this puzzle is to say that what the rat has learned isn't a set of movements with some end. What it has learned is where the food usually is. But this means it has learned something about the world—something that can be expressed in a proposition ("the food is at the end of the left alley"). To have been learned, this fact about the world must be *represented* in some state or other of the rat. We may not want to call this a state of belief about where the food is, but it is still an intentional state of some kind. Now if this is the only way to identify the behavior that the rat has learned, then we are in exactly the same boat with respect to operant behavior as we are with respect to action.

The same suspicion arises for the notion of an environmental stimulus. This is supposed to be an observable feature of the environment that leads to an operant response that can be or has been reinforced. In the case of a pigeon, it may be that the pigeon is reinforced for pecking when a button is lit, but not otherwise. In the case of animals under experimental conditions, it is relatively easy to identify stimuli. They are changes in the environment that are correlated with reinforced responses in accordance with the law of effect. If we can train a pigeon to discriminate shapes, then shapes are environmental stimuli. If we cannot train a pigeon to discriminate odors, say, by reinforcing whenever ammonia is presented and the pigeon pecks the key, and never reinforcing when it pecks the key in the presence of gasoline, then these odors are not stimuli. But notice, we are now using [LE] to test [LE]. That is, in order to establish the initial conditions that together with the law of effect explain the discriminatory behavior of the animal, we need to identify the feature of the environment that controls the behavior, what the animal discriminates. And the way we do this is by applying the law of effect to that feature in order to see whether it controls behavior. If it does, then it's a stimulus. If it doesn't control behavior, then it isn't.

Now, as we've seen with [L], this is permissible (though it weakens the testability of [LE]), provided we have some alternative means of identifying environmental stimuli. This will be especially important when we leave the laboratory and turn our attention to human behavior. What are these alternative means of identifying stimuli? Obviously, something is a stimulus if the organism can perceive it, see it, hear it, taste it, feel it, and so forth. But this can't mean simply that photons from the object fall on the retina or waves of air pressure strike the inner ear. For many things impinge on an organism's sense organs this way without being *registered* in the mind. To see a red apple is not simply to have the required sensations, it is to classify them under the right categories, such as "red" or "apple." But this looks like another case of bringing something under a description, that is, coming to have something like beliefs about it. And now we are faced with a choice between intentionality or circularity again. For if behaviorists argue that seeing a red apple is just overtly responding in an appropriate way (say, reaching for it and taking a bite out of it), then they have not provided an alternative means of identifying stimuli; they have merely redescribed the operant behavior the stimuli "control." And if behaviorists admit that seeing a red apple is bringing it under a description, they embrace the very sort of intentional theory behaviorism repudiates.

When we come to reinforcement, the situation is perhaps clearer. A reinforcer is whatever changes the organism's response rate. And again in the laboratory it is easy to vary the presence and absence of varying conditions to learn whether they are reinforcing. The results are quite remarkable, for the range of reinforcers is very broad. Included is food, of course, but saccharin too; even the opportunity to look out of a window is a powerful reinforcer for monkeys. Indeed, monkeys have been trained to solve puzzles when the only reinforcement present seems to be solving the puzzle. And the range of items humans find reinforcing is staggering. What do all these reinforcers have in common? What makes them all reinforcers? The tempting answer is that organisms, animals, and people want them, desire them, find them satisfying, et cetera. But this is not a permissible means for the behaviorist to identify reinforcers independently, for it rests on an intentional notion of want or desire.

Of course somewhere deep in the brain all reinforcers must have something neurological in common. In fact, rats in which electrodes have been implanted at the midbrain will literally work themselves to exhaustion if a bar they can press closes an electric circuit that stimulates this part of their brains. James Olds, the psychologist who undertook this particular experiment, has hypothesized that all reinforcement may operate through connection with this portion of the brain, which he called the pleasure center. But this hypothesis, like the rest of neuroscience, cannot provide any immediately useful means of identifying what is a reinforcer, and thus cannot help operant behaviorism improve on the attainments of folk psychology in the explanation and prediction of human behavior.

Without denying the important accomplishment of behaviorism in the explanation of aspects of the behavior of laboratory animals, our conclusions about this theory as an alternative to folk psychology cannot be optimistic. The motivations of behaviorism in the history of scientific progress may well be correct, and its aim of avoiding intentionality may be the right one for providing a science of human behavior. But at a minimum, this goal appears more difficult to attain than the behaviorist supposes. For the obstacles behaviorism must surmount seem identical to the ones it charges folk psychology cannot overcome. And behaviorism seems too much like folk psychology to succeed where the latter has failed. This leaves the naturalistic approach to human action no better off than it was before the behaviorist offered to solve its problems. In Chapter 4 we shall see how the antinaturalist deals with these problems. Meanwhile, we need to trace out the influence of behaviorism in economics and political science, disciplines in which "behaviorism" labels a slightly different approach to the search for improvable laws about human behavior. We shall see that in these disciplines, "behaviorism" raises more issues than it settles.

Behaviorism in the Theory of Rational Choice

Many of the motives for advocating behaviorism have force for economic theory and for aspects of political science that employ economics' theory of *rational choice*. To begin with, these disciplines need to come to grips with the problems outlined in Chapter 2, for, as we will see, rational choice theory is just folk psychology formalized. Thus the theory faces the same problems that bedevil [L]. For this reason economic theory has traditionally been accused of being either false or vacuous and untestable. We have seen that the more accurate charge these criticisms reflect is that it seems unimprovable in respect of explanatory power and predictive precision. Unlike psychological behaviorists, economists have not sought a substitute for folk psychology.

Instead they have tried either to make it more precise or to give it a new behaviorist interpretation that would undermine these criticisms.

The theory of rational choice is most easily understood from a historical approach. This approach will also make clear how economic theory responded to charges of falsity versus vacuity, by changing its claims about human action and its aims as a social science. In the nineteenth century, economists known as "marginalists" systematized economic activity on the basis of a theory of utility. They held that every economic agent could derive a certain amount of utility or satisfaction from any quantity of any commodity; and subject to the limitations of the available resources and information, each agent acquired that collection of commodities that maximized his utility. Rationality was thus defined as the maximization of available utility, and all agents were assumed to be rational. In effect utility theory was a way of ordering desires. It enabled us to dispense with the clause in [L] excluding overriding wants. It also provided a more precise, apparently quantitative theory of the strength of different wants and of how they are combined and reconciled.

These economists and their successors typically assume that agents have full information about the world, that is, they have true beliefs about all the facts relevant to their circumstances. By making this assumption, economists are able to determine agents' choices just given their utilities. Recall that given [L], we can derive action from desire, if we can hold belief constant. The full information assumption is a means of holding belief constant. For example, if a person knows all the ice-cream flavors available to him, and if we know which one he likes best, we can unerringly predict which one he chooses.

(Once economists had explored the ramifications for desire and action of holding belief constant, they shifted to holding utilities constant and considering how action was affected by variation in belief from full information to probabilities [risk] to ignorance [uncertainty]. This strategy is expounded below.)

Economists provide another restriction on [L]. They limit its application to economic actions only: choices made in the light of costs and benefits, as measured by prices. But the power and elegance of the economist's theory of choice have led economists and others to expand its range of application to all actions explained originally by [L]. They have done so by extending the notions of cost and benefit to ends and goals that don't have money prices, but still involve trade-offs and therefore "shadow prices": the cost of one action as measured by the value of another action I must forgo to do the first one. Thus, if you have to choose between two potential marriage partners, the "cost" of one is determined by what you must give up in not choosing the other. By this extension to the explanation of all human action, the theory of rational choice has come to be explicitly advocated by some as a formalization of folk psychology.

The marginalists held that the utilities associated with commodities are measurable in real units that enable us to say that an agent prefers something twice as much as something else and to say that one agent prefers a commodity more than another does because he derives more utility from it than the other does. This view is called "cardinal utility" theory. The name derives from the hypothesis that utility, like mass, comes in amounts that can be measured in *cardinal* numbers: zero units, one unit, two units, et cetera. From the assumption of cardinally measurable utility, economists were able to derive important results about how individuals' demand and supply of commodities varied with their prices. Suppose, as seems reasonable, that the amount of utility derived from an additional unit of a commodity—the so-called marginal utility—declines as more units of a commodity are acquired. For example, if you crave an apple, the amount of utility derived from an apple may be large. If you have already had two or three, the amount of utility derived from the fourth will be much smaller. If marginal utility declines, then the individual's demand for commodities will decline as their price increases. If you're hungry for apples, you will pay a fairly high price for the first apple. But if the price of the second apple is the same or higher, you will be less inclined to buy it, for the utility it provides is less than that of the first one.

The marginalists also showed that the amount of a commodity an individual would be willing to produce and sell—its supply—rises as its price increases, provided that the individual seeks to maximize profit. But this of course is just what a utility maximizer will seek do to if income can be used to purchase goods that increase utility.

Now, for each individual, we can plot on graphs the relation between price and supply and between price and demand (with price as the ordinate), and the curves will cross each other, the demand-price curve going downward and the supply-price curve going upward. But the entire market for a particular good is just the sum of the supply and demand for that good by all the individuals in the market. By adding the individual supply-and-demand curves, economic theory can derive supply-and-demand curves for an entire economy and thus show how prices work as a signaling mechanism, informing producers how much to produce of each kind of commodity and informing consumers what the real cost of consumption is for each commodity.

Marginalists not only held that utility is cardinally measurable, but they also assumed that it was "interpersonally comparable." That is, it makes sense to say how much more one person desires something than another person, for utilities give the amounts in which we can measure the strength of these desires. Marginalists were never able to show how we can interpersonally compare the utilities people derive from goods, but they assumed that this was at least in principle possible. The technicalities were to be left to the psychologist.

Utilities that come in definite units and that can be compared between people are important not only for their apparent explanatory power. They also enable the economist to make strong judgments of welfare and to advise on the distribution of benefits by the state. If utilities are measurable and if, as marginalists held, the amount of utility each successive unit of some good provides—the marginal utility—declines, then $1,000 provides fewer units of utility to a millionaire than to someone at the poverty level. Thus, a government with $1,000 to spare, committed to maximizing total utility, would be justified in giving the money to the poorer person. The notion that $1,000 gives more utility to a poor person than to a rich one seems obvious—indeed, it is another piece of folk psychology. But it cannot be true unless the difference it makes to people's levels of satisfaction is measureable in cardinal units.

Now the trouble with the claim that all economic agents are cardinal utility maximizers is that it just seems false. People frequently seem to do things that preclude the maximization of their utility. Consider acts of altruism or charity or our frequent willingness to settle for good enough when the best is available. Of course, we can defend the theory by saying that these appearances are deceptive. Altruists really enjoy their good deeds, and philanthropists receive nonmonetary rewards, and so forth. When we settle for less than the best or make a mistake, it is because the costs of finding the preferred alternative, or of performing the correct calculations required to select it, are too high. But these ploys open up the theory to the claim that it is unfalsifiable. The real nub of this problem is one we have faced before: We cannot really tell which, if either, of these criticisms is correct because there seems no way to measure cardinal utility so as to test fairly the theory that people always maximize it.

To begin with, we have here another case of a generalization's being employed to establish the initial conditions to which it is applied. For the method marginalists offered to establish cardinal utilities already assumes that people are rational. We begin by giving an agent, say, ten apples. We then stipulate that the tenth apple the agent received provides one unit of utility. Now we see how much orange juice he would trade for the apple. This amount—say 150 ml—must then also be worth one unit of utility to the agent. By giving him the juice and repeating the experiment, we can determine how much juice is required to provide a second unit of utility. The marginalists held that more than 150 ml of orange juice would be required to get the agent to give up the tenth apple: Marginal utility declines. Marginalists often grounded this declining marginal utility in introspection: You can try the thought experiment on yourself to confirm it. But notice, this method will only work if the agent is rational, that is, maximizes utilities.

Moreover, the amount of utility a good produces depends on the availability of other goods. The utility of mustard for a person may be quite low in the absence of a hot dog, and the utility of a hot dog may be quite low in the absence of mustard. Together, each has a higher utility than separately, and they may have a still higher utility if beer is available, or if they are consumed at a major league ball park . . . under sunny skies . . . with his favorite team playing . . . and winning . . . by a large margin . . . in the seventh inning. . . .

The point is that we cannot undertake the experiment to measure the cardinal utility of each commodity by "pairwise" comparisons because the amount of utility we measure depends on a vast number of other goods present or absent. Economists sometimes expressed this problem by saying it is impossible to "operationalize" the notion of cardinal utility; that is, no practical measurement procedure for it is possible. And if measurability is required for a legitimate scientific quantity, cardinal utility is in serious difficulty.

What is more, the theory seemed far too psychological for economists. The notion of declining marginal utility and the appeal to introspection that often supported it were an embarrassment to rigorous economic analysis. Fortunately, by the early part of the century, mathematical economists were able to show that most of the important results of theoretical economics could be derived from a much less psychological theory of rationality: one that required only that commodities be rank ordered—best, second best, and so on, and not numerically weighted in units. This is the theory of *ordinal* utility or preference. It holds:

1. For all possible pairs of commodities, the rational agent prefers one to the other or is strictly indifferent between them (the assumption of comparability).
2. For any three commodities, *a, b, c,* all rational agents who prefer *a* to *b*, and *b* to *c*, prefer *a* to *c* (the assumption of transitivity).
3. Rational agents choose the available commodity that they prefer most, that is, that maximizes their preferences.
4. Economic agents are rational—they act in accordance with 1–3.

There is no assumption here that commodities provide numerical units of utility, only that there is a rank order of utilities provided by goods: the most utility available, the second most utility, the third most, and so on.

This approach to rationality enabled economics to derive all the same theoretical results about choices that the cardinal theory provided, without the dubious excess baggage of cardinal utilities. But there was a price. Economic theory had to forgo its claim to justify certain apparently attractive social welfare policies. Thus, economic theory could no longer sanction giving $1,000 to the poor man instead of the rich man on the grounds that the poor one would get more satisfaction from it, for ordinal utility does not allow for interpersonal comparisons the way that marginalism did. We cannot say that one person prefers a commodity more than another person does, according to this approach, because we have no units in which to count the strength of either one's desire. The result has been to read modern Western mathematical economics out of large parts of the ethical debate about economic equality and exploitation. This is an important subject to which we shall return in Chapters 5 and 6.

Though it circumvented the charge that economics was wedded to an antique psychological theory, ordinal utility did not after all allay the nagging doubts about the falsity or vacuity of rational choice theory. After all, consider how this theory bids us to measure preference. We present a large number of different pairs of commodities to an agent, and on the basis of his choices, we construct a preference ranking. Of course we cannot present all possible pairs to the agent, but we don't need to. We can extrapolate pretty safely from our experiment. This method will work, provided that, first of all, the agent we are testing is rational and, second, that his tastes do not change over the period of the test or after it.

But now suppose that a person behaves irrationally, suppose he violates the second condition above, the requirement of transitivity. People *seem* to do this frequently, and if they do, then the ordinal theory is disconfirmed, either because people are after all irrational, or because even rational people make mistakes. But of course it is easy to defend the theory by claiming that apparent violations are not real violations, but rather changes in taste. For instance, when I was a boy, I chose bubble gum over licorice and both over peppermint. Now I choose peppermint in preference to licorice and both over bubble gum. Yesterday I chose escargots over oysters; the day before, oysters over clams; today, I choose clams over escargots. My choice is not irrational; my tastes have changed. The trouble is that there is no way of distinguishing *within* economic theory between change in taste and irrationality. And there seems to be no way outside of economic theory if it is folk psychology formalized. For the way we actually tell when people have made a mistake as opposed to changing their tastes is by asking—by using [L].

The problem of distinguishing taste changes from violations of the principle of rationality is a rarefied theoretical one. But it reflects the fact that for all its formalization, rational choice theory is no better at explaining and predicting the details of particular economic agents' choices than folk psychology is. And this fact has led economists to fundamental reinterpretations of the aims and claims of economics: one, an approach that excuses economics implicitly from the task of explaining individual human action, and another, a reinterpretation that does so explicitly.

The implicit excuse is founded on a self-consciously behaviorist interpretation of rational choice, the "theory of revealed preference." The trouble with ordinal utility theory was, some economists said, that it was still too psychological. We do not wish to make any assumptions about what goes on in the heads of agents; we don't even want to use the notion of utility, no matter how minimally interpreted. And we don't need to. The only assumption we require is that behavior be consistent, no matter what its causes are. These we leave to psychology. Consistent behavior means merely this: If an agent chooses *a* over *b* when both are available, then he does not choose *b* over *a* when both are available. On the basis of his choices, we can build up a preference map for the agent, but we need not attribute this preference map to him. All he does is make consistent choices that reveal a consistent pattern. The psychological machinery behind this consistent pattern is a matter of indifference to economics, and its theory of choice should be silent on the question. The agent's behavior is described as "revealed preference," but this is a misnomer because there is no commitment to a preference revealed by choices that is independent of them. There is just the consistency of choices, and that is all we require to derive all the standard results in the theory of consumer choice. The doctrine of revealed preference was said to free economics from the very notion of preference and from all dependence on the concept of utility.

It is indeed an interesting fact that almost all the results in economic theory that were once thought to require cardinal utility as a foundation, and then thought to require ordinal preference, turn out to be derivable from an extremely weak assumption that makes no claim whatsoever about the psychological causes of individual choice. This really is behaviorism of the most thoroughgoing sort. One important thing to note is that adopting revealed preference theory limits the domain of economic theory even more than surrendering cardinal utility does. Recall that the shift to ordinal utility excluded interpersonal comparisons and thus severely restricted the scope of economic judgments about welfare. Now, with revealed preference, we surrender the age-old economic aim of explaining individual choice by assuming people are rational.

Revealed preference theory in effect tells us that the starting point of economics is the consequences of, and not the causes of, individual choice. To explain individual choice we need to make some assumptions about what produces this behavior. But if economics declines to assert the existence of a preference ordering that the individual actually has, *independent* of his behavior, then it cannot explain this behavior.

This may indeed be viewed by economists as a solution to the problem their theory shares with folk psychology: the problem of being unable to provide improvable explanations and predictions of individual action. The solution is that economics does not aim at such explanations and predictions. Its concern is only with the consequences of choice, not choice itself. Taken seriously, this attitude means that talk about preferences revealed in behavior is just a useful fiction, a handy instrument. It is the most convenient description of the behavior from which all the interesting results about markets and economies follow.

It is easy to complain that changing the subject does not provide a solution to the problem of explaining human action. Moreover, the new claim that agents are rational just in the sense that their choices are consistent does not really avoid the problem of falsity versus vacuity that haunts [L] either. One reason for this is the following: Consistency in choice among three goods implies transitivity, and we have seen that there is no way to distinguish violations of transitivity in choice from changes in taste. Revealed preference theory has no room for the notion of taste, but short of being disconfirmed every time a person's tastes do change, it needs some qualification or ceteris paribus clause to remain plausible. The obvious qualification of assuming no changes in taste is tantamount to surrendering the claim that revealed preference theory is a purely behavioral doctrine, with no commitment to the psychological sources of consistency in choice behavior. For now we have admitted tastes—desires—into the economist's theory.

Furthermore, consistent choice behavior is only rational if tastes remain unchanged and if beliefs do as well. If there are changes in my beliefs about the commodity bundles between which I must choose, then sometimes the rational thing to do is to choose *b*, even though in the past I chose *a*. Now, this possibility does not arise so long as we maintain the economist's standard assumption of perfect information. Once this assumption is relaxed and beliefs must enter explicitly into determinants of choice, the whole behaviorist's pretense of revealed preference theory must be surrendered. For there is no way to read my beliefs off my behavior, except against some background assumptions about my preferences. This is the point of the conspiracy theory of beliefs, desires, and actions (see Chapter 2).

Indeed, the most fertile and influential theory of economic choice under conditions of uncertainty, the theory of "expected utility," originated by John Von Neumann and Oskar Morgenstern, involves this very triangular relationship among beliefs, desires, and actions. Its central role in contemporary economic theory has reinforced both that theory's commitment to explaining individual action and its character as a formalization of folk psychology.

The theory of expected utility begins by resurrecting cardinal utilities, though not interpersonally comparable ones. It does so by a subtle use of the conspiracy theory and the assumption that people are utility maximizers. The method works like this: We offer a rational agent choices between, let us say, a 100 percent chance of getting $100 and a lottery ticket providing an 80 percent chance of winning $200 and a 20 percent chance of receiving nothing. If the agent chooses the certainty of $100, its utility must be greater than that of the lottery ticket. If he is indifferent between $100 and the lottery ticket, then their utilities must be the same. Assume he is indifferent. Therefore, an 80 percent chance of $200's worth of utility plus a 20 percent chance of nothing equals a 100 percent chance of $100's worth of utility. That is, $.80 \times$ (utility of $200) $+ .20 \times$ (utility of $0) $= 1.00 \times$ (utility of $100). By simple rearrangement, the utility of $200 $= 112.5$ percent of the utility of $100 to our agent.

So, if we stipulate that a 100 percent chance of $100 provides our subject with one unit of utility, then we can determine the amount of utility that any other commodity will provide him. We simply offer him choices between $100 and lottery tickets in which we vary the probabilities of getting the other commodity or nothing, until he says he's indifferent. Then we calculate what the utility of the commodity must be to make him indifferent between the $100 and the lottery ticket.

Once we have identified the cardinal utilities of the agent by these means, we can explain and predict choice under conditions of uncertainty. By combining his cardinal utilities and his incomplete information—his probability beliefs—we can derive the rational agent's utility-maximizing actions. But to apply this recipe to actual choice under uncertainty, we need to establish what a person's beliefs about the probabilities are. How do we do this? We use the conspiracy theory and the same lottery method we employed to measure his utilities. Only now, given his cardinal utilities for commodities, we offer him choices between certain outcomes and lottery tickets for known utility values with the probabilities left blank. Whenever he expresses indifference between the certainty and the lottery ticket, we can use the same formula, with the utilities as data and the probabilities as unknowns, to calculate what his beliefs about them are. Thus we can either work back from choices and beliefs about probabilities to utilities, or from choices and utilities to beliefs about probabilities. This theory of choice under conditions of risk is truly folk psychology formalized to a very high degree.

But we cannot adopt it as a refinement of the economist's theory of rational choice if we take seriously a behaviorist's interpretation of economics that simply reads individual choice out of its domain. Since eliminating (real) psychological choices does not seem to solve the problems of economics in any case, the behavioral interpretation is not much of a reason to forgo expected utility theory. Moreover, its prospect of accommodating economic theory to the fact that people do not ever have the sort of complete information usually assumed by economists is in itself a strong reason to embrace the theory of expected utility. Additionally, its employment by political scientists, operations researchers, and students of management seems to have improved our abilities to explain and predict behavior beyond the powers of unformalized folk psychology.

However, it is evident that people do not seem to act in strict accordance with the theory of expected utility, and its claims to have increased explanatory unification and predictive precision are controversial. And after a certain point there will be serious limits on its further improvement because of the impossibility of measuring utilities and probabilities independently of assuming the truth of expected utility theory and the truth of [L]. And at this point the theory of expected utility will face the same problems that bedevil folk psychology.

Instrumentalism in Economics

Difficulties in the employment of rational choice theory to explain and predict the behavior of economic agents have led economists to adopt a strategy for reading individual choice out of the domain of economic theory. As with other aspects of economic method, this one too has found favor among noneconomists who have adapted rational choice theory to their own subjects.

Some economists hold that their discipline isn't about actions of individuals at all. It's about markets, industries, and whole economies. On their view, rational choice theory is just a calculating device, a convenient *model* that helps us systematize our expectations about markets, industries, and economies. Its truth or falsity as a set of claims about what makes individual agents tick is irrelevant to the intended domain of the theory. Doubts about the truth of its highly idealized assumptions about individuals are simply misplaced. A theory is to be judged, not on the truth of its assumptions, but on the confirmation of its predictions for observations in its "intended" domain, that is, aggregate economic behavior. And the reason for this is that predictive success, in the "intended" domain, is the sole goal of science.

This strategy is a well-known one in the philosophy of science: instrumentalism. According to this doctrine, scientific theories do not need to be treated as literally true or false claims about the world but rather as devices for systematizing our observations. The claims of scientific theories about unobservable entities and forces that underlie observable phenomena may be viewed as heuristic devices, useful fictions, which help us predict observations but are not to be treated as referring to existing things and processes. A somewhat weaker version of this approach holds, not that theories work by postulating fictions, but rather that we can never know whether their claims about unobservable reality are correct because our knowledge extends only as far as observation. Thus, we should be agnostic about the theoretical claims of science, merely using those theories that work, without committing ourselves to their truth. It should be evident how much of a motivation instrumentalism has provided for behaviorism, both in experimental psychology and in economics. It lets us use words like "expectation," "preference," "information," "uncertainty," without having to take them seriously.

There seems much to be said for this approach to rational choice theory and for the exploitation of intentional theories in general. Of course, not all agents are rational all the time, or perhaps even much of the time. But from the unrealistic, idealized assumption that people are rational, many important large-scale economic phenomena can be derived, explained, and predicted. So the argument goes.

We must distinguish this view from an alternative that holds that although no one behaves rationally all the time, the individual deviations from rationality are distributed in such a way that the average of all individuals' behavior falls close enough to rationality for it to explain and predict aggregate economic phenomena. If this view is right, there is no special mystery about why rational choice theory is explanatory in the large, even though it is false or quite weak in its explanations and predictions of individual behavior.

But if this were the case, we would naturally seek an explanation of why individual deviations are so conveniently distributed. The distribution cannot be accidental, and one suspects that the individual divergences should be explainable by appeal to a finite number of different interfering forces, deflecting individuals to greater or lesser degrees away from the optimally rational choice. If we could find these factors, we could add qualifications to our theory of rational choice that would enable us to improve our explanations and predictions of individual behavior. We could do so by measuring the degree to which these interfering forces were operating in any given case. This defense of rational choice theory is far from an instrumentalist one. And if it could be substantiated, it would establish the credentials, not only of the economic theory of choice, but also of the whole strategy of providing intentional explanations of action. Of course, we have already repeatedly run up against obstacles to identifying these disturbing forces that infect the measurement of belief and desire and that block attempts to improve such theories.

If economic agents' behavior simply deviated from the rational in a regular and replicable way, then there wouldn't be any obstacle to interpreting rational choice theory as a set of statistical regularities. And the instrumental interpretation of the theory would be gratuitous. But the instrumentalist wants a justification for using rational choice theory even where there is no evidence that individual behavior is on average rational in the economist's formalization.

Thus, the instrumentalist claims that the only basis on which to assess the rational choice assumptions of economic theory is their consequences for observations of aggregate phenomena dealt with by econometricians: Are the predictions of this theory about the effects of a rise in the price of oil on aggregate demand for that commodity borne out by evidence? Are its predictions about how the stock market responds to a change in the interest rate, or in the money supply, confirmed? If we employ rational choice theory in order to predict the effect of an excise tax or a monopoly, and design public policy around such a prediction, will our policy goals be attained? These are the sorts of questions that concern economists. If the theory of rational choice gives us the right answers about these large-scale economic questions, then this is all the justification it needs. The theory will have proved itself as a reliable tool in the service of economists' scientific aims.

If, as some economists write, the theory of individual behavior is just a stepping-stone to the economist's real interest in groups of individuals, then perhaps the best view to take of the theory is that of a convenient fiction, or a calculating device—a black box, whose contents do not interest us, but that provides output in the form of predictions about market processes for input in the form of data about initial conditions obtaining in the market. In fact, the idealizations and unrealistic as-sumptions of economic theory about the rationality of agents, their complete information, the infinite divisibility of commodities on the market, the absence of returns to scale, the existence of a futures market for every commodity, and other esoterica are essential to the theory's instrumental success. A more realistic theory studded with qualifications and ceteris paribus clauses, introducing more and more of the factors that obtain in the real world, would be impossibly complicated to employ, would provide no clear-cut predictions, and would fail to connect and unify diverse phenomena into a manageable system. Thus unrealistic models are essential to economics, as they are to the rest of science. And the most important of these is the theory of rational choice. Questions about its truth or about its explanatory and predictive power for individual action are beside the point so far as economics is concerned. This conclusion will be seconded by political scientists, some sociologists, and even some historians, those who focus on the behavior of groups and attempt to explain it by appeal to this theory.

The adequacy of instrumentalism about economics hinges on many issues: One is the philosophical issue of whether instrumentalism is a tenable approach to the nature of scientific theories. This question will give little pause to working economists. They are no more interested in philosophy than experimental psychologists usually are—in fact less! A more immediate question is whether economic theory in fact has been as successful in systematizing and predicting aggregate economic data as this argument requires. For unless the economist's predictions about aggregate economic phenomena are in fact well confirmed, or at least improving, the claims on behalf of his black box, the theory of rational choice, will be moot.

Before an unrealistic theory can be accepted on instrumental grounds, it must be shown to be actually a good tool, to do things that other theories cannot do, to improve the accuracy of our expectations about the future, given information about the past and present. Has the theory of rational choice met this instrumental test? This is not a question on which a text in the philosophy of social science can take sides. It is a factual matter to be decided largely by economists. But the accuracy of economic predictions employing the theory of rational choice is a necessary condition for the cogency of this instrumentalist defense. In what follows let's assume this condition is met. The result is an argument against an instrumental reading of rational choice theory.

The most disturbing issue this approach to economic theory faces is the question of why the theory of rational choice and the rest of the idealized and unrealistic assumptions of economic theory are so useful in systematizing and predicting aggregate economic phenomena. We may illustrate the problem by appeal to the ideal gas law, $PV = rT$, according to which the temperature of a gas is a function of the product of its pressure and volume (where r is a constant of proportionality). There is a highly unrealistic model in the kinetic theory of gases that systematizes this regularity along with several other generalizations of thermodynamics. It is the well-known "billiard ball" model of a gas: Gas molecules are assumed to behave like billiard balls on a table. Like such balls, the molecules obey Newton's laws of motion, and the aggregate values of their mechanical properties are identical to the entire gas's thermodynamic ones. Thus, the temperature of the gas is equal to the average kinetic energy of the molecules it contains. But kinetic theory is highly unrealistic. For PV = rT follows from the model only on two highly unrealistic assumptions: that molecules are point masses—they have mass but no volume; and that there are no intermolecular forces acting between the molecules—they just bounce off each other with perfect elasticity.

No one will reject the kinetic theory of gases just because it embodies unrealistic assumptions. And thus the example seems to be an analogical argument in favor of retaining other theories that are predictively successful even though their assumptions are unrealistic. But we must ask ourselves, why does the billiard ball model function as a good instrument for accommodating the behavior of gases? Obviously, because the two unrealistic assumptions are pretty close to the truth. Evidence for this comes with improvements in the data of thermodynamics and improvements in kinetic theory. Thus PV = rT seems to hold for moderate values of pressure, temperature, and volume; at great pressure, low volumes, and very high temperature, it is strongly disconfirmed; gases no longer obey the formula. But by adding assumptions to kinetic theory about the small but finite volume of molecules, and the infinitesimal intermolecular forces that actually obtain, we can derive an improved and only slightly more complicated version of PV = rT that does accommodate this new data. This new, more realistic model explains why the old, simple one worked so well. In fact, it constitutes an argument for continuing to use the old model out of convenience when dealing with gases at moderate values of P, V, and T.

Therefore, the explanation of why the billiard ball model is a good instrument is that it is pretty close to being true and that there is another model, remarkably like it, which is closer to being true, and the latter explains why the former is a good instrument. This should be no surprise. For nothing is a good instrument *by accident*. For every good instrument, whether a hammer, a computer, a linear accelerator, or a theory, there must be an explanation of why it works so well. The simplest explanation in the case of a theory is that it is true or close enough to the truth.

This is not an explanation the advocate of an instrumentalist interpretation of rational choice theory can accept. For the initial motivation of this interpretation is to be able to employ rational choice theory in spite of the fact that it is *not true* or close to true.

Of course, following the advice of instrumentalist philosophers, economists can block this argument by refusing to answer the question of why their black box works well. This, they insist, is not a question that the science of economics, or any science, has to answer. For answering it does not increase the predictive power of the theory, and that increase in the end is the sole goal of science.

This assertion is a distinctively philosophical one, just the sort of claim many economists wish to avoid. Near the end of Chapter 2 we came to the conclusion that the social scientist wedded to intentional explanation must eventually come face to face with the fundamental philosophical problem of the relation of the mind and the body—as reflected in the problem of intensionality versus extensionality. Psychologists' and economists' attempts to circumvent that problem bring them face to face with another one—this time, a fundamental epistemological problem. For their assertion that science has but one goal and that predictive success is that goal is not to be settled by factual findings in any of the individual sciences. The question of what the goal of science is ultimately comes down to what counts as *knowledge*.

Most people agree that knowledge is the ultimate goal of science. Perhaps the only ones who don't agree are the instrumentalists who claim predictive success is its sole goal. And these instrumentalists make common cause with philosophers and social scientists who hold that predictive success is at least a necessary means of certifying scientific knowledge, not a substitute for it. By contrast, when social scientists and philosophers hold out another goal, like intelligibility, as the one we should pursue, they implicitly or explicitly endorse a different epistemology. Ultimately the choice between naturalistic social science and interpretative social science comes down to a decision about epistemology, as we shall see by the time we have finished the next three chapters.

What we have seen so far is that behaviorism's attempt to deal with the problems of an intentional social science has not succeeded. The problems facing naturalism remained, and progress did not seem any faster after the advent of behaviorism. In Chapter 4 we examine the way interpretational or antinaturalistic approaches to social science have dealt with the same problems. But the reader must not be left with the impression that behaviorism proved a fruitless dead end. For not only did it spawn technologies for the control and prediction of behavior among "lower" organisms and among people in highly restricted settings, but also by working through its limitations, experimental psychology emerged ready to face the problems of understanding the mind, and to face them with new tools, forged during behaviorism's heyday.

Introduction to the Literature

The most vigorous exposition and defence of behaviorism is to be found in B. F. Skinner's *Science and Human Behavior*. A useful

introduction to the experimental psychology influenced by Skinner is
H. Rachlin, *Introduction to Modern Behaviorism*. Behaviorism in sociology
is associated with the work of George Homans, *The Human Group*. See
also an anthology of writings in the areas edited by R. Burgess and D.
Bushell, *Behavioral Sociology*. J. C. Charlesworth (ed.), *The Limits of
Behavioralism in Political Science*, treats the impact of this movement. It
contains an influential paper by D. Easton, "The Current Meaning of
Behavioralism in Political Science."

The two most sustained attacks on behaviorism are to be found in
Charles Taylor's *Explanation of Behavior* and in Noam Chomsky's well-
known "Review of B. F. Skinner, *Verbal Behavior.*" The effect of these
criticisms has been to encourage the transformation of behavioral psychology into "cognitive science." See D. C. Dennett, *Brainstorms*, and P.
Churchland, *Matter and Consciousness*, for an exposition of these developments.

Important discussions of the nature of teleological analysis and explanation by philosophers are to be found in E. Nagel, *The Structure of
Science*, Chapter 12, and C. Hempel, "The logic of functional analysis,"
in his *Aspects of Scientific Explanation*. A recent criticism of their views
is R. Cummins, "Functional Analysis," *Journal of Philosophy* 72(1975):
741–764. L. Wright, *Teleological Explanations*, is the most relevant analysis
of teleology for the behavioral and social sciences. It offers an important
counterweight to C. Taylor's arguments in *The Explanation of Behavior*
that biological and behavioral teleology is both ineliminable and causally
inexplicable.

Any textbook of microeconomics provides a useful introduction to
rational choice theory, under the name of the theory of consumer behavior.
An excellent history of the changes in utility theory is M. Blaug, *Economic
Theory in Retrospect*. For an informal introduction to the theory of
expected utility, consult B. Skyrms, *Choice and Chance*. An exposition
of the theory, with applications to political science, is W. Riker and
P. Ordeshook, *Introduction to Positive Political Theory*. The thesis that
rational choice theory can explain everything of interest about human
behavior is defended and illustrated in Gary Becker, *The Economic
Approach to Human Behavior*. Becker's theory involves a novel interpretation of the conventional theory, an interpretation that he claims
circumvents conventional criticisms of it, including those treated in this
chapter. A. Rosenberg, *Sociobiology and the Preemption of Social Science*,
both expands on these criticisms and assesses Becker's "new" theory.
An extract from Becker, together with other important papers on rational
choice theory and Herbert Simon's notion of satisficing or "bounded
rationality," can be found in J. Elster (ed.), *Rational Choice*. H. Rachlin,
"Maximization Theory in Behavioral Psychology," *Behavioral and Brain*

Sciences 4 (1981): 371–418, not only explicitly applies the theory of rational choice to animal behavior, but thereby reveals the close similarity between revealed preference theory and operant behaviorism.

Instrumentalists in economics and others who wish to insulate the discipline from methodological scrutiny appeal to a famous paper by Milton Friedman, "The Methodology of Positive Economics," from his *Essays in Positive Economics.* The paper has been widely reprinted and is available in A. Ryan's anthology, *The Philosophy of Social Explanation.* This anthology also contains an important criticism of Friedman's views by Ernest Nagel. D. Hausman's anthology, *The Philosophy of Economics,* also reprints Friedman's paper, together with other influential documents on the nature of economics. Hausman's introduction to the subject is especially helpful. M. Blaug, *The Methodology of Economics,* gives a convenient history of the controversy that followed Friedman's paper. Blaug's book and Hausman's anthology contain invaluable bibliographies. A relatively advanced, but important, recent discussion of rational choice theory is to be found in two papers by A. Sen, "Rational Fools" and "Behavior and the Concept of Preference," both reprinted in his *Choice, Welfare and Measurement.* The former is also to be found in Jon Elster's anthology.

4

Intelligibility

As a predictively improvable theory of human behavior, folk psychology leaves much to be desired. Behaviorist redefinitions that seek to circumvent its weaknesses do not seem to do much better, nor do approaches that reject intentionality altogether in favor of some allegedly more experimental approach. This may be because human behavior is fundamentally undetermined by causal factors. For all we know, people have "free will"—their behavior is beyond the purview of any predictive theory because it is *uncaused*. Opponents of a scientific approach to human behavior have occasionally endorsed this view. Some employ it as a premise in their arguments that no causal laws about human action are forthcoming: For example, because we have free will, human actions cannot be predicted with ever-increasing accuracy. But such improvements in accuracy are what causal theories provide. Therefore, no causal theory of human behavior is possible. Others consider the doctrine of free will too tendentious to figure as a premise in any such argument. They recognize that there may be philosophically far less controversial explanations of why we cannot improve on folk psychology's predictions. These people are nevertheless motivated to find arguments against a causal science of human behavior by the conviction that we have free will and/or by the concern that such a science would threaten that conviction.

However, what is striking about the prospect that we might have this kind of causally undetermined free will is this: Even if we did, our intentional explanations of our actions would continue to be intelligible and accepted as illuminating them. This suggests that such explanations are not causal claims at all. If so, we should not treat folk psychology as an incipient causal theory or protoscience, to be improved upon by the employment of experimental methods. We need to view its claims and its aims in quite a different light. What is more, if we can find the right way to approach the theory, perhaps the problems and puzzles that daunt it on a causal interpretation will disappear. They will turn out to have been "pseudoproblems" generated by a mistaken presupposition, namely, that in social science our aim is causal knowledge or predictive improvement.

Here the reader may recall the interpretationalist position set out in Chapter 1, "Understanding and Intelligibility," which constitutes a preamble to the antinaturalistic argument this chapter will examine. First we will sketch out the approach to explaining human action in terms of its meaning, then we consider from the interpretationalist's perspective whether this explanatory strategy can be reconciled with a causal treatment of desires and beliefs. From there we turn to how the interpretationalist parlays the importance of meanings into an entire theory, not just about social science, but about society itself. At the end of this chapter, we will see how wide the gulf is between naturalism and interpretative social science.

The Hermeneutics of Human Action

Human action is explained by *interpreting* it, that is, by giving its *meaning* or *significance*. This is not a new thesis, indeed Plato argued for it explicitly in the *Phaedo* (99 a-b). But "hermeneutics" is a relatively new name for the science of interpretation. Because explaining action is a matter of meaning, it follows that the methods of social science must reflect much more fully the influence of the distinctive human capacity for *language* and the learning of it than the purely physical character of behavior captured in causal regularities.

Desires and beliefs explain action by making it intelligible, revealing its meaning or significance. This claim is often made in a metaphorical way. We often phrase a request for explanation of an action in the words, "What is the meaning of this?" But then we also ask what the meaning of that ominous cloud in the West is: "Does it mean rain?"

But hermeneutics takes the appeal to meanings quite literally. Finding the meaning of an action is equivalent to deciphering a text. Deciphering a text requires that we understand the language in which it was written. The language in which it was written consists in a series of practices that follow *rules*. If the text is a poem, then we need also to identify the rules that govern its character—blank verse or rhyme, Italian or English sonnet, sacred or profane, and so forth. Once we have learned all the rules that govern the text, we can give it a meaning. There remains but little that the specific intentions of the author can add to our understanding of the text. Why the work was produced on one day rather than another may be of interest to the biographer and the literary historian, and doubtless knowing the rules that govern a text's meaning cannot give us this information. But because our aims are not to predict when a poem will be produced but to understand it once it has been written, this information is of passing interest only. All the action is in discovering the rules.

On this view, social science seeks the meaning of actions and events composed of them. Thus, it needs to identify the rules that give these things their meanings, and it is far closer to an activity like literary criticism than to natural science. This explains why desires and beliefs are what we seek when we set out to account for actions; it explains the commitment to folk psychology and its imperviousness to "scientific" criticism or "improvement." Recall the logical-connection argument of Chapter 2: Desires, beliefs, and actions are logically connected in virtue of their intentional content, for the content of each implicates the others. This does not preclude the existence of a causal connection among them, as we saw, but it makes clear that the connection among them hinges on the sentences they contain and thus on our use of language. Moreover, the causal connection is a sidelight to the intelligibility such linguistic connections provide.

In fact, the very notion of linguistic meaning can be articulated in terms of desires, beliefs, and actions. The idea that actions are explained by giving their *meaning* reflects a basic fact about meaning in general. And this shows that far from being metaphorical, intentional explanations are the basis of linguistic meaning. When I nod my head in answer to your question, "Are you thirsty?" why does that *mean*, "Yes, I am thirsty"? First, because I want you to believe that I am. But I could have gotten you to believe that by making you notice the sweat on my brow, my parched lips, and my swollen tongue. And those phenomena don't *mean* "I am thirsty," they are just evidence for it. So, meaning requires more. The nodding means "I'm thirsty" because it got you to believe I am, because it got you to believe that I *wanted* you to believe I was thirsty, and finally, because I wanted the nodding to get you to have both beliefs: that I was thirsty and that I wanted you to believe I was. It's hard to keep these nested beliefs and wants straight, but each part is necessary to distinguish *linguistically meaningful action* from symptoms, signs, and indications of what we believe and want.

This analysis, however, leaves something crucial out. Why did I choose nodding my head, instead of, let us say, shaking it, to express assent to your question? Because I believed correctly that there is a *rule* in our language: Expressions of assent are given by nodding; expressions of dissent are given by shaking. And though the story about the nested beliefs and desires is crucial to my actions' having the linguistic meaning of assent, the most significant factor in my nodding was my recognition of this *rule*. And this rule, like all the rules of language, reflects a fact about my linguistic community, one that anyone who hopes to understand my language needs to learn and can only learn by living in my community.

Here then is the key to understanding human action, that is, meaningful behavior. We need to identify the rules under which it falls because they are what give its meaning. The rules under which actions fall are reflected in the intensional content of the desires and beliefs that lead to them, and that's why desires and beliefs explain action. Human action is thus a matter of following rules, and the aim of social science is to uncover these rules.

Rules are facts about communities: Linguistic rules are facts about members of a linguistic community; chess rules are facts about the community of chess players; traffic rules are facts about drivers, pedestrians, police officers, judges, and others. Rules range from the obvious, such as everyone drives on the right, to the esoteric, such as paintings of the Annunciation of the Virgin must alway show her on the right. They range from the specific, like "*i* before *e* except after *c*, or when sounded like *a* as in neighbor and weigh," to the general, like [L]: "If you want *d*, and believe that action *a* is one means to attain *d*, then do action *a*."

To the extent that [L] governs behavior, it does so as a rule and not a law. How do we know? Like all rules, [L] has two features that no causal law has: First, we can break it; and second, breaking it is punishable. These two properties of rules are related, of course, for if we could not break a rule, there would be no need of a punishment to encourage compliance. In the case of many rules, the punishment is obvious. Break the traffic rules, and you are liable to fines or worse. Break the rules of bridge, and you will lose points. Break the marriage rules in your tribe, and you will be ostracized. The punishment for breaking [L] is less obvious: You will be stigmatized as irrational, as subject to weakness of will or to some other mental malady.

The fact that rules can be broken and come with enforcement provisions is reflected in their grammatical mood. Rules are often expressed in terms like "should" or "should not." They are imperatives. There are also rules that permit, instead of precluding or requiring, although they are of less interest than the stronger imperatives because mere permissions don't explain so much as prohibitions or obligations do. It is because rules have enforcement provisions that they are facts about a community, for it takes a community to see to it that people comply and are punished for failing to comply.

The explanatory power of a rule rests on enforcement of some kind or other, and thus on a community that recognizes the rule and ensures compliance to at least some limited extent. For example, on days that I teach, I wear a tie. Why? Suppose I respond, "Well, I have a rule I impose on myself: On days that I teach, I have to wear a tie." But you will rightly complain that this doesn't explain why I wear a tie when I teach. At most it identifies the behavior as an action. What if I add that when I violate this self-imposed rule, I fine myself $10, by tearing up a $10 bill. Does this explain my behavior? No. You want to know what forces this action upon me, and this must be some community-based sanction. But if I say the college has a rule, and the fine is $10, then my behavior is explained.

Keep in mind that though the rule has explained my action, it can be broken at the cost of $10. Sometimes I break it and get away unnoticed by the proctors, but imperfect enforcement does not deprive the rule of its explanatory powers with respect to days I teach and do wear a tie. This is an important difference between explanation by rules and explanation by causal laws. The rules retain their explanatory force even though they are sometimes broken and even though violation is not always detected or punished. By contrast, a generalization that is violated as often as a rule is loses its causal explanatory force even for those cases that are in accord with it. But someone else's violation of a rule, even repeated violation, doesn't deprive my compliance with the rule of its meaning as an instance of rule following. That's why his violation doesn't affect the rule's explanatory power with respect to my behavior, even if he doesn't get caught.

In fact, imperfect enforcement may be essential to the claim that explanations of human action cite rules and not laws. Imagine a rule that was always successfully enforced, one that could never be violated without the perpetrator's being punished. In such a case we would have an exceptionless generalization: The "rule" is always followed or the violator is punished. In fact, we wouldn't need the rule to explain the behavior. We could just cite the general law, for instance, that teachers always wear ties or are punished. But this is just the sort of generalization that interpretationalists deny we can ever find in human action; it is just the sort of thing that naturalists search for. Now, a perfect record of rule enforcement could only be attained by nonhuman agencies, superhuman ones, or purely mechanical ones. A human enforcing any rule would himself have to do so as a rule follower. But any rule could be broken, and the record of perfect enforcement could be interrupted as well. If this is correct, rules must necessarily suffer from imperfect enforcement. But this means that showing someone getting away with violating a rule does not deprive that rule of explanatory force for another person. That is, violation cannot deprive rules of their explanatory force, if they have any to begin with.

Only few of the rules we follow are consciously before our minds when we are following them, and there are others that many of us could not formulate correctly even though we follow them scrupulously. Other rules are so evident that they may never have formed themselves into words in our minds. Some of them are silly, like "Don't spread peanut butter on the soles of your shoes before vacuuming the carpet"; others are complex, like the rule that governs the use of "who" and "whom," a rule few can state, though many obey. Nevertheless, those that explain our actions must somehow be "represented" within us. Rules would not explain our behavior if we merely acted in accordance with them, by accident, or through the operation of some kind of nonintentional causal mechanism. If rules do explain our behavior, it must be that we act out of a recognition of them, though it may be nothing more than an unconscious recognition. It must be the case that we could formulate the rule, given the right setting and enough time and thought. Otherwise, how could rules work to give meaning to the actions they explain? Thus, rules will have to have some sort of "intensional" representation or existence in our minds. Moreover, any other kind of existence would make it hard for us to "break" them— to ignore them. A "nonmental existence" would turn a rule that most people followed into an incipient causal generalization, ready to be refined in the direction of an exceptionless law.

Can We Reconcile Rules and Causes?

It is tempting to suppose that the fact that rules must somehow be represented in us makes for a possible line of reconciliation between the explanation of action as meaningful and its explanation as caused. It must somehow be that our recognition of the rules governing our behavior is at least part of the cause of the behavior. Thus, when social scientists search for the rules that make behavior meaningful, they are also engaged in a causal inquiry, within limits. The fact is that deciphering the rules that govern peoples' behavior increases to some extent our ability to predict it. How could it do so unless in learning what the rules are that govern an activity, we are learning at least something about its causes?

It is certainly true that learning the rules governing a practice or a form of life enables us to improve predictions of the behavior of those acting in accordance with it. So determining the meaning of actions provides some knowledge of causes. Moreover, we cannot identify the rules that give an action meaning without presupposing that recognition of the rules is part of the cause of action.

But, the interpretationalist argues, these concessions *miss the point* of the social scientist's interest in rules. Improvement in predictive power with respect to human actions is a relatively unimportant by-product of our study of human behavior, and our dependence on minimal causal hypotheses reflects nothing of importance about the kind of knowledge social science aims at.

Understanding the meaning of a stranger's actions provides predictive knowledge only up to the limits of our own quite weak powers of predicting a familiar one's actions and is, in any case, not the aim of such understanding. Consider the way anthropologists proceed in the attempt to understand the behavior of an utterly foreign people. They begin of course by trying to learn the language, that is, the rules governing the speech acts of their subjects. To do this, anthropologists must first assume that the noises the subjects emit are actions, that is, that the natives are following the rule expressed by [L]. But this is not a very restrictive hypothesis. Whether treated as a causal generalization or as a rule, [L] is pretty vacuous. This is a serious problem for the former interpretation, as we have seen: A vacuous generalization that can be embraced come what may in behavior has no casual explanatory power. But this is no problem for the view that treats [L] as a rule usually followed but sometimes violated. In fact, if we set out to learn the subjects' language, we must attribute [L] to them, and no evidence could lead us to deny [L] is a rule of their language. [L]'s vacuity is thus essential to its function. To see this, suppose that without the aid of a translator, we begin to learn our subjects' language, but that our translations of their remarks always come out as falsehoods. For example, the sun is shining, but our translation of their words is "It's raining." Someone who has just had three helpings of a dish and cleaned his plate each time says something that gets translated as "What a revolting dish. That tasted terrible. It must have been spoiled, and it was too spicy to eat." Obviously the fault lies with our translation. Either that, or these people are fundamentally irrational—that is, we cannot identify the meaning of their actions. Because social science commits us to treating actions as meaningful, it commits us to [L], and the fault must lie in our translation. We have not yet learned the natives' language.

Because learning their language is a precondition to learning all the other rules that make their actions meaningful, [L]'s role as something we would not give up, come what may, is crucial to the method of social science, as opposed to being a liability for it. As we learn more of the language, we find ourselves able to learn more of the rules that govern behavior in the society. Finally, we reach the point where we can predict every step in the religious ritual of the leading cult among our subjects. The rules we have learned not only make each of the actions in the ritual meaningful, but they also enable us to make quite precise predictions about their order, duration, topography, location, and so on. But notice that these predictions are no better and no worse than those that natives have always been able to make about this ritual. In fact, they are exactly the same as native predictions. Our anthropological inquiry has brought us to the point of knowing the folk psychology of our subjects. Beyond this point improvement is not possible, and more important, it is not necessary. For the success of our explanations is not judged by predictive success or its improvement.

The search for causes and the search for meanings part company at this point. Our own folk psychology and that of other people reach a certain level of predictive precision and stop. A naturalistic approach, which seeks causal knowledge, cannot stop with folk psychology but must continue to demand improvements in predictive knowledge. Such improvements are the marks of further discoveries about the causes of behavior. But such improvements are secured, if at all, by approaches that forgo the *meaning* of action. As such, they are of no interest to a science of interpretation.

Rule-following action is indeed caused by beliefs and desires, in which the rules are represented. But as we have seen, there are no natural laws connecting beliefs and desires with actions, either at the level of the greatest generality—[L]—or at the level of the narrowest precision, like traffic rules. This means that when I explain someone's stopping for a red light by appeal to his beliefs and desires, his recognition of the authority of the traffic rules they reflect, I am committed to *no laws* about traffic rules and behavior, beliefs that the light is red, and desires not to violate the law, invariably causing applications of the foot to the brake pedal. Indeed, I am certain that there are no laws about events that fall under these descriptions, for I know that people run red lights all the time, even people with the right beliefs and desires. I admit that there may be some large number of generalizations in neuroscience about how my brain, my perceptual apparatus, and my central nervous system work that connect the beliefs and desires to the action on any particular occasion. But the set of such laws will differ from occasion to occasion. More important, they will not connect the beliefs and the desires to the actions under their descriptions as beliefs, desires, and actions. They will connect them under descriptions of electrochemical and molecular changes in the brain and movements of the limbs. And such connections cannot show the *meaning* of applying the brake. Of course, there is a causal mechanism underlying human action, but knowing everything there is to know about it won't elucidate the significance of actions. And this is what makes even the minimal reliance of meanings on causation irrelevant to meaning's explanatory function. The reliance is no grounds for a reconciliation. For all the causal mechanism does is to justify a singular causal judgment that the desires and beliefs the agent had on that occasion were part of the cause for the action he then undertook. It does nothing to throw light on the meaning of what he did.

The philosophers who advanced the logical-connection argument we examined in Chapter 2 provided a similar argument for this claim that causal information plays no role in explaining action, even when we accept that actions are caused. They held that to identify something as an action in and by itself precludes the very possibility of a causal explanation of it. This isn't quite the radical thesis of free will that our actions are uncaused. It's the claim that they are not causally *explainable*.

The argument that causal explanation of action is impossible proceeds by example. The favored example is the action of signing a check. Every time I do this, the action is caused. But there can be no law or laws that cover every case of check signing and connect it to some invariable prior event. Why not? Because I can sign a check in a vast number of different ways: with my left hand, my right hand, my left foot, in block letters, in script, with a pentagraph, ink, pencil, red pencil, large signature, small signature, and every size in between. Any way I do it, it will still count as a check signing. But each of the different ways is a different movement of my body, and as such, it will be caused by a different set of prior events. Remember the maxim: Same cause, same effects. Its contrapositive operates here: Different effects, different causes. If each act of check signing is caused by different sets of prior events, it must be linked to them by different laws, and if there are an indefinite number of different ways of signing a check, there must be an indefinitely large number of different causes of these different effects and an equally large number of different laws required to connect them. But this means that there can be no finite set of generalizations or "covering laws" connecting the general class of events of check signing to any other general class of prior events, no causal laws of check signing, and no causal explanations of it. A fortiori, the explanations of what I am doing when I sign a check are not causal and don't hinge on any causal regularities.

Like the logical-connection argument examined in Chapter 2, this one is too strong, but it still makes an important point. At most it shows that actions cannot be causally explained *as actions*. That is, once we have described a movement of the body as an action, or for that matter described its failure to move as a refraining from action, we cannot, on this argument at least, give it a causal explanation (because the causes of what happens in and to the body do not explain the action *as an action*). Every event, however, has more than one possible correct description, and any event described as an action can also be described in terms that do not bring it under that category but simply treat it as a physical event. As such, it is open to a causal explanation and perhaps a simple one at that. The last time I signed a check, the action was identical to a particular movement of my arm under specified circumstances. The movement of my arm was subject to a purely physiological explanation. The next time I sign a check, the movement of my arm will differ, and the resulting shape of the signature will be different. Because the event to be explained differs, the causal explanation will differ too, both in initial conditions—the prior state of my body—and perhaps also in the particular physiological laws involved. And if the number of ways the action of check signing can be accomplished is *finite*, then there is in principle a single causal explanation for all cases of check signing: Just put together all the different causal explanations of the finite number of movements that exhaust the ways I can sign a check. To block this possibility, it must be possible to sign a check in an infinite number of different ways, not just an indefinitely large number.

But this is a hollow victory for the reconciliation of causes and meanings. Because the number of ways of discharging any action is at least vast, though not infinite, the complete causal explanation of an action will be too long and complicated to be of any use—it will not help explain an action because it will be too complicated to absorb. More important, it will not improve our predictive powers beyond those of folk psychology because it will be too difficult to establish the neurophysiological initial conditions or to complete the complex calculations from these conditions to the predicted movement of the body before it actually takes place. Thus, the causal explanation of action is not after all logically, conceptually, philosophically impossible; it's just physically, technologically, practically impossible.

Nevertheless, we do actually succeed in explaining actions. And we do so by citing the rules they fall under. These rules explain because they render the actions *intelligible* to us. But how and why does knowing the rule under which an action falls make it intelligible to us? And what does intelligibility consist in anyway? These are two abstract philosophical questions that social scientists may think they can neglect. By the end of this chapter we shall return to them and show that they cannot be avoided and that answering them brings us face to face again with the central problems of epistemology.

Rules, Roles, and the Social Construction of Society

Social science is more than the study of individual actions. In fact, to the extent that actions are the result of following rules, they must involve other people. For rules come with enforcement clauses, and enforcement requires others. Many sociologists and some philosophers hold that by putting together rules that we learn about in examining a society, we can identify the particular *roles* and *institutions* that characterize it. And more important, once we recognize that institutions and social roles are composed, indeed constructed, out of rules, our whole attitude toward society must change. And some go on to argue that with this change, the goals of social science must change as well.

Societies differ in their institutions. But an institution is not a building or a physical entity of any sort. It emerges out of the actions of individuals, and it persists through their actions. One of the things the anthropologist uncovers about the societies studied is their distinctive institutions. The anthropologist does so by identifying the rules individuals obey and determining how the rules combine with one another in order to generate roles, like police officer, or bridegroom, or father, and how these roles combine with others to generate institutions like law courts, wedding ceremonies, and families.

This sort of information may strike us as obvious and uninteresting. Indeed, much of what the sociologist or anthropologist can tell us about our own society seems *banal*. And what is exciting to us in reports about societies elsewhere would seem quite banal to members of the society whose character is reported to us. This charge, that when we have found the meanings interpretationalists seek, we have learned only obvious platitudes and nothing really new and deep either about ourselves or about others, is a serious one. Dissatisfaction with the interpretationalist defense against such a charge is probably the leading motive for the adoption of naturalism and, indeed, behaviorism. But in identifying the roles and institutions characteristic of our society and the different ones characteristic of others, sociologists and anthropologists may have aims beyond mere description of the obvious, and in these aims lies the defense against the charge of banality.

One of these aims is to attempt to settle a debate among social scientists about the inevitability of social arrangements: whether social institutions represent the operation of forces beyond individual control, whose origins are not in human choice, whose continued existence is also beyond our control, and whose character controls and constrains our social behavior; or whether the features that characterize a society are creatures of the choices and actions of its members, so that by choosing differently, we may change society. Those who hold the latter view often describe social roles that appear to constrain people as "constructions" or the results of "negotiation." The conception of institutions and roles as resulting from the interaction of human actions is often thought to substantiate this view. Action is "voluntary." That is, we can violate the rules that give its meaning. Indeed, acting together, people can change the rules that give their actions meaning, and thus, they can change the institutions that result from their interactions. In this sense, then, social institutions are not "inevitable"; they are constructions, albeit, often unnoticed ones, that we mistake for facts fixed independent of human decisions.

Many social scientists believe that answering this kind of question about the nature of social phenomena is central to the aims of their disciplines. For them questions of predictive success are either marginal or even irrelevant to the tasks of social science. On this approach to social science, these disciplines seem much more "philosophical" inquiries than "scientific" ones. The question of whether a social institution is "real" or merely a construction is like the philosopher's question of whether numbers are real or merely human constructions. Numerals, like "2" or "II" or "dos" or "10 in the binary code" are of course constructions, names we use in accordance with rules to refer to the number two. When the philosopher asks whether this number is real, he is asking whether there is an entity that these numerals name, in particular, one that exists independent of our thoughts. The philosopher's method of answering these questions seems quite different from the empirical scientist's method of answering the question, "Are there quarks or monopoles?" For the philosopher's method involves the analysis of the concepts we employ in making mathematical claims instead of the design of experiments. Are the statements in which the numerals figure best interpreted as committing us to the existence of the number? Can we translate statements about the number two into, say, statements about sets of objects? The philosopher's focus is thus on language, both ordinary language and the specialized language of mathematics.

Similarly, the social scientist who considers most central questions about what kind of thing social institutions are also proceeds by focusing on the analysis of language, ordinary language, and the language of social science. These inquiries, both the philosophical ones and those of interpretationalist social scientists, are distinctly nonexperimental and nonobservational. These are just the sorts of inquiries that are forced upon us if we take seriously the demand that social science explain the meaning and significance of action.

Of course, there are many who are likely to be impatient about such absorption with language. The results of an examination of ordinary language must perforce appear banal: telling us what we already know about our own language and nothing new. And the study of the jargon of sociology or anthropology will seem a species of self-indulgence. Both may be viewed as a distraction from the serious problems of social science. Skeptics about this approach are also likely to complain that such questions about the reality—the "ontology"—of social concepts are no more answerable than are many of the traditional problems of philosophy. But what others may see as an inordinate interest in philosophical arcana is a direct consequence of the decision to take *meanings* seriously. For these social scientists the philosophy of language is as important as the study of differential equations is for physics.

To say that social institutions are "constructed" means roughly that they do not exist independent of people's action, beliefs, and desires—their reasons for acting. On one interpretation, this claim may not be controversial, for all will grant that without people there is no society and thus no social roles to be filled by people. The claim becomes controversial when we add to it the idea that people can do otherwise than what they in fact have done hitherto, that they can violate the rules that constrain their actions, that they can construct new rules. This makes social institutions that we may have thought to be *natural* and unavoidable look *artificial* and revisable. If this is a fact about society that human agents haven't noticed, then it is far from a banal fact, and bringing it to the attention of people may have profound effects on them and society. Moreover, all this follows, not from empirical investigation, but from conceptual reflection on the nature of human action, the concept of rules, and the analysis of social facts.

One of the main targets of this approach to social science has been naturalistic social science, which it opposes. To undermine naturalism in social science, this approach attempts to show that the methods of natural science are constructs as well and not reflections of objective reality. The institutions of natural science are expressed in norms and rules demanding controlled experiment, observation, causal hypotheses, "objectivity," and predictive success as a test of knowledge. The "constructivist" holds that in fact these rules do not reflect any independent truths about nature. They are simply social constructions, consciously or unconsciously contrived and inculcated, but lacking in any foundation independent of human thought and action. Once we have recognized that the scientific method, like other social institutions, is a human construction with no special claims to objectivity, we will be freed from the mistaken belief that this is the only way to acquire knowledge or even the appropriate way to do so in social science.

Thus, the reply to the charge of banality combines two claims: first, that the ultimate aim of social science is not simply to discover the rules that give our actions' meaning but to show what the nature of social phenomena really is. Second, discovering their nature helps explain why naturalistic social science is so sterile: why, on the one hand, it has failed to provide a "science" of human behavior, and on the other hand, why such a science would not answer to our human interests in the meaning of our actions anyway.

Pursuing this debate may seem to onlookers to be simply another digression from social science into philosophy, this time the philosophy of science instead of the philosophy of language. But it would be a mistake to view this as a digression, say the sociologists who pursue this subject, for science is one of the most salient and imposing of our institutions. Indeed it may be the most distinctive institution characteristic of Western civilization. Accordingly, it must be of the first importance to the social scientist. And if its proper study makes debates in the philosophy of science central to the social sciences, then this can hardly be termed a digression.

One of the most effective ways of showing the arbitrariness or artificiality of features of our society that people take to be immutable and unchangeable realities is provided by cross-cultural anthropology. By showing that an institution characteristic of our society has very different features in another otherwise similar culture or does not even exist there at all, the anthropologist offers a powerful argument for the institution's dependence on our choices and actions. Ethical, epistemological, theological relativism is the chief legacy of twentieth-century cultural anthropology. Merely by showing that other societies have survived with institutions different from our own, anthropologists have called into question the "objectivity" of these institutions. Now that it has become more difficult to undertake anthropological studies in Third World countries, cultural anthropologists have turned their attention to Western domestic subcultures, especially ethnic minorities, hoping to explain differences in behavior as the result of differences in the way these subcultures construct their social realities.

But sometimes anthropologists discover similarities between different societies in human action, similarities that seem best explained by assigning them meaning or significance that the agents do not themselves recognize. For example, anthropologists report that many tribal societies around the world employ complex, but strikingly similar, marriage rules. Indeed, the study of such rules is one of the chief concerns of the discipline. We shall consider a detailed example of such rules and their explanation in Chapter 6. For the moment, we must examine the sociologist's claim to discover that behind the meanings people identify as explaining their actions, there is a *deeper* set of meanings that explain the actions in a more profound way. The existence of such deeper meanings is the most powerful reply to the charge that focusing on meanings can only provide banalities we already know or don't need to know.

Critical Theory

Many of these methods, motivations, and morals are combined together in a philosophy of social science that describes itself as "critical theory." This theory shares with others that focus on meaning a rejection of naturalistic approaches to human behavior, which it labels as "positivism." Unlike some exponents of interpretative social science, critical theorists treat empirical methods—positivism—as adequate in the physical and biological sciences. They reject its claims about method in social science because the subject matter of social science differs crucially from that of natural science. People can come to be aware of the findings of the social scientist about people and their behavior, whereas inanimate objects and nonsentient creatures cannot. A science of human behavior must accommodate this possibility; it must be, in their terms, "reflexive." A science proceeding by positivist methods cannot be reflexive.

There is a fairly well-known problem of "reflexiveness" in the social sciences, and it is a potentially serious obstacle to predictive success in these disciplines. But as we shall see, it is not clear that the problem is either insoluble or due to a misguided commitment to methods appropriate only in natural science. And this suggests that there is something more involved in the critical theorist's claim that social science is reflexive and natural science is not.

The phenomenon of reflexiveness is easily illustrated. An economist surveys farmers' costs and the current price of wheat and, plugging these data into his theory, predicts that there will be a surplus this fall and that the price will decline. This prediction, circulated via the news media, comes to the attention of farmers, who decide to switch to alternative crops in expectation of lower wheat prices. The results are a shortfall of wheat and high prices. Here we have an example of a suicidal prediction. The dissemination of a physical theory has no effect on its subject matter, but the dissemination of a social theory does. It is reflexive (recall the notion of reflexive verbs describing things that one can do to oneself).

If the prediction had not been disseminated, it would have been confirmed. Thus, in making such predictions, the social scientist must take into consideration a variable reflecting the degree to which the prediction will become known to its subjects and the degree to which they will act on it. Doubtless this complication makes prediction more difficult but certainly not impossible. Indeed, in recent years, economists known as rational expectations theorists (because they attribute rational expectations about the future to the subjects of economic theory) have held that the failure of governmental policies based on macroeconomic theories is the result of reflexiveness. Businessmen are acquainted with the same theories the government uses and change their behavior in ways that falsify the theories used to shape economic policy. Some rational expectations theorists hold that reflexiveness makes macroeconomic policy (and even theory) impossible.

But critical theorists have something quite different in mind when they claim theory is reflexive. What they really seem to mean by their demand for "reflexive" theory is social science that has a moral dimension, that does not merely describe the way the world is, but that provides positive guidance about the way the world *ought to be*. Such a theory is reflexive in a stronger sense than the one we have just discussed. Its dissemination not only *can* affect action, but also it *should*. It prescribes the direction in which action should be taken. And it is clear that methods employed in natural science could never produce such a theory, for these theories are limited to description and make no claims about prescription.

Critical theorists hold that the aim of a social science is not just intelligibility of human actions but also enlightenment as to their true meanings and emancipation from false beliefs about the nature of society and their morally unacceptable effects on people. We shall return to the normative dimension of critical theory in Chapter 7. For the moment we need to focus on the deeper meanings that this theory finds in human actions.

It is characteristic of many contemporary theories in social science seeking to find the *meaning* of human action and of human events that they embody moral dimensions conspicuously missing from theories in natural science and from theories about human behavior that either avoid intentional explanations—like behaviorism—or are embarrassed by them—like modern economic theory. The source of this prescriptive element is easy to find, according to some philosophers and social scientists. It is a consequence of the intentionality of social explanations. It arises from the language in which agents express the rules that guide, explain, and justify their behavior. Thus prescription is an inescapable dimension of folk psychology. It must explain actions by describing them in morally evaluative terms. These terms figure in the rules people act on and are the starting point of the social scientist's inquiry.

Consider [L]. It is a rule that helps determine what counts as rational. But it is not all there is to rationality, for to describe some act as rational is to praise it. What is more, rationality extends beyond the appropriateness of means to ends that [L] reflects. It reaches as far as the assessment of the appropriateness of ends themselves as permissible, obligatory, or prohibited as irrational. Thus, a morally neutral social science is impossible—or at any rate, one that treats people as agents must either wear its moral commitments openly or disguise them.

Critical theorists will identify a good example of this sort of morally contemptible deception, or better, self-deception, in the twists and turns of the bourgeois economists' theory of rational choice. Recall that the shift from cardinal and interpersonal utility to ordinal utility precludes the economist's making interpersonal comparisons of welfare. Among economists this self-denying ordinance has ossified into the claim that such comparisons are unintelligible. This belief goes hand in hand with a strict injunction, in economic methodology, of value neutrality: Economists can describe, but they cannot evaluate; their discipline is positive, not normative. Here the overt rationale is the desire to be scientific, to be like natural science.

The covert *meaning*, however, of the events that reflect these principles is quite different and essentially normative. First, the surrender of interpersonal comparisons effectively blocks arguments for redistribution, expropriation, and other tactics for improving social welfare. Accepting this theoretical restriction has great social consequences and represents a moral decision that welfare inequalities are permissible, when this decision is reflected in the dubious claim that they are indeterminable. By attempting to adopt the value neutrality of natural science, economics is trying to absolve itself of the obligation to search for a replacement for cardinal utility theory that could reach conclusions about manifest injustice. This tactic enables economics to turn the normative concept of rationality into a positive, descriptive *shell*, a concept that cannot be used to adjudicate between the rationality of ends and that is restricted to assessing the rationality of means, when it has any intentional content at all.

This kind of unfavorable appraisal of alternative conceptions of social science is characteristic of critical theory and of other philosophies of social science that combine a methodological critique of alternative philosophies with a moral critique of them. But the moral critique rests crucially on finding meanings in events that the participants did not see in them. No critical theorist accuses F. Y. Edgeworth or Vilfredo Pareto, the founders of ordinal utility theory, of consciously adopting the theory because of its prospects for rationalizing the political status quo of early twentieth-century Britain. Nor does any critical theorist suggest that the developers of modern welfare economics were engaging in a nefarious game to obstruct the forces of egalitarianism. Though critical theorists seek the *meaning* of these economists' work in such results, they do not seek these meanings in the conscious intentions of individuals. However, they expect that once people become aware of the real meaning of their actions, their actions will change. Social science is reflexive.

But what kinds of meanings can explain human action and be neither already known to the agent nor reflected in folk psychology? In identifying these meanings, critical theory and other theories like it escape from the charge of banality. But as we shall see, they do so at the risk of losing their anchor in rules, language, and the reasons that embody them and explain human behavior as action.

Freud and the Analysis of Deep Meanings

The twentieth century's two favorite theories of hidden meanings are Marxism and Freudian psychoanalysis. One problem with them is that each is an incipient causal theory. At a minimum, each was intended by its originator to provide a predictive science of laws. Freud viewed his theory as a temporary stand-in for neuroscience. Marx identified his theory as "scientific socialism"; it is said that he sought to dedicate *Das Kapital* to Darwin (who declined the honor). Marx certainly thought he had uncovered the iron laws of historical change. But both Freud and Marx have had a special fascination for those who seek meaning in human affairs, for the theories of both of them explain by appeal to meanings—hidden or deeper ones not immediately accessible to human consciousness. And both are "reflexive" in the critical theorist's sense of the term. That is, both embody prescriptions about what people should do as well as descriptions about what in fact they do; both hold that once (some) people have learned the truths these theories convey, their actions will in fact change in a prescribed direction. But both of these theories also face the critical theorist with a potential embarrassment, for those who embrace them as noncausal theories must show that Marx and Freud mistook the very essence of their own creations. Critical theorists have to provide an alternative interpretation of these theories as well as a diagnosis of their originators' errors.

The literature on what Freud and Marx really meant and on the details of their theory is vast. No one should consider the discussion of these two figures that follows to be anything more than a very rough sketch, and a controversial one at that. Bear in mind that our interest is in how such theories are employed to identify the deeper meanings of human affairs. Anyone with a serious interest in these theories must look elsewhere for a fuller view (some sources are mentioned in the introduction to the literature at the end of the chapter).

Freud's theory was an attempt to account for individual behavior by appeal to forces that he believed to be biological but that, pending advances in neuroscience, had to be described in an intentional way. He identified three components or forces driving human behavior: the id, the ego, and the superego, which among them determine elemental human goals and means. The id—source of impulses, drives and wants— is channeled by the ego—the source of information about the world and about available means for satisfying the id. The superego—which embodies the norms and rules of the agent's social environment—sets constraints on how the ego goes about satisfying the id's demands. The underlying model is clear: The id, ego, and superego work together to produce behavior just as desires and beliefs work together to produce action. For a generalization like [L], Freud substituted a "pleasure principle" and a "reality principle." The former claims that acts are undertaken to derive immediate pleasure or reduce dissatisfaction, and the latter claims that the immediate drive for pleasure is reconciled with the prospects of greater pleasure postponed. So far then, only the labels are different.

However, according to Freud, much of the interplay between ego and id is unconscious, as are most of the id's "desires." So, behind our consciously expressed desires and beliefs, there are unconscious ones, which give a deeper account of the meaning of our actions. These unconscious desires are largely sexual, and the unconscious beliefs are about how they are to be controlled and when they can be expressed and fulfilled. Psychopathology results when the interaction of the id and the ego becomes unbalanced. Neurosis reflects the unhealthy repression of the id by the ego; psychosis, the overwhelming of the ego by the id.

For purposes of social science neurosis appears the more important notion. In fact, Freud attempted to explain the character of many social institutions, and of historically important events, in terms of repression. And he suggested that social life could be ameliorated if we only recognized this unhealthy repression. Unhealthy repression of the id by the ego forces the id to seek alternative means to satisfaction of its desires. The result is neurotic behavior—inappropriate and ultimately unsatisfying actions that produce unhappiness and worse. Society is in part responsible for individual neuroses, because its norms and directives are impressed on the ego by the superego. In turn, social institutions can be identified as neurotic to the extent that they are the joint products of the neurotic behavior of the members of society.

The reflexiveness of Freud's theory enters with his concept of psychotherapy, the aim of which is to restore the balance between id and ego. Because the interaction between them is unconscious, therapeutic methods must focus on the manifestations of the unconscious in behavior—reports of dreams, free association, nondirective personality testing. And the therapist must *interpret* this behavior so as to determine the *content* of unconscious desires and beliefs. The cure hinges on the patient's coming to recognize these unconscious wants and beliefs. Once patients learn the deep meaning of their behavior, they will either come to accept their behavior without distress or, more likely, surrender some of the desires as unhealthy or some of the beliefs as false. Mental health, according to Freud, requires that the id's drives—that is, our basic unconscious desires—be "sublimated," channeled into healthy directions. Neurosis is the result of "repression"—the unhealthy imposition of false and ungrounded beliefs and unnatural social values, taboos, and restrictions represented in the individual's superego. Once the patient recognizes these for what they are, they lose their force, and his behavior should cease to be neurotic. Thus, the theory is "reflexive" in the critical theorist's strong sense of this term.

It is clear why Freud's theory has held such a tight grip on the popular imagination for almost a century: It is easy to understand, for its explanatory strategy is that of folk psychology, a theory we are already comfortable with; unlike other theories, such as Skinner's, it does not deny that human action is meaningful; rather, it seeks a deeper meaning; it is a debunking theory, one that allows us the opportunity to diagnose as unhealthy the orthodoxies of our culture; and it is sexy.

In part because of its popularity, Freud's theory has been the focus of controversies in the philosophy of social science over several generations. The classical objection is that the theory is unfalsifiable and therefore scientifically empty. Often this charge is said to hinge on the theory's reflexiveness. A patient is cured once he has learned the real meaning of his behavior, just by learning its real meaning. Therefore, if a patient has undergone a course of psychotherapy and has not been cured, it is always open to the defender of the theory to assert that the patient has not yet learned the real meanings of his acts, the therapy is incomplete, or the therapist is incompetent. This essential component of the theory is alleged to deprive it of any scientific respectability.

This sort of attack is already familiar from its appearance in the treatment of [L] and other intentional theories of behavior. It has called forth two sorts of replies. On the one hand, those who wish to defend psychoanalysis's credentials as a scientific theory (even those who hold it is a false one), point out that no theory is strictly falsifiable. Every theory is tested only in the company of auxiliary hypotheses (recall the role of hypotheses about the expansion of mercury in a thermometer that is assumed in any test of $PV = rT$). On the other hand, philosophers and social scientists who reject the demand that their theories meet tests appropriate to natural science welcome the untestability of psychoanalytic theory, or at any rate they are indifferent to it. In fact they claim it shows that Freud did not really understand his own theory, for he thought it had to be verified by clinial trials.

Freud considered his theory to be ultimately reducible to neuroscience, but it is clear that this is quite impossible. For one thing, the theory is evidently intentional. Though the id and the ego operate in largely unconscious ways, nevertheless, their states represent the way the world is or could be, they have propositional content, as the philosopher would say. This is why the theory provides deep meanings, and why some insist it cannot be causal. What is more, the theory is reflexive, and no theory in natural science is reflexive. So, the criteria of appraisal drawn from natural science, like testability, are irrelevant to its assessment.

Some interpreters of Freud claim, contrary to Freud's own view, that his theory is essentially "historical." To find the meaning of contemporary behavior we must search the events of the patient's childhood. But, they note, scientific theories are not historical in this way. To explain the present state of a gas, we need only to know about the current states of the molecules that compose it, together with the kinetic theory of gases. To explain neurotic behavior, we need to know about events in the patient's infancy. Finally, unlike inanimate objects, patients can talk, and what they tell us is a source of confirmation for psychoanalytic theory that no merely physical theory can boast. All these arguments have been offered by critical theorists to defend their use of Freud's theory. Each of them raises serious questions to which philosophers of science have devoted much attention. As we shall see, many of the same things have been said on both sides of the controversy about Marxism.

If the critical theorist is right, then in effect, Freud was profoundly wrong about the character of his theory, and he produced something quite different from what he had intended to provide. This possibility is sufficiently disconcerting that much scholarship has been devoted to identifying Freud's true intentions and the meaning of his own claims about the theory. And of course, much attention has been paid to a philosophical analysis of both his own theories and those of his psychoanalytical disciples, followers, and opponents.

Despite its fervent defense of Freud against charges of pseudoscience (by insisting that it is nonscientific), critical theory is not really wedded to the details of Freud's theory. Infantile sexuality, the Oedipus complex— these details are less important to critical theory than the Freudian conception that some beliefs are unfounded illusions foisted upon us by others, intentionally or not, from which we must emancipate ourselves. Crucial also to critical theory is the technique of psychoanalysis, which the critical theorist wishes to adapt to identifying and curing social ills. Just as Freud's theory requires the analyst to identify a "text"—a story— in the apparently random and undirected behavior of the patient, so too the critical theorist examines unintended features of culture to find the real meaning of social institutions. By identifying this meaning, the critical theorist hopes to produce changes in culture.

Meaning and Marxism

An interest in producing changes in society also makes Marxian theory particularly important to the search for deeper meanings. But the attempt to accommodate Marx to a philosophy of social science that sacrifices prediction for meaning is even more difficult than the attempt to so treat Freud.

To begin with, Marxism styles itself a "materialistic" theory, one that identifies the causes of change in beliefs, attitudes, values, roles, laws, institutions, and whole societies, in physical facts about the nature and prerequisites of human existence. In particular, it is facts about the "modes" of production, the means people employ in order to survive and perpetuate themselves, that dictate the characteristics of all the rest of society. The means of production Marxians call the "base" or the "substructure." All the rest—marriage rules, legal principles, moral precepts, aesthetic standards, literary styles, religious dogma, political constitutions—are parts of the "superstructure." Thus, the explanations of social institutions, roles, rules, relations among people, and so forth are to be found in fact about the means of production. Which facts are these? Ultimately, they are the ways the means of production must be organized at any given time in their development in order to ensure survival of society.

Society goes through stages of social organization determined by the levels of development that the means of production have reached at any given time. For example, the shift from hunter-gatherer organization to agricultural modes of production in Europe induced feudalism as the concomitant social organization. All the rights and duties of the feudal lord, vassal, master, journeyman, yeoman, and serf are supposed to have been causally determined by the factors necessary for agricultural production. Elsewhere, in Mesoamerica, for example, agriculture required vast irrigation systems and highly centralized production, storage, and distribution. So, a different set of social relations emerged. In Europe, feudalism gave way to the nation-state because the feudal mode of production gave way to commercialization.

Each of these stages is characterized by a particular form of ownership and property. These forms, expressed in legal writ and social norms, are essential to the society's survival. But like other aspects of society they are dependent for their existence on the means of production. Property provides individuals with interests, a stake in production, and these interests clash. As the means of production shift, the classes legally endowed with property rights become weaker or stronger. Eventually, when one system of production replaces another, the ruling class in that society changes. Thus, as the factory replaced agriculture, the landed classes—the nobility—lost power to the mercantile classes. In consequence, political organization changed from monarchy to bourgeois democracy. Marx predicted that continued changes in the modes of production, economies of scale, for example, and automation, would cause further centralization in industrial organization, and this centralization in the means of production would eventually shift the balance of power from the interests of the entrepreneurs to the workers, thus ushering in socialist forms of political organization.

According to many, Marx's theory, like Freud's, is reflexive. It not only prescribes the transition to socialism but also holds that the acceptance of Marxian analysis by the proletarian class will precipitate the shift to socialism the theory predicts. This part of the theory relies on a more detailed account of the meaning of human institutions, again a theory of deeper meanings than those provided by common sense. It is a theory of ideological analysis and criticism, whose basic concept is a clearly evaluative, morally appraising one: alienation.

According to Marx, humans find meaning and value in their lives through productive activities. By creative interaction with nature man makes his environment meaningful. Here "meaningful" does not just reflect human aims and beliefs, it also expresses approval of these hopes and purposes as valuable. But capitalism exploits labor, both in the sense that capitalist profit is unjustly derived by paying labor less than the value of its output, and in the sense that capitalism deprives the laborer of a meaningful relation to his productive activities. By measuring man's productive work in money, instead of a socially valuable product, homogenizing his relations to his fellow worker into a dollars-and-cents connection, making work obligatory instead of voluntary, replacing its values with commercialized distractions, capitalism makes us strangers to our own products, to our fellowmen, and to our own essence as a productive agent. Making someone feel like a stranger is "alienation."

The means by which capitalism does this is through the superstructure, which creates the values, ideals, laws, social norms, and institutions people live with. These features of society constitute an *ideology*—a "form of consciousness" that legitimizes and supports certain social institutions, despite the fact that they do not serve the general interest, but ensure the domination of society by a part of it. Ideologies often persist after the means of production have begun to undermine them, they hinder the social changes these substructural forces set in motion, and they divert attention from these changes.

Although strictly speaking almost everything in the superstructure of society is an ideological rationalization determined by the means of production, in fact, the term "ideology" is usually restricted to a pejorative characterization of views, both factual and normative, with which the

Marxian disagrees. Once a belief has been traced to its ideological roots as an instrument for the maintenance of capitalism, the question of whether the belief is true may be hard to take seriously. Once the interests served by an idea are identified, once we know that only some classes of society, say, the bourgeoisie, benefit from other classes' accepting an idea, we can be pretty confident that the idea is false, baseless, and unwarranted.

The ultimate object of *exposing* (another value term) the ideological character of ideas, beliefs, expectations, theories, religions, et cetera, is to secure a revolutionary set of social arrangements that will put an end to human alienation, as well as more pedestrian forms of misery. But the immediate aim of the critique of ideology is reflexive. By revealing to ourselves both the artificiality of a social institution and whose interests are served by it, we are freed from illusions about it and from its hold on us. There is in this notion a close similarity to tenets of Freudian therapy. Once the blinders are drawn from our eyes, little or nothing more need be done to create a revolutionary consciousness, to be emancipated.

This sort of *Ideologiekritik* is probably the most important thing critical theory has taken from Marxism. It is illustrated in the critical theorist's attack on modern bourgeois economic theory outlined above (Chapter 4, "Critical Theory"). By means of *Ideologiekritik* we can discover our real *interests* and the interests of those who encourage ideological delusion, even when they themselves do not realize what these interests are. And this *Ideologiekritik* can of course be severed from the details of Marxian theory. In fact some critical theorists are eager to do this, for several reasons.

One reason why critical theory as a whole has not adopted more of the Marxian theory is that among critical theorists there is considerable disagreement about its interpretation and its truth. This disagreement mirrors general controversy on the subject. Marxian theory has been at least as fruitful a source of methodological problems for the philosopher of social science as Freud's psychoanalytic theory has been. In fact, many of the same questions that daunt Freud's theory trouble Marx's as well.

Both men advanced theories that they held to be causal, yet both traded heavily in intentional notions. So both theories have been the scene of debate about whether intentional theories can be causal. Both have also been targets and benchmarks for claims about testability and falsifiability, independent of the problems that intentionality makes for such requirements on scientific theory. Just as Freud's theory is accused of being held true come what may, Marx's theory suffers from the same accusation. For the disconfirmation of its most important predictions, about the impoverishment of the proletariat in capitalist society, about the place and circumstances of socialist revolution, about the creation of socialist man, and so forth, do not seem to have shaken the theory very much, or even to have led to widely agreed upon modifications.

Much of the passion behind apparently abstract issues about folk psychology, like those treated in Chapter 2, reflects the recognition that these issues will have consequences for whether we can embrace imposing theories like Freud's and Marx's as scientific or not. In general, those philosophers who spurn Freud for philosophical reasons have little confidence in Marx, for the same reasons—that their theories do not seem to be "scientific." And those who appeal to either one, to find the deep meanings behind banal ones, are usually comfortable with the other and do not need to assess the theories they embrace on standards drawn from natural science.

Marxism was for a long time the focus of much philosophical analysis. The reasons are obvious: its political importance and its claims to lay the foundations for "scientific" socialism. Even more than to Freudian psychoanalytic theory, it was to Marxism that philosophers of science applied their tools and conceptions in order to demonstrate that the theory was or was not really scientific. During the heyday of logical positivism, according to which meaningful statements had to be verifiable or falsifiable, the verdict on Marxism was largely negative. The theory as a whole was stigmatized as both unverifiable and unfalsifiable. And its details were attacked as false or unscientific or caricatures of scientific practice.

For example, Marx's labor theory of value denies, in contrast to bourgeois microeconomic theory, that the real value of commodities is a function of market price. Instead, Marx argued, the amount of labor that goes into the production of a commodity determines its value. Capitalist exploitation of the worker rests, in Marx's view, on paying the market price of labor—the wage—instead of its full value. The trouble is that there seems to be no way to measure uniformly the amounts of different types of labor that go into production, except by its wage, which is a function of market demand. Without such a means of calculating the "real" value of commodities, it is difficult to apply or test Marxian theories about the nature of capitalistic exploitation, and its future. In contrast, most of the suggested ways of measuring the value of labor independent of its wage are either unsatisfactory or lead to the disconfirmation of Marxian claims about capitalistic exploitation. The continued commitment of Marxians to this theory is therefore criticized as methodologically unwarranted.

Another issue to which philosophical reflection has been devoted is Marxian claims about the historical inevitability of successive stages of economic and social organization, and the laws that determine these stages. The inevitability of socialism and the unavoidability of prior stages of economic development, like capitalism, are likely to breed both resignation and complacency among revolutionaries. Their actions cannot hasten the revolution, for that will occur when the time is "ripe." Moreover, the substructural determinism of Marx's theory makes it difficult to see how Marxism can even be "thought of" and influential before the breakdown of capitalist society. The theory's reflexive character requires that agents be free enough from the constraints of their economic substructure to embrace Marx's theory, and to act on it. Yet if it is indeed reflexive, then its claims about the determination of thought and action by the means of production are jeopardized. Can we reconcile the deterministic element in Marx's theory with its prescriptive force?

As we saw in the case of Freud's theory, Marx's is also sometimes interpreted, defended, and attacked as "historicist." A theory or method is historicist, roughly, if it holds that in order to understand and to predict subsequent states of a system—whether a whole society or an individual person—we must have detailed knowledge of the past states of the system. Even to predict the very next "stage" in the development of a neurosis or an economic system, we need to know about events long past in the life of the individual—usually the patient's infancy— or the society—sometimes even its prehistory.

Deciding whether Marxian or Freudian theory really is historicist or not is important, in the view of some, because theories in natural science are not historicist. If Freud's theory and Marx's are, then on the one hand, naturalists will reject them as unscientific, and on the other hand, antinaturalists will cite their historicism to buttress the claim that the human activities they explain require nonscientific explanatory strategies. The problem raised by historicist theories is about causation. In astronomy, all we need to predict and explain future states is a description of *present* ones, plus the dynamical laws of mechanics. Given the present position of the planets, we can predict all their future positions, and all their past positions too. We don't need to know their past positions to predict their future ones because all the causal forces determining future position are present and detectable in the current state of the system. In other areas, biology for instance, we sometimes need to know about the past in order to project the future, but this is presumably because we do not know the dynamical laws that govern systems under study. It's not because the distant past continues to exercise an independent causal force on future states.

When Marx's or Freud's theories are described as essentially or unavoidably historicist, what is meant is that past events really do continue to exercise control over future ones, and not just because they have brought about the present. We need to study the past, not as an alternative to studying the present (because we don't know what features of the present state of a person or a society will determine its next state), but because over and above features of the present state, there are causes in the distant past.

Thus, in Freud's theory, especially as critical theorists treat it, we cannot use the present neurophysiological effects of infantile experiences to predict psychopathology. We must identify those experiences themselves. And, in Marx's theory, we need to know the particular stages through which a society has passed, in order to determine its future. Studying the effects of these past stages on the present is not enough.

This sort of causation bears the same problems as teleological causation. Recall, as discussed in Chapter 3, the problem of future events, which don't exist, bringing about present events. Historicism requires that past events, which no longer exist, bring about future events, *without* doing so going through present ones. But if past states do not leave on the present a mark that we could identify and employ to chart the future, then however they determine the future, it cannot be through causal means known to the rest of science. For causation does not work through temporal gaps any more than it works through spatial gaps. There must be chains linking the earlier to the later; and a complete knowledge of the intrinsic causal properties at any link, together with laws, should be enough to determine the character of future effects, without adding information about earlier links.

If understanding and predicting the future requires unavoidable appeal to events of the distant past, then the explanations such knowledge involves will not be causal. This is another reason philosophers of science have raised grave doubts about Freud's theory and Marx's, when interpreted in the way their originators wanted to treat them—as scientific theories.

By and large the debate in the philosophy of science came out against the conclusion that Freud and Marx's theories were scientific, in the strict positivist sense of that term. Therefore, positivist philosophers read the theories out of the corpus of legitimate knowledge. In contrast, these same arguments were employed by antipositivists and exponents of interpretative social science as reasons why these theories are not to be judged by the standards of causal theories, and why the study of deep meanings they reflect need pay no heed to strictures inappropriately drawn from natural science. After all, faced with the choice between surrendering the intelligibility of human affairs that Marx and Freud as well as common sense provide, and ignoring the strident claims of logic choppers, it seemed obvious which alternative should be endorsed. Thus, a countercharge arose against positivist philosophers of social science and social scientists eager to be as "scientific" as possible. To the epithet of "pseudoscience," the defender of meanings replies with the label "scientism"—an exaggerated and ideologically explainable respect for a certain mistaken image of science. Indeed, two of the most remarkable figures to have been in thrall to "scientism" were Freud and Marx themselves, whose own theories must be reinterpreted in order to free them from this incubus. So critical theorists and others sympathetic to interpretation as the method of social science will argue.

Impasse and Epistemology

On one side are those few philosophers and social scientists who have held that meanings can't be causes, that the knowledge social science seeks must be causal knowledge, and that therefore we must turn our backs on meanings. On the other side there have been a larger number of social scientists and philosophers who have agreed that meanings cannot be causes, but that they provide knowledge, so that the aim of social science cannot be causal knowledge. Between these camps has stood a body of writers advocating reasonable compromise, holding that the arguments of neither side are right, that there is no logical incompatibility between meanings and causes. Therefore, there is no forced choice between intelligibility and prediction. We can have them both, in principle. If we have rather more intelligibility and less prediction, well, this is a practical problem of complexity and difficulties of research. It is surely not one that makes epistemology unavoidable.

Reasonable compromises, however, are always unsatisfying. Those who demand improvements in prediction will insist that their opponents show that meanings really do provide intelligibility and not just a psychological feeling of intelligibility. What after all is the test of intelligibility? Is it really just the *feeling* that were we in the place of the agent whose behavior is explained, with the same beliefs and desires, or in the grip of the same neurosis or ideology, we would do the same thing? Why should this feeling be a mark of knowledge? How can it certify the explanation offered and the principles behind this explanation as *true*? Feelings are a notoriously poor guide to knowledge, as Freud or Marx would himself attest. We feel nothing more firmly than that the Earth is at rest. Yet this belief, despite the feeling that it must be true, is quite false—we are hurtling through the universe at a high velocity. If we had allowed this feeling to serve as a mark of knowledge, we should still be in the grip of Aristotle. It is just possible that the feeling of intelligibility is equally mistaken. Perhaps it too can be explained *away* as a mistake, just as the feeling that we are at rest can be.

The real test of intelligibility, this argument continues, is not a feeling but the application of the information that produces the feeling to successful prediction. This application certifies the information as reliable, as knowledge. As for the feeling of intelligibility, well, it is at best and only sometimes a by-product of such successful prediction.

The fundamental assumption in this argument is epistemological: It is the claim that propositions count as knowledge only if there can be independent objective evidence for them, evidence based on observations of phenomena independent of our feelings and thoughts. This is some sort of empiricism. And it leads inevitably to skepticism about a science of human action.

Observations of human behavior alone can never decide between competing intensional theories, whether Marxian, Freudian, common-sensical, et cetera, not even in principle, when everything else is known about the rest of science (including neuroscience), and when all the data about behavior are in. All this information will still not enable us to choose unambiguously between two different combinations of belief and desire, combinations that have exactly the same vague and imprecise consequences for behavior. If meanings then are ultimately underdetermined by all the evidence, the appeal to them cannot constitute knowledge of any kind that the empiricist will sanction.

Against this argument there is another powerful one with an equally fundamental epistemological starting point. The argument begins with a claim of René Descartes, the founder of modern epistemology: Some things I know for certain, directly, and immediately. I know them without evidence, or they are self-certifying, or the evidence for them is more powerful than anything that could justify my other doubtable beliefs. Among these things that I know with certainty is my own existence (*Cogito, ergo sum,* "I think, therefore I am"). I cannot doubt my own existence, for the act of doubting requires a doubter—and that's me. Similarly, at least sometimes when I myself act, I know why I act. I cannot doubt that my basic *actions*—raising my arm, for example—stem from desires and beliefs, which give them meaning. My direct awareness of the "phenomenology," the sensory awareness of what is going on inside of me, guarantees this. The feeling of intelligibility is based on this immediate certainty about why I act, in my own case. And this conviction requires no further evidence, for it cannot be doubted, any more than I can doubt my own existence.

Thus, the reason that a proposition like [L] seems like an irrefutable definition is that it is an a priori truth or at least a proposition I know to be true from my own case, by introspection, and with far greater assurance than I know any further fact about the world beyond my immediate experience. Of course whether the other human bodies that make up the social world are just like me "on the inside" is another matter. But if they are, then the intelligibility of their behavior is certified as knowledge by my direct awareness of the truth of [L].

Here of course we are faced with epistemological rationalism as the final arbiter of method in the social sciences. Meanings provide knowledge, regardless of their predictive limits, because they produce intelligibility and intelligibility, not prediction, is the mark of knowledge.

Shall we give up social science, at least until this question of empiricism versus rationalism is settled? If we do, we shall probably never take it up again, for we are not likely to settle soon this epistemological dispute, which goes back to the Greeks. But if we don't take it seriously, then aren't we sleepwalking, no matter which side we take? In Chapter 5 we explore some alternatives to the unpleasant prospect of sleepwalking or giving up social science altogether.

Introduction to the Literature

The notion that human action is explained by meanings goes back along a continuing thread of intellectual history to Plato. See his dialogue *Phaedo*. The view has animated much of the philosophy of history from the nineteenth century to the present. For a discussion see R. G. Collingwood, *The Idea of History*. Among social scientists, the same position is advanced by Alfred Schutz, whose key papers are reprinted in M. Natanson's and D. Braybrooke's anthologies. Schutz's view of the primacy of ordinary concepts in the explanation of human action, and of their differences from explanatory concepts and strategies in natural science, has animated a long series of methodologies, especially in sociology and social psychology. Some of these approaches are outlined in N. Smelser and S. Warner, *Sociological Theory*. Recent influential social science in this tradition includes M. Sahlins, *Culture and Practical Reason*, R. Schweder and R. Levine (eds.), *Culture Theory: Essays on Mind, Self and Emotions*, H. Garfinkel, *Studies in Ethnomethodology*, C. Geertz, *The Interpretation of Cultures*. D. W. Fiske and R. Schweder, *Metatheory in Social Science*, includes several essays by leading figures in social psychology, defending this approach against methodological criticisms. R. Harré and P. Secord, *The Explanation of Social Behavior*, connects the substantive theory of interpretative social science with a philosophical foundation.

Among philosophers who have elaborated this idea and have made the notion of a rule central, the most well-known work is P. Winch, *The Idea of a Social Science*. Winch attributes this view to L. Wittgenstein, *Philosophical Investigations*. Students interested in Wittgenstein's treatment of rules and meaning are urged to start with S. Kripke, *On Rules and Private Language,* an accessible introduction to Wittgenstein's aphoristic text. D. Braybrooke's *Philosophy of Social Science,* Chapter 3, contains a condensed treatment of recent thought about rules in the explanation of action.

The most well-known reconciliation of action explanations and causation is Donald Davidson, "Actions, Reasons and Causes," originally in *Journal of Philosophy,* 1963, widely reprinted, and in Davidson, *Essays on Actions and Events.* A. Rosenberg, *Microeconomic Laws: A Philosophical Analysis,* Chapter 5, applies these arguments and others to defend a causal interpretation of rational choice theory against the logical-connection argument. Neither provides more than a formal reconciliation proving the logical coherence of such an interpretation. The problems surrounding really useful generalizations about reasons are treated in P. Churchland, "Eliminative Materialism and the Psychological Attitudes," S. Stich, *From Folk Psychology to Cognitive Science,* and A. Rosenberg, *Sociobiology and the Preemption of Social Science.*

In addition to the works by social scientists cited above, P. Berger and T. Luckman, *The Social Construction of Reality,* is a well-known development of the notion that social phenomena consist in our collective interpretations of the actions of ourselves and others. Of special interest to philosophers of science is the attempt to apply this theory to conclude that scientific findings are social constructions themselves. See B. Latour and S. Woolgar, *Laboratory Life: The Social Construction of Scientific Facts,* and K. Knorr-Certina, *The Manufacture of Knowledge: An Essay on the Constructivist and Contextual Nature of Science.*

The general problem of reflexive predictions in social science is examined in papers by R. Buck and by A. Grunbaum reprinted in L. I. Krimerman's anthology.

Among critical theorists, the most influential figure for social science is J. Habermas, *Knowledge and Human Interests.* T. McCarthy, *The Critical Theory of Jurgen Habermas,* is recommended as an excellent introduction to Habermas's thought. See also R. Geuss, *The Idea of Critical Theory,* a particularly lucid exposition of the theory. Accounts of Freud's theory are widely available, but it is best to read Freud himself, for instance, *New Introductory Lectures on Psychoanalysis.* A. Grunbaum, *The Foundations of Psychoanalysis,* is a philosophical critique of Freud's theory, with special reference to the critical theorists' reinterpretation of it. R. Schmitt, *Introduction to Marx and Engels,* provides a general treatment of Marxian social science. D. Braybrooke, *Philosophy of Social Science,* is in part devoted to vindicating critical theory's application of Freud and Marx, both predictively and as interpretative theories.

Two works giving priority to introspective knowledge of why we act as we do are R. Taylor, *Action and Purpose,* and S. Hampshire, *Thought and Action.*

5

Macrosocial Science

PROBLEMS OF INTENTIONALITY seem to haunt the explanation of individual behavior. But not all social science is devoted to the explanation of human action. There are those who hold that what is characteristic about social science is that it deals with a range of facts about people, facts that have nothing to do with the psychological factors explaining individual human action. These are facts about human social institutions, like families or businesses, and facts about large aggregations of people, like social classes, religious groups, or even whole societies. Following Durkheim, let us call these facts "social facts." Suppose there are social facts, and their character and/or their existence is not just the result of adding up the psychological facts about individual agents, their behavior and its causes. As we shall see, the supposition is a widely held one among social scientists. But first, what are the ramifications? To begin with, we might have a way around all the problems canvassed in the four previous chapters. For perhaps a theory that explains and predicts the relations among social facts, and that does so without reference to psychological facts, need not concern itself with problems of intentionality or even make use of an explanatory principle like [L].

Indeed, the existence of a range of such facts may provide a new explanation for the predictive weakness of social sciences: Perhaps the problem is that we have been attempting to construct a theory about the wrong sorts of objects. If we change our perspective, we will discover an improving social science staring us in the face. Consider a parallel from physics. Imagine trying to frame a theory about the thermodynamic properties of a gas—temperature, pressure, volume, et cetera—by focusing on the behavior of the molecules that make it up. If we could observe them, we would see nothing but a buzz of random motions and nothing that could help us understand the gas or, for that matter, the molecules either. The proper way to proceed is to search for macroscopic regularities among observable features of the gas and then later frame hypotheses about individual molecules that might explain them.

Mutatis mutandis for the social sciences. The behavior of the individual looks random. We can't seem to frame any laws about the individual. But what if we examine the aggregate of individuals? Then we might— indeed, it has long been argued that we will—find laws about these aggregations of individuals. And having found them, we may be able to turn back to discover hypotheses about individuals that explain their behavior. And even if, as some hold, there are no such hypotheses, at least we have discovered laws or perhaps other important facts about macrosocial phenomena.

The name usually given in philosophy of social science for those who advocate the possibility or the actuality of social facts is "holists"—from the Greek *holos*, meaning "whole." Their thesis is often associated with the doctrine that the whole is more than the sum of its parts: Society is more than the individuals who make it up—whence the existence of independent social facts.

There are, however, philosophers and social scientists ready to produce arguments that no such range of irreducible social facts exists to be found or explained. These opponents of "social facts" are known as "methodological individualists" or "individualists" for short. They stand ready also to demonstrate that any example given of such a fact is best described or fully explained in terms of the behavior of individuals, or is not a fact of any kind, but a figment of the holists' imagination or research program. The modifier "methodological" is attached to the name of this view in order to reflect the fact that its exponents adopt a methodological dictum always to search for individual descriptions and explanations to substitute for "holistic" ones.

It will perhaps be surprising to some social scientists that there could be a philosophical question about whether there are social facts inde- pendent of individual ones, for such facts seem the sum and substance of many of the social disciplines. And whether such facts obtain or not seems to many social scientists a substantial matter of fact, not to be decided by considerations from philosophy.

However, there is (especially, but not exclusively) among naturalists in social science and philosophers of science a long tradition of doubting whether there could be any such facts not reducible to facts about individuals. In part this skepticism stems from a suspicion of theoretical entities—things, forces, or features that are not directly observable by the scientist. Some scientists and philosophers have raised doubts about the existence of microphysical entities, such as electrons, quarks, and photons, just because we cannot observe them and thus cannot justify our theories about them. Similarly, we can only observe individual agents, so that facts about things "larger" than people are equally suspect. There is another reason naturalists are dubious about social facts. The very idea of a range of facts distinct from ones about individuals seems intrinsically mysterious and unempirical to them. For such facts smack of the doctrine that the whole could be more than the sum of its parts, or that above and beyond the individual consciousnesses that govern behavior there is a "collective consciousness" of the society as a whole. Even holists who reject both of these doctrines are sometimes accused of commitment to them willy-nilly.

Holism is also controversial because it is connected to another feature of social science that raises serious methodological questions: functionalism—the strategy of identifying and explaining features of society in terms of the purposes they serve, not for individuals, but for the society as a whole. This strategy is widespread in social science. And as we shall see, holism provides a natural motivation for it. However, functionalism has itself been a problematical strategy, in part for reasons we have already examined in the discussion of behaviorism and teleology (Chapter 3).

In this chapter we explore arguments for and problems raised by holism, as well as its concomitant commitment to explaining things by uncovering the social functions they serve. Part of the argument for holism derives from the motive of showing sociology to be an "autonomous science"—one distinct from and independent from psychology. This motive parallels a similar one among psychologists, who hope to show that their discipline is independent of more fundamental ones in the life sciences, like neurophysiology. The arguments that these two disciplines offer are so similar that we can examine them together and draw conclusions about both subjects. We will then turn to the connection between holism and functionalism and the methodological individualist's critique of both. In Chapter 6 the strategy of methodological individualism, particularly in economics and in sociobiology, will be examined further.

Holism and Human Action

How is the existence of social facts to be established? One argument for holism is narrowly philosophical and turns on the analysis of the terms we use to describe individual human actions. A second argument is more clearly factual and therefore more convincing to social scientists than the philosophical one. Before moving to it, we examine the philosopher's argument, with the warning that like most philosophical arguments, it is pursued at a very high level of abstraction.

Consider the conceptual machinery of intentional explanations. Merely by reflecting on notions like language, meaning, rules, roles, institutions, and so forth, we can deduce the existence of such social facts. Describing something as an action and explaining it in terms of beliefs and desires seem already to commit us to social facts. Consider the example of my cashing a check. How is such behavior explained? In order not to miss aspects of this explanation suppressed because of their banality and obviousness, imagine that I am explaining this behavior to someone who does not even understand the concept of money. To do so, I need to explain the significance of my action to me and the teller, and doing this brings in the entire monetary and banking system. The teller and I are operating under rules—enforced by society—that give the exchange its meaning. But these rules are unintelligible except against the background of rules with compliance conditions, that is, institutions of persuasion and enforcement. My actions are explained in terms of the status of the teller as a *teller*, independent of any other facts about him. His behavior as a teller can only be described by reference to other roles in the bank, and so on. We cannot break out of this circle of institutions into descriptions of mere behavior. Similarly, an account of the beliefs and desires that give the meaning of each of our actions must make reference to one another's roles and the rules governing them. Because we cannot characterize these beliefs and desires without reference to the concepts like teller and customer that give their content, reference to social facts is unavoidable in individual explanations.

The methodological individualist's traditional counter to this argument was an objection from considerations of testability. Individualists held, quite rightly, that the only test of a statement that purports to refer to social facts is to be found in observations about individuals. Therefore, such statements had ultimately to be translatable, at least in principle, if not in practice, into claims about individuals. Any residue in such translation was meaningless metaphysical excrescence. The trouble with this argument was that it proves too much. For, by the same standards, all the theoretical claims of science must be translatable without residue into statements about observations, and this cannot be done short of depriving scientific theory of its explanatory power. If "electron" must be translated into observational terms, we can no longer explain observations by appeal to the behavior of electrons. We'd just be redescribing the observations.

What this point shows, however, is that statements that transcend observation are to be judged on their explanatory power, not their testability. Therefore, the argument that ordinary language descriptions of human actions presuppose social facts does not carry much weight. For such statements merely describe phenomena that need to be explained. Perhaps the best explanations will involve first redescription of the events in terms that do not presuppose social facts. A description of the sun as "setting" seems to commit us to the geocentric hypothesis: The sun goes around the earth. An explanation of the sunset, however, makes no such supposition. It begins by implicitly redescribing the sunset as an earth turn. Similarly, whether there are social facts or not cannot rest on descriptions we employ to identify events to be explained. It must rest on arguments that the best explanation of individual actions presupposes social facts.

Therefore, it is not enough simply to show that our *descriptions* of individual actions presuppose social facts. The argument for the existence of social facts rests entirely on the adequacy of an explanatory theory of human actions, one that adverts to social facts in order to explain the character and content of the beliefs and desires that result in actions.

But the methodological individualist will not accept as adequate any such an explanatory theory adverting to social facts. The individualist holds that there is a crucial disanalogy between the unobservable theoretical facts of physics and the unobservable social facts of the holist. For the existence and interaction of individuals are not only necessary for the existence of society and of social facts but are also *sufficient* for their existence. Both holists and individuals agree that people are necessary for the existence of society. Individualists argue that in principle claims about social facts should be reducible to claims about individuals, because the existence of individuals is also *sufficient* for the existence of society and social facts. If all we need to produce social facts is for people to exist and behave in certain ways, then it is hard to see how these facts can consist in more than people's behavior.

If it is difficult to see this, then the comparison between theoretical facts of physics and social facts breaks down. The truth of claims about observable phenomena of physics is necessary for the truth of statements about the theoretical facts that physics postulates. That's how we test them. But such confirming observational predictions are not sufficient for the truth of theoretical claims. Otherwise, we *could* translate statements of physical theory into sets of statements about observations for which theoretical claims are both necessary and sufficient. And then, when statements about, for instance, electrons, are equated with descriptions of observations, the power of such statements to explain observations is a real mystery. By parity of reasoning, if aggregating individual behavior is sufficient for social facts, then the social facts cannot explain the individual ones.

Now, one way holists can restore the parallel is to claim that the whole is more than the sum of its parts: Somehow, putting people together *creates* new things that, together with people's behavior, constitute society and make for social facts. These new things then are the theoretical entities of sociology to which we must appeal to explain the behavior of individuals in society. Few philosophers or social scientists will want to take this idea seriously, except as a last resort. For in the end, this hypothesis is not so much an explanation of a social fact as an admission that it can't be explained. How the whole could be more than the sum of its parts is just a mystery.

But consider the alternative, namely: There are two sets of facts, one about society and one about individuals. The first set is wholly dependent on the second set and yet not identical with it. The dependence is not accidental; it's at least causal and perhaps logical: without people, no social facts; with people, social facts. Moreover, these social facts, whose existence depends only on the existence and interaction of people and on nothing else, are an essential part of the explanation of their behavior. It's not just that subjective and perhaps false beliefs about social facts explain behavior, for the social facts are needed to explain beliefs, true or false, on the holist's view. Perhaps the hypothesis about wholes being more than the sum of their parts is more attractive than first supposed. For it seems no more mysterious than the complete dependence of one set of facts on another set, even though the dependent ones explain the independent ones.

In the end, the argument for holism from the terms in which we describe action is not very appealing. And if the intentional explanation of action really requires social facts, as this philosophical argument holds, then holism—with its mysteries about wholes greater than the sum of their parts—will also have to bear the methodological problems of [L] and intentional explanations generally. As such it would fail to provide what we advertised at the beginning of this chapter: a way out of the dilemmas of naturalism and interpretationalism. So, it's pretty clear that holism needs an argument that is both more convincing than this philosophical one and independent of the problems of intentional social science. As we shall now see, there are more powerful arguments for holism, arguments that in fact undermine intentional theories of human action.

The Autonomy of Sociology

Among speculative philosophers, and in various religious traditions, holism is an ancient doctrine. But holism became an issue of importance to social science with the work of Durkheim in the late nineteenth century. Durkheim did more to establish sociology as an independent discipline than anyone else. But Durkheim was as hard-headed an empiricist about methodology in social science as one is likely to find. He was quite explicit in claiming that the methods of sociology must be the same as those of the natural sciences. But as to the subject matter of sociology, that he held is quite distinct and different from the subject of any other discipline.

In fact the existence of a range of social facts was Durkheim's most powerful argument for the distinct existence of a science of sociology, at a time when sociology was struggling for its autonomy from psychology (and philosophy, for that matter). In the 1890s, even psychology was not yet viewed as a discipline distinct from philosophy. And what better argument for establishing a discipline's autonomy than *showing* there are facts that no other discipline even takes note of, let alone can explain?

The term "social facts" was coined in *The Rules of the Sociological Method*, but the most powerful argument for them was not methodological. It was factual. In *Suicide*, Durkheim uncovered some startling statistics. Among the most well known are the fact that the number of suicides per 100,000 differs radically for Catholics as opposed to Protestants; even when we control for all other reasonable factors, Catholics had a much lower suicide rate. The numbers differ also between men and women, married and single, army officers and conscripts, newly wealthy and steadily impoverished, between the summer and the winter, during meal times rather than between meals. These statistical regularities cry out for explanation.

Durkheim noted that the reasonable thing to do is to search the reasons for suicide and see how they vary between the differing classes, Protestant and Catholic, officer and conscript, and so on. For suicide is an action and, accordingly, the result of desires and belief. In fact, coroners had already been doing this throughout the nineteenth century, citing the presumptive causes of suicide under headings like poverty, family troubles, debauchery, physical pain, love, jealousy. Leave aside the difficulty of correctly identifying these reasons from case to case, under the reasonable assumption that errors will cancel each other out. What do we find? Well, in certain parts of Europe the suicide rate rose 100 percent between 1856 and 1878, and not gradually either; rather, it remained at the lower level for some years, then suddenly jumped to the higher level and remained there. But now examine the coroners' reports: The proportion of each of the "presumptive causes" of suicide— illness, poverty, jealousy, and so forth—remained almost exactly the same. But this means that either the incidence of each of these reasons for suicide increased in exactly the same proportion or else they were not the causes at all.

Now, consider the methodological maxim, same cause, same effect. This principle tells us that like effects must have like causes, and unlike effects must have unlike causes. Between 1856 and 1878 the effects—the number of suicides per 100,000—were unlike: There was a 100 percent difference in the number of suicides. So, whatever caused the rate in 1856 cannot also be identified as the cause in 1878. Because the reasons cited in coroner's reports remained the same, in proportion, they cannot have been the causes. From this Durkheim concluded that even if each individual suicide is caused by a psychological fact—the suicide's reasons for committing suicide—the change in the *rate* per 100,000 cannot be caused by such facts. This statistical fact is a social fact, Durkheim held, and cannot be explained by psychological facts. To explain this social fact we must seek other social facts that cause it and that also cause the psychological facts. For the stability of reasons for suicide over time must itself be explained by forces external to and independent of the individual.

Here is an argument for the existence of social facts independent of a theory that hypothesizes them. And once we grant on the basis of an empirical argument that there are such facts, there is nothing methodologically suspicious about hypothesizing further social facts to explain the ones whose existence we have already proved "theory-free." And this is exactly what Durkheim did.

The theory is a paradigm of twentieth-century sociological theorizing. Durkheim treated the suicide rate as a social indicator—a measure of the health of the society as a whole. Beyond some baseline level of suicides per 100,000, which we can determine by comparing time-series data, a rise in the suicide rate represents something gone wrong in the society. The members of a society are governed by social forces that exist independent of them and that determine the degree of social integration of a society's members. The behavior of individuals is determined by norms of conduct of which we are not aware but which are imposed on us by social institutions. Thus, suicide is lower among Catholics because they are bound more closely to one another and the guidance of the church than are Protestants. And suicide is higher among army officers than conscripts because they are bound even more tightly to their units and sacrifice themselves to "the good of the service" if required. The newly wealthy, whose means are now beyond their needs, are made normless and more inclined to suicide than perpetually poor folk, whose social norms remain undisturbed. In fact, Durkheim identified three different sorts of suicides in terms of three distinct social causes: egoistic suicide, resulting from too little social integration; altruistic suicide, resulting from too much; and anomic suicide, resulting from great and rapid changes in the degree of social integration that leave agents normless and disoriented.

Thus we can explain each of the social facts about differences in suicide rates by a social fact about differences in the degree of social integration. There is an optimal level of social integration at which the baseline level of suicide is maintained. But one may ask, optimal for whom, and for what? For the society as a whole, its well-being and survival. Each of the institutions of society has a *function* to fulfil, and its behavior is explained by this function. Thus marriage, religious organizations, family structure, legal and business institutions, political organization, everything of interest to the social scientists, has a function in the operation of society. When these institutions are oppressively overbearing, the society functions poorly, as manifested by a high suicide rate and by other social ills as well. When institutions are not sufficiently powerful in their effect on individual behavior, the same symptoms of social disorder are manifest. Durkheim viewed society as a vast organism, a unity reflecting its organization. Thus, the function a social institution serves is not for individuals but for the society out of which they are composed. This is holism with a vengeance, and no shame about entities above and beyond individuals.

Durkheim was not embarrassed about the apparent commitment of his theory to a doctrine of "organic wholes" and its concomitant thesis that the whole is greater than the sum of the parts. There were two reasons for this. First, along with other late-nineteenth-century writers about method, he supposed this principle to be substantiated in the relation of physics to chemistry, and of both to physiology. That is, chemical phenomena could not then be explained wholly in terms of physical theory, nor physiology be explained fully in terms of chemistry. This now seems far less clear than it did in Durkheim's day.

But, in any case, Durkheim seems to have held that along with individuals, society is also made up of an *âme collective*, which is usually translated as "group mind," though we should beware of literal translations. It is unclear how much Durkheim really required this notion in order to expound his theory. What is clear is that neither it, nor the social regularities it was called upon to explain, were in Durkheim's view *reducible* to psychological processes. Therefore, sociology had to be an independent and autonomous discipline. It had its own facts and it had its own law. What more could a science want? Its own distinct method? No. Durkheim held to the thesis that logical positivists later called the unity of science, that disciplines were distinguished by subject matter and not method, for method is determined by the requirements of knowledge, which are the same everywhere.

In fact, according to Durkheim, psychology must surrender some of its domain to sociology. His proof that social facts exist is also an argument that at least some individual behavior, that appears to be determined by psychological factors is not caused by them. To begin with, as Durkheim recognized, social forces must work through individuals. So he held that such facts constrain and direct individual behavior, even when this behavior seems entirely "voluntary," in his words. And Durkheim has an argument for this conclusion: If there are social forces that determine the suicide rate, they can only do so by determining individual suicides. What the psychologist identifies in individual cases are either mediating links in a causal chain between the social forces and suicide or else, as Durkheim sometimes seemed to indicate, merely by-products, produced along with suicide by social forces.

Here then is a more powerful argument for holism, and not just about the social suicide rate. For Durkheim and his sociological successors have employed similar arguments to assert the existence of a wide range of such facts, more than enough to provide an entire scientific discipline with plenty to occupy itself. And this type of argument is one that claims to be well within the naturalistic camp, at least as regards scientific aims and methods. It claims to be an argument no different from those that stand behind the autonomy of biology or chemistry from physics. Just as there are biological facts, whose existence we recognize without having already bought into biological theory, so too there are sociological ones, whose existence can be established without question-begging appeal to a theory that already assumes them. But once we recognize the existence of some social facts that cannot be explained by psychology, it is evident that the explanatory power of the theory of autonomous social factors, which best explains them, provides further evidence for the truth of holism.

Holism and Reductionism in Psychology and Sociology

There is however at least one loose thread in this argument. It's the relation between autonomous sociological facts and psychological ones from which they are autonomous. Consider the psychological facts about individual suicides, for example. How can we decide the question of whether psychological factors are causal links or by-products? The question is important for Durkheim's claims about the autonomy of sociology and the existence of social facts.

In fact, the question is a crucial issue for an autonomy argument, like Durkheim's, that justifies the autonomy of a discipline on the existence of distinct entities and laws for that discipline to study and to discover about these entities. If it can be shown that these laws can be explained by laws of another more fundamental discipline, then the argument for the autonomy of the discipline seems seriously weakened. It may then be claimed that the facts the discipline deals with are not autonomous but consist of facts described and/or explained by the more fundamental discipline. This argument has always seemed especially threatening to sociologists and anthropologists, for without an argument for holism, their disciplines seem in danger of being swallowed up by psychology. Otherwise what else is there to society but people, whose behavior it is the business of psychology to explain? Sociologists and anthropologists therefore frequently quote Durkheim's injunction, "Whenever a social phenomenon is directly explained by a psychological phenomenon we may be sure the explanation is false." We need to consider whether this thesis is defensible and what sort of autonomy from psychology it is that sociology needs or can secure.

Suppose that psychological facts are causes of suicide in individual cases. Then presumably there will be generalizations linking these factors to suicide, perhaps even intentional generalizations of [L]'s form. If there are such generalizations, then by simple arithmetic aggregation of the explanation of individual suicides, these generalizations should also explain the aggregate fact of the number of suicides per 100,000. Working backward from the psychological causes of suicide should bring us to the social facts that determine these psychological causes. In effect, then psychological facts would be part of the explanation of why social facts obtain, and psychological laws would help explain sociological laws linking the degree of social integration to the suicide rate. But this result threatens the autonomy of sociology. For it makes it look as if sociology is "reducible" to psychology. All we would need is to show that social integration is itself the result of psychological factors or the behavior of people toward one another.

The alternative is to treat psychological factors as by-products, "epi-phenomena," which have no causal role in suicide, as merely "joint effects," along with suicide, of purely social forces. But this claim flies in the face of a causal principle that no empiricist like Durkheim could ignore: the principle that there is no "action [that is, causation] at a distance." One of the legacies of the success of mechanical explanations in science is the doctrine that one change cannot cause another unless they are in spatial and temporal contact or unless there is a chain of such contacts between them. Now, for a change in the degree of social integration to cause a change in the suicide rate, there must be such a causal chain, and it must pass through people. Unless it can do so without passing through their thoughts, psychological processes cannot be a mere by-product of suicide's social cause.

The same argument seems available for any generalization connecting one social fact with another. The causal chain must pass through individuals, and this threatens the autonomy of disciplines that deal with such facts, even if we grant their existence. Furthermore, showing the dependence of social laws on psychological processes may lead to the conclusion that the social facts are ultimately psychological too. This conclusion in fact mirrors an influential image of the nature of scientific progress and the structure of scientific knowledge, an image that seriously threatens arguments for the autonomy of distinct social sciences, especially ones without well-established records of success in the discovery of laws.

This image is unabashedly reductionist. It claims, first of all, that the history of scientific progress is the history of reductions of narrower theories to broader ones. Once a science discovers its first improvable generalizations, progress comes in the formulation of deeper laws and theories that both explain the initial generalizations and improve on their accuracy. Thus, Kepler's laws of planetary motion and Galileo's laws of terrestrial motion were the break with Aristotle that produced modern physics. It took Newton to show that both were derivable from a single set of laws, a set of profound economy and simplicity, to which over the next three hundred years many other regularities were "reduced." That is, these regularities were shown to be special cases of Newton's laws or deducible from them when we added certain assumptions about the mathematical values of parameters and constants, et cetera. And Newton's laws not only enabled us to systematize disparate generalizations, they enabled us to improve the generalizations, explained their exceptions, and showed us what further forces need to be taken into account in order to improve their predictive powers. But scientific progress eventually led to the reduction of Newtonian mechanics to still more fundamental principles that explain it and its exceptions: the theory of relativity and quantum mechanics. We can deduce Newton's laws from these theories by adding the false assumptions (embedded in Newton's theory) that the speed of light is infinite, and that energy comes in a continuum of values, instead of discrete quantities—quanta.

What is more, in addition to reducing Newtonian mechanics to more fundamental theory, modern science seems to reduce thermodynamics, electromagnetism, and large parts of chemistry to fundamental physical laws. In fact, important parts of biology, like genetics, enzymology, and parts of physiology, have been reduced to chemistry. And this suggests not just that science progresses by reduction but that the edifice of scientific theories is reductive as well. Thus, chemistry seems reducible to physics and, increasingly, biology to chemistry. But where do the social and behavioral sciences fit into this picture? The picture is a deeply antiholist one. It tells us that biological systems are nothing but chemical systems, and chemical systems nothing but physical systems. So, psychological systems—organisms with minds—must themselves be biological and, ultimately, just chemical or physical systems. Social systems—groups of individuals—must ultimately be composed of psychological ones. More precisely, if there are psychological laws, they should be derivable from biological ones; if there are sociological laws, they should be derivable from psychological ones.

The methodological moral reductionist draw seems twofold. First, propositions not explainable by reduction to laws of a more fundamental discipline are, not laws, but either falsehoods or local descriptions of initial conditions to which real laws may be applied. Second, any discipline that has not yet secured laws is unlikely to do so, unless it follows the guidance of methods that have secured laws in other disciplines and employs descriptive language common to these successful disciplines.

This view has profound ramifications for psychology that we must address before returning to their bearing on holistic arguments for the autonomy of sociology. As we have seen, intentional psychology seems irreducible to neurophysiology. Neuroscience is an extensional discipline: The vocabulary of this theory does not have "content" in the way that intensional sentences do. Substitution of equivalent descriptions in any sentence of neuroscience will not change a truth to a falsity, or vice versa. The same is true of the rest of science. This means that intentional descriptions of our brain states can't be equated with neurological descriptions of them. But just such equations are necessary conditions for reduction. For example, we can deduce the gas law, $PV = rT$, from theory about molecules only if we can identify the temperature of a gas with properties of molecules that make it up. Reducing thermodynamics to molecular mechanics hinges on the fact that the temperature of a gas is *equal* to the mean kinetic energy of the molecules that compose it. This kind of equivalence is just not going to exist to link belief, for example, and any description of brain states—it's logically precluded by the intensionality-extensionality difference.

The conclusion some philosophers, psychologists, and social scientists draw is that intentional psychology is a dead end, that there are no laws of intentional psychology. For any such laws would not be reducible to the rest of science, and that's impossible. Why? Because intensionality blocks the unity of science.

According to the unity-of-science view, all our scientific theories should be coherently interconnected with one another and arranged in a hierarchy from the most fundamental to the most derivative, and the derivations must be deductive. This will explain why no one has found any laws in psychology, why [L] is so close to vacuous and has so little predictive content, and most of all, why [L] hasn't undergone any improvement in all of recorded history. It can't be improved because improvement requires being linked to a broader reducing theory, just what is impossible for intensional statements. And the problem is the descriptive terminology we have always employed in attempting hypotheses in psychology. Intentional concepts don't link up neatly to the rest of science because they don't "carve nature at the joints."

Recall the point about the concept of "fish" in Chapter 1, "Progress and Prediction." Any attempt to frame generalizations about how fish breathe, and to improve these generalizations or explain them, will be frustrated by the fact that "fish" is not a "natural kind" term. Though its origins in ordinary thought are clear, it has no place in biological science, just because it cannot be linked up in laws with other general categories. So, biologists give up the ordinary category of "fish" as aquatic animal and either redefine the term or break up the class of fish into several homogeneous categories to which they assign Latin names.

Psychologists who embrace this view have turned their attention to neuroscience or artificial intelligence, or have tried to make a go of Skinnerian behaviorism. This line of argument has the following implications for the rest of social science. First, to the degree that other social disciplines are intentional too, they have no more prospects of reduction than psychology. Like psychology, they will not be reducible to extensional science. What is more, their commitment to intentionality explains their failure to have identified laws and theories reflecting the continuing derivation and improvement characteristic of science.

On the one hand, if intentional psychology is a will-o'-the-wisp, then of course a macrosociology irreducible to it is untouched by its problems. On the other hand, intentional psychology must on the reductionistic picture link up with the rest of science somewhere, either through a nonintensional psychology, or, what is less likely, through some direct connection to biology. Either way, on this argument, sociology will turn out to be reducible to, not autonomous from, the rest of science. This is of course a heads-I-win-tails-you-lose argument against holism and autonomy. If sociology is not reducible, then it's a scientific dead end, like intentional psychology. And if it is reducible, then it's not autonomous.

The argument, however, has several weaknesses. To begin with there is its picture of the history of science as cumulative progress by successive reduction, and its image of a deductive hierarchy of scientific theories. If the picture ever was an uncontroversial account of the history and present status of scientific theorizing, it is no longer. Both historians of science and some philosophers have repudiated the picture as a simple-minded reconstruction. First, there have been detailed attempts to show that the deductive relation claimed to hold between successive theories in physics does not obtain. Nor do such relations obtain, it is claimed, between theories in different sciences: Biological theory is held to be autonomous from chemistry, even at the level of molecular genetics, but especially between evolutionary theory and the rest of natural science. Secondly, and more radically, it has been claimed that in fact theories once viewed as related by reduction are in fact "incommensurable"—not just logically incompatible, so that no deduction between them is possible; they are not even intertranslatable. Third, this incommensurability has been extended from factual theories to scientific methods, so that the fact that a method works in one discipline or theoretical research program is no reason to think it will work in another.

All of these ideas stem from Thomas Kuhn's *Structure of Scientific Revolutions* and especially from interpretations of it. No work has been taken more to heart by proponents of the autonomy of social sciences from each other, and from natural science's findings and methods. If the *most radical* of these methodological writers is correct, then there are few problems in the philosophy of social science. Certainly none of the ones we have dealt with will turn out to be serious, for they all involve attempts to decide between irreconcilable viewpoints, when no such attempt is even intelligible. No attempt to solve problems in the philosophy of science is intelligible because every attempt presupposes some theory or other. But all theories are incommensurable with one another. Any attempt to bridge the gap between theories is just covert mistranslation. And any conclusion in favor of one methodology will beg the question against some other equally acceptable methodology.

Let us therefore consider the least radical of these objections to the reductionist's picture. Biology is certainly a respectable science, one that adopts to a large extent the causal methods of physical science and that searches for laws to explain its phenomena. Moreover, it has had some important nomological successes: evolutionary theory, population genetics, molecular biology, to name the most imposing. Yet, biological theory is not as yet reducible to chemistry or physics. And even when it is, no one will begin to deny the reality of biological organisms.

Sociologists and intentional psychologists can take considerable comfort in these facts, for they suggest that irreducibility is not a symptom of pseudoscience or sterility and frustration. Moreover, even if sociology were reducible to psychology, and/or psychology reducible to neuroscience, it would not follow automatically that there were no sociological facts or no psychological facts after all, would it?

In fact the question of whether biology is reducible to physical science may be instructive for the holism/autonomy question. For one thing, it suggests that the really interesting issue is not whether there are social facts or not, but whether there is a distinctive discipline couched in the language of such facts. That is, almost all biologists are prepared to admit that their research subjects, whether species, populations, organisms, organs, tissues, cells, or macromolecules, are "nothing but" physical matter, albeit organized in distinctive ways. No one thinks that each of these levels of description refers to a distinct and different entity greater than the sum of its parts. Rather, biologists seek interesting and useful generalizations at each of the various levels of organization they identify—in the case of organisms and organs—or hypothesize—in the case of species or macromolecules. One way of saying that there are such generalizations at any level is to say that there are facts about species or macromolecules distinct from facts about individual organisms. And such a claim need have no mysterious metaphysical or ontological connotations.

Similarly, the autonomist may argue, the question of whether there are social facts is the question of whether there are interesting generalizations couched in language that purports to refer to such facts. The rest is "mere" philosophy. Let the philosophers fight about whether the terms in a well-confirmed law refer to real objects or not. (Notice that this is not a version of the instrumentalist view broached in Chapter 3, "Instrumentalism in Economics," for it begins with the assumption that these statements about social facts are well confirmed, independent of anything they might explain.) Like the claims of biology, sociological laws must ultimately be explained by psychological ones or by whatever theory best explains individual human behavior. But that doesn't mean there are no interesting generalizations about social facts, generalizations that can be used to explain and predict social phenomena, and some cases of individual behavior for that matter too. This is not a view Durkheim would have been comfortable with, perhaps, while fighting for sociology's life. But now that its life is not threatened any longer, we may relax and adopt it as the cognitive content of the claim that there are autonomous social facts. This is a view we might describe as "methodological" or "instrumental" holism, according to which the autonomy of a discipline hinges not on whether a special range of facts exists, but on whether the discipline can come up with interesting generalizations.

Functional Analysis
and Functional Explanation

Methodological holism goes hand in hand with another "ism"—functionalism. Not only does functionalism go along with holism, but as an analytical strategy and an explanatory one, it too was first advocated, explained, and exploited by Durkheim. And we may easily adapt Durkheim's arguments for functionalism to support the methodological holism sketched above as a substitute for his sterner version.

Functionalism as an explanatory strategy is fairly obvious and common both in ordinary life and in biology. We often explain something's character or even its very existence by citing the function it serves. "What's that rock doing in front of the door?" "It's a door-stop." "Why does the heart beat?" "In order to circulate the blood." As we have seen (Chapter 3, "Behaviorism's Attack on Teleology"), both of these sorts of explanations are problematical: the ordinary one, because it is intentional; the biological one, because it isn't! That is, explaining something's purposes in terms of our desires and beliefs introduces all the problems of intentionality—how do our beliefs and desires represent things, have content? Explaining something in terms of purposes that no person has seems to require God, or some intelligent agent that modern science would rather not have to invoke.

Problematical or not, both sorts of explanations are commonplace in ordinary life and in biology. More important, leaving aside ordinary contexts, it is almost unarguable that such explanations are legitimate in biology. The philosophical puzzle is not to decide whether they are legitimate but to give an analysis of biological method and theory that explain why they are indispensable. In the absence of such an explanation, no one is going to withdraw his assent to William Harvey's great discovery about why the heart beats. And a philosophy of science that delegitimizes functional explanations in biology, instead of justifying them, must be wrong.

Along with explaining, appeal to functions has another purpose. It is used for "individuating" and classifying things, for identifying units or wholes, for tying together disparate and apparently unconnected things into a large system composed out of them. By discovering the common function that many disparate things serve, we can begin to frame interesting generalizations about them, generalizations that would have escaped our attention otherwise. For example, consider the functional concept "clock," meaning a system for telling time. Now consider the incredibly diverse set of physical objects that have this function. There are first of all the many different kinds of watch mechanisms—escapement wheels, tuning forks, quartz mechanisms, microprocessors, et cetera. Then there are atomic clocks, cesium clocks, pendulum clocks, sundials, water clocks, hourglasses, marked wax candles, the sun, leaves that change color with the season, tree rings, blood vessels that pulse, and so forth.

What is it that all these things have in common that makes them clocks? Certainly no physical mechanism (except perhaps at the ultimate level of quantum mechanical description). What enables us to identify them all as clocks is their function, or the uses they can be put to. And we would be unable either to calibrate one clock mechanism against another mechanism or to improve on the accuracy of any without the general functional category of clock, which enables us to bring this physically heterogeneous collection together in one theory that explains their common behavior. The functional concept of clock permits us to do something else. If we are given a collection of "junk" on a workbench, simply learning that the objects go together to make up a clock will help us to figure out how to put them together, what each of them does, what sort of a thing they compose, and so forth. And in contrast, if we know little about the physical makeup, or construction, of things, the best way to begin to learn this is to see what they do, what function the parts go together to perform, if they have a function.

Now, autonomous macrosocial science requires this sort of functional analysis just because it claims to be autonomous from psychology and the rest of science. The claim of autonomy is the claim that knowing about the behavior of individuals can't tell us much of anything about the social facts, because psychological theory is no help in discovering sociological theory. But if this is correct, the only route to such theory is through functional analysis. We have to ignore the problem of "composition" or "structure," the question of what social facts are composed of because knowing this information won't help us identify social facts or discover any generalizations about them. This leaves only the study of how they work, what they do, in short their function, as a source of sociological theory. And we can neither identify the social facts nor discover the regularities that systematize them without *assuming* that they have functions.

Methodological holism thus begins with the reasonable hypothesis that what we have learned about individual behavior provides little direct insight about the character of macrosocial phenomena. Once we have discovered systematic regularities, if any, about social facts, then a psychological theory may be called upon to help explain these regularities. But psychology will not help us identify the basic units and kinds of social facts that are regulated by social forces.

Nor will ordinary language. The divisions that it identifies reflect functions, but not necessarily the ones we seek, or even the real functions, and certainly not the basic functions of social institutions. Thus, for example, the jury system is identified in ordinary thought as the institution with the function of determining matters of fact in legal proceedings in nations employing the English common law. This, however, may be quite a superficial functional analysis, one that obscures some other deeper functional role or disguises the fact that the jury system shares important functional properties with other institutions. Both of these possibilities are important, because identifying "deeper" functions, or wider functional categories, is essential to uncovering interesting sociological generalizations. Thus, some Marxian sociological analysis may hold that the real function of the jury system is "ideological"—to encourage public acceptance of decisions made elsewhere on the basis of class interests, instead of on the basis of real guilt or innocence. The institution is thus to be explained in terms of its "real function," that of sustaining the ruling classes. Or, alternatively, if the jury system's role is described more widely as that of "peaceful conflict resolution," then it will be classified together with other social institutions having the same role. Subsequently, the sociological theorist will attempt to frame generalizations about conflict-resolving institutions, generalizations that can be tested by further examination of the jury system and other institutions with the same function.

This difference between apparent and real functional roles is often described in terms of the distinction between *latent* and *manifest* functions. The manifest functions of a social institution are those it was, as it were, intentionally designed to accomplish, and which it is recognized by its participants as accomplishing. Latent functions are those it serves unwittingly, without the recognition of its participants. Such unnoticed functions are held to be more important and more systematically significant than the manifest functions of the institution.

For instance, the manifest function of marriage is to legalize domestic and sexual relations and regularize the duties and rights associated with them. But, according to Durkheim, marriage has other, latent functions. It is one of many institutions that protect the members of society from suicide. Its latent function is that of maintaining the optimal degree of social integration. In that respect it is to be grouped with other social institutions that may seem quite different from it, the jury system, for example, or the institutions of the Catholic parish.

Identifying things by their functional role may also enable us to recognize the artificiality of boundaries between social institutions, boundaries that prevent us from recognizing generalizations that may explain them. For example, the functions of the police, as the agency of law enforcement, and of the courts, as the agency of factual determinations in legal questions, may seem quite distinct. Yet the sociologist who views the latter as an institution for rationalizing class interests may bring the courts together with the police into one institution with a single latent function, an institution that operates effectively by making it appear as though both its parts have distinct identities and separate functions.

Individuating social institutions by function and framing explanatory theories about them go hand in hand. We would be unable to discover any generalizations about functionally identified social institutions unless we first identified them in terms of their functions. But just to identify something as an instance of a functional category is to advance a generalization about it. To identify marriage as a socially integrative mechanism involves asserting that in general it encourages social integration. This is a generalization as well as a classification. It enables us to lump marriage together with other such institutions and then to see whether we can frame hypotheses about them, for instance, the generalization that they reduce the individual's probability of suicide. In fact Durkheim's claim that there are three different types of suicides— egoistic, altruistic, and anomic—is based on a prior identification of social institutions into functional types and an examination of the consequences of three different ways they can break down in their function of maintaining an optimal degree of social integration.

So functionalism is both an analytical strategy for identifying socially significant institutions and an explanatory strategy that accounts for their characteristics by appeal to their effects for society as a whole, instead of by appeal to the behavior of constituent individuals who compose them.

If holism is correct, either as a doctrine about the independent existence of social facts or as a methodologically reasonable practice, then functional analysis and functional explanations are obviously appealing. In fact they are more than appealing. They are indispensable. That is why holists are functionalists. However, functionalism is a method with some serious potential problems, upon which methodological individualism has seized in its counterarguments against holism, both ontological and methodological.

Methodological Individualism
Versus Functionalism

The commitment to functionalism represents everything that is wrong with holistic social science, according to the individualist. It is held to be complacent at best, immoral at worst, and sterile when it isn't untestable altogether. Besides, individualists charge, it rests on a false view about the nature of society, the view that society is some sort of organism, as opposed to a collection of "atomic" individuals. Accordingly, individualists recommend we turn our backs on its methods completely, search for explanations of social phenomena that appeal only to the behavior of individuals; and when we fail in the employment of this strategy, we should blame our own lack of scientific ingenuity and not twist the facts to explain our failure.

According to the individualist, functionalism works as a method in biology because the subject matter of biology is organisms—and their organs, tissues, cells, et cetera, which have indisputable functions with regard to the survival and well-being of the organism. Holism and functionalism are tenable only on the assumption that society is some sort of superindividual organism, made up of institutions and individuals. But, individualists insist, society is not an organism, and there are scientific and moral dangers even in the metaphorical treatment of it as such. Therefore, these "isms"—holism and functionalism—encourage cognitively and morally dangerous suppositions.

First consider the individualist's morality charges: At its worst, holism is hand in glove with totalitarianism of the right and the left. By according social institutions a life of their own and according them functions with respect to the needs of the society as opposed to the needs of the individuals who compose it, holism and functionalism threaten the priority of personal liberty and individual human rights. For example, we hold that the jury system has the function of ensuring the rights of the accused. The suggestion that it has some other deeper, latent function undermines the priority of the protection of rights as its real function and encourages us to view this institution as serving some other needs with social priority over the protection of individual rights. If the real function of elections is, as Marx put it, so that the proletariat can regularly pretend to decide which among the capitalist classes will exploit it, then someone who adopts this theory is unlikely to respect the process or outcome of "free elections."

It is regrettably true that, from Plato onward, totalitarian political philosophies have subordinated individual rights and advantages to the needs and well-being of society. They have justified this subordination on a holistic theory of social organization, one that makes society as a whole into an agent with rights, claims, and interests. But it is also clear, to many holists at least, that this misuse of a version of their methodological prescription is no reason to condemn all uses of it. For, as some of them are keen to argue, their theories are value free, neutral on moral and political applications, and certainly embody no prescrptions about how society should be organized.

Nevertheless, individualists reply, holists and functionalists must be inclined by their doctrine to be complacent about social arrangements, and their theory is at least an unintended bulwark against social change. For the identification of social institutions in terms of their function carries with it the implicit suggestion that they fulfil a *need* of society, and on the latent-function theory, a need we may not have recognized.

As such, one must be leery of replacing institutions or changing them considerably, for the change may adversely affect society's ability to meet its needs. Conservatives often point to the unintended consequences of social change, which often overwhelm the foreseen ones. Functionalism is grist for their mill because it holds that beyond the things institutions do directly for individuals, they do things for the society that social planners often fail to take account of when they set out to make "improvements."

This is a charge that may have more substance than the complaint that holism is akin to totalitarianism. For functionalists are likely to seek support for their method in an evolutionary approach to society, one that identifies institutions as adaptations. To call something an adaptation certainly seems a way of commending it.

And this brings us to the cognitive objections individualists offer against holism. Treating society as an organism, even metaphorically, and taking latent functions seriously force the holist to make difficult choices. He must either opt for Durkheim's "âme collective"—the group mind—to explain how society arranges institutions to meet its needs, or embrace a Darwinian evolutionary view, according to which all long-lasting social institutions arose through variation and selection for their beneficial functions. This is an alternative to which we shall return, in the discussion of sociobiology (Chapter 6). The individualist considers either of these alternatives unattractive enough to reject holism, even as a methodological convenience.

In some ways functionalism is a natural development of the strategy of finding *meaning* in human affairs. One reason it is so appealing a strategy is its similarity to folk psychology's approach to explaining individual behavior in terms of purposes. Moreover, by finding latent functions we do not recognize, it pursues the strategy of other theories that seek deeper meanings. Thus, it can help defend the search for meanings against the charge of banality. It is in some respects a far more appealing approach to deeper meanings that psychoanalytical theory, and it is a natural way to interpret Marxian theories. Functionalism is widely preferred to Freud's account of deep meanings because it has far less specific content. One can still search for deep meanings even if one repudiates psychoanalytical approaches to them. Instead of investing unconscious psychological states with unrecognized purposes to explain action, one invests social institutions with such purposes and then shows how they constrain, overwhelm, or inform individual action with a deeper meaning, derived from the institutional function.

The attractions of functionalism cum holism as a way of interpreting Marx's theory are evident. Society is to be viewed as a system composed of classes competing for supremacy. The institutions of society are analyzed in terms of their functions in fulfilling the needs of the competing classes. *Ideologiekritik* provides the meaning of aspects of the ideological superstructure in terms of the interests, not of individuals, but of social classes that these aspects serve. The whole society is itself viewed as a superorganism, composed of these classes, which changes over time in ways that perpetuate itself. Of course not every aspect of Marxian doctrine can be easily accommodated to this approach. In particular, it is difficult to reconcile functionalism with the reflexive character of the theory in which critical theorists set so much stock. But it is not impossible. Still we can leave this matter to Marxian scholarship, for there are both holist and individualist strains in Marx's writings.

The question the individualist raises is who or what are these meanings for? Not for individuals, for the meanings of institutions are not to be found in their subconsciouses or in their immediate interests. If functions provide the meanings that explain institutions, then we need an intentional agent in which to "locate" these meanings unless, of course, talk of meanings is metaphorical or figurative in these contexts. For Durkheim in *Suicide*, at least, there was such a consciousness, and his arguments for it are far from derisory. Nevertheless, few have followed him.

So, we need another rationale for the attribution of functions. But functional attributions and explanations are teleological: A system's functions are its effects, in particular those effects that meet a need, either its own or that of a larger system that contains it. So functional explanation is explanation of causes by their effects. Now, as our reflection on the problem of teleology (in Chapter 3) shows, the only way to ground talk of functions is the way biology does—by overt or covert appeal to natural selection.

If a functional theory is to be a causal one, then it cannot allow later effects to explain earlier causes. But functions are *later effects*. Marriage's function is in part the prevention of suicide because it *results* in the reduction in suicide's incidence. Results, however, cannot cause their antecedents, and therefore results cannot causally explain them. And of course some married persons commit suicide, so that in these cases marriage did not have the usual effect; yet this does not detract from the functional analysis.

The solution in biology is, as we have seen (Chapter 3, "Behaviorism's Attack on Teleology"), to appeal to the mechanism of evolution. "The function of the heartbeat is to circulate the blood" implicitly *means* that over the course of evolution random variations in heart configuration that fostered circulation were selected for because of their contribution to fitness. Thus, a heart that circulates the blood is an *adaptation*. And functional claims turn out to be only apparently about immediate effects and really about ultimate causes in the long evolutionary past.

Well, why can't sociological functionalism help itself to a theory of the natural selection of societies, in which variation produced an assortment of social institutions with diverse effects for the future of societies? Among these institutions some were adaptive, some were maladaptive, and others neutral. Those societies with adaptive institutions flourished, those with maladaptive ones extinguished themselves, and those with adaptively neutral institutions were overwhelmed in competition with the better adapted ones. By a succession of refinements, through the mechanism of variation and selection, there arose societies with the institutions we recognize today. And this entirely causal account underwrites the functional analyses and explanations the holist requires.

The individualist may recognize this theory as an abstract possibility, but he will reject it as a solution to the teleological embarrassment of holism. To begin with, whatever evidence there may be for this theory in biology, there is none in sociology, or at any rate not enough to justify functionalism as a research strategy. Second, there are crucial disanalogies between biological evolution and the sort required to underwrite sociological functionalism. Third, the theory of natural selection has problems of its own, and its applications beyond biology are too controversial to lend much weight to sociology. Fourth, many important functionalists reject and repudiate a biological approach to their discipline. And fifth, even if it were true, an evolutionary account of our social institutions would not answer the really pressing questions that social science must answer about them.

Biology has had several billion years in which to evolve complex organisms through selection and variation. But clearly, there has not been enough time, it is argued, since the appearance of Homo sapiens or some social predecessor for blind variation and selection to have evolved the social institutions we recognize around us. Many of them are undoubtedly the result of evolution, but not blind evolution, rather, foresighted design and cultural transmission. Moreover, the diversity of cultures emerging in the face of the same selective forces is left entirely unexplained by this theory. Why, for example, should very different and quite complex marriage rules emerge among societies of almost the same size, state of development, and environmental conditions?

Then there is the disanalogy between biological selection and societal selection. Nature selects for individuals, and the mechanism it employs is differential reproduction. An adaptive variation enables the individual who carries it to leave more offspring, more copies of itself. The sociological employment of this theory requires a parallel sort of reproduction, whereby a society with adaptive institutions, in competition with others, leaves more offspring societies than the others do. But there is no evidence of such multiplication of offspring societies, or any credible analogue to differential reproduction in biological evolution. There was among evolutionary biologists in the 1960s a brief fascination with group selection, as opposed to individual selection, but even this notion involved the leaving of more successor groups than competitors. Subsequent biological research has shown that group selection even under the best of circumstances is only a bare possibility (see below, Chapter 6). And these circumstances are not realized in the competition among human societies.

Moreover, the biological theory of natural selection is alleged to have infirmities of its own and thus can provide no support for an even more controversial theory. The most famous exponent of methodological individualism, Karl Popper, was among those who held that the theory of natural selection is a vacuous and empty tautology. According to Popper, the theory claimed that evolution proceeds by the survival and reproduction of the fittest, but it defined "the fittest" as those who survive and reproduce the most. This turns the theory into the empty claim that the fittest are the fittest, or those variations that survive and reproduce are the ones that survive and reproduce. If this criticism is correct, then functional analysis will be in serious trouble in biology as well as in sociology.

There is much to be said in response to this charge, which turns out to be profoundly confused as an argument against the theory of natural selection. But it does reflect a serious problem for functionalism outside of biology. Evolutionary biologists do in fact have a way of identifying adaptations independent of rates of reproduction, so that they need not define fitness in terms of it. First, they have independent ways of determining what the needs of organisms are: food, oxygen, water, warmth, and so on; these are all needs that must be fulfilled by any organism that survives. Second, biologists have means of determining the extent to which varying behaviors, organs, tissues, cells, and so on, contribute to meeting these needs in different environments. They can explain in detail why arctic organisms like polar bears have a larger volume-to-surface-area ratio than their conspecifics in more temperate zones: the polar bear dissipates heat less, and this is important in meeting his need for warmth.

Without such evidence biologists can easily fall victim to the "just-so-story" temptation of explaining every feature of an organism as having evolved because it fills some adaptive need, known or unknown, of the organism. This approach would condemn evolutionary theory to uninteresting vacuity. But, the individualist argues, it is exactly the situation in which functionalism finds itself. Unlike the biologist, the functionalist has no independently established list of needs every society must meet in order to survive. Nor does he have a means of determining the extent to which alternative social institutions might meet such needs, so that he can plot a course of successive adaptations and winnowings by competition between societies bearing different institutions. In effect, the functionalist is guilty of the errors of Voltaire's Dr. Pangloss, who saw function in everything—including the bridge of the nose, which he thought designed to support eyeglasses. But, the individualist argues, to be compelled to seek a function for every long-standing institution and, failing to find one, to be compelled to keep looking reveal the evolutionary approach in social science to be an empty one. Nothing will refute the hypothesis that the institution has some function or other.

The individualist may even note that many functionalists reject an evolutionary foundation for their theories. They do so in large measure because they reject the naturalist's claim that teleology, real or apparent, requires an underlying causal mechanism. Indeed, some functionalists deny that their findings about latent functions are to be given a causal interpretation of any kind. But of course, this position is one individualists are even less comfortable with than an evolutionary approach to holism. It hardly strengthens the case for functionalism to reject without argument the demand for an underlying causal mechanism, for it leaves the teleological character of functionalism utterly unexplained.

Finally, even if we could adapt an evolutionary theory to underwrite functionalism, such an approach simply wouldn't tell us what we want to know about society anyway, claims the individualist. For evolutionary analyses and explanations only reveal to us something's *origin*, not its *mechanism*. At most, they tell us where something came from, not how it works *now*. For to attribute a function is to announce that sometime in the evolutionary past, a certain variation proved adaptive. What social science is interested in, however, is the present, not the inaccessible past. And for this we must forgo function and turn to structure, to the individuals who make up the institutions whose alleged function explains their existence.

At this point, individualism has probably gone too far in its attack on functionalism and methodological holism. For it is now ignoring the point, made by Durkheim at the origin of this debate, that in order to understand how an apparently random collection of pieces interact, the most useful thing to know may be what function they go together to serve. To complain that this approach begs the question in favor of functionalism is to mistake a hypothesis of considerable heuristic value for a dogmatic assertion. In pursuing scientific inquiry, we must begin somewhere. Wherever we begin may appear question begging until our hypothesis is either confirmed or surrendered. In the next chapter we will find the individualist accused of question begging by holists, for there we pursue the positive arguments, among economists, anthropologists, and sociobiologists, for methodological individualism. What we have seen so far is that even if holism does provide a way of avoiding the problems of intentional social science, it raises equally serious difficulties of its own.

Introduction to the Literature

The three principal anthologies, M. Brodbeck's, L. I. Krimerman's and A. Ryan's, all contain important papers arguing for and against holism, by M. Mandelbaum, J. Watkins, E. Gellner, M. Brodbeck, and S. Lukes. A particularly sophisticated recent version of the philosophical arguments against methodological individualism is to be found in H. Putnam, *Meaning and the Moral Sciences.*

E. Durkheim's views are expounded in his extremely important manifesto, *Rules of the Sociological Method,* and they are illustrated in *Suicide.*

Contemporary debates about holism and reductionism focus on the relation of psychology to neuroscience but recapitulate and extend the sociological debate. See especially the papers by Putnam and by J. Fodor in N. Block, *Readings in the Philosophy of Psychology,* vol. 1. These papers and others in Block also treat functionalism as a research strategy in cognitive psychology, which is continuous in many ways with its sociological application.

After Durkheim, the most prominent early advocates of functionalism in sociology are B. Malinowski, *A Scientific Theory of Culture,* and A. R. Radcliffe-Brown, *Method in Social Anthropology.* In U.S. sociology, the method is closely associated with the work of Talcott Parsons, *The Social System.* The latent/manifest function distinction is due to R. K. Merton, *Social Theory and Social Structure.* Problems for functionalism in sociology are lucidly identified by C. Hempel's "Logic of Functional Analysis," in his *Aspects of Scientific Explanation.* These issues are identical with those surrounding teleology (see Chapter 3).

The most vigorous opponent of holism and advocate of methodological individualism has been K. Popper. See especially *The Poverty of Historicism* and his attack on the moral foundations of holism, *The Open Society and its Enemies,* vols. 1 and 2. Popper's doubts about holism and functionalism extend even to evolutionary theory, and to Freud as well as Marx.

Much of the debate about the propriety, logic, and foundations of functional explanations has been carried out in the philosophy of biology. For an introduction to this debate see A. Rosenberg, *Structure of Biological Science,* and an anthology of significant papers, E. Sober (ed.), *Conceptual*

Issues in Evolutionary Biology. Some social scientists embrace a functional approach although explicitly abjuring any causal mechanism to underlie it. See R. Needham, *Structure and Sentiment.*

Further references relative to the holist-individualist debate are to be found at the end of the next chapter.

6

Two Kinds of Invisible Hands

THE METHODOLOGICAL INDIVIDUALIST attempts to explain large-scale social phenomena—what the holist describes as social facts—by a strategy that goes back to Adam Smith, the eighteenth-century founder of modern economics. This strategy explains large-scale social phenomena as the unintended and/or unexpected consequence of the behavior of individuals. In *The Wealth of Nations* Smith held that the unrestrained pursuit of individual economic interest by each person in competition with all others results, not in conflict and frustration, but in outcomes for the whole economy that benefit all, though no one intended them. It is as though an "invisible hand" leads individual action in directions that attain advantages for the whole society.

The best-worked-out examples of the operation of Smith's invisible hand are the ones most impressive to economists: Free trade and competition among self-interested individuals will lead inexorably to the widest availability of goods people actually want at the lowest prices that will sustain the goods' continued availability. Compared to the inefficiencies, surpluses, and shortages of a centrally planned economy, the successes of an unplanned economy need explanation, and the aggregation of apparently anarchistic, uncoordinated competitive activities gives it one.

This invisible hand strategy has been exploited elsewhere of course, most notably in evolutionary biology. Thus, in the absence of a designer, we need to explain the extensive adaptation and coordination of varying species within an ecosystem where each has a niche, where the populations remain unchanged over long periods, and where no resource is depleted. Evolutionary theory cites the invisible hand of variation and selection, often in the form of competitive struggle, between individual organisms to maximize their reproductive success, and the selection of the fitter among them from generation to generation. In recent years this sort of biological invisible hand explanation has been applied increasingly by sociobiologists to human social behavior and social institutions.

As such, it has begun to compete with the traditional methodological individualist's employment of rational choice theory to provide invisible hand explanations of social phenomena. And both, of course, compete with the holists' explanations of what they allege to be irreducible social facts. In this chapter we examine the alternatives to holism that these two economically and biologically inspired versions of individualism advance. We shall do so in part by comparing the explanations all three of these approaches provide for a single anthropologically central phenomenon: marriage rules and kinship systems.

In many small and isolated tribal systems there are complex rules of marriage: These rules often proscribe, sometimes merely permit, and occasionally prescribe permissible marriage partners. Of course our society has a few such rules: Incest is prohibited, including marriage between first cousins in some jurisdictions. But in tribal societies the rules are more numerous and far more complex. And among anthropologists at any rate, these rules often seem to be the most interesting aspects to have been discovered about such tribal societies. Like Durkheim's suicide rates, such rules have often been held to be irreducible social facts that brook no nonsociological explanation.

Let's examine one such rule more closely. Anthropologists note that among small tribal groups across Asia, Australia, the Pacific, and elsewhere, marriage with "cross cousins" is encouraged or prescribed. A boy's cross cousin is his mother's brother's daughter (his maternal uncle's child) or the boy's father's sister's daughter (his paternal aunt's child). Now, there are two interesting facts about these rules: First, about three-quarters of the tribes encourage marriage with the maternal uncle's child, and only one-quarter, with the paternal aunt's child. Why this proportion, instead of the 50 percent ratio that randomness would lead us to expect? Second, among the one-quarter of tribal systems in which marriage is expected between boys and their paternal aunt's daughters, almost all are "matrilineages"—societies in which descent is traced through the mother's family instead of the father's.

The most widely embraced anthropological explanation for these facts follows Durkheim. It is both "holistic" and functional. Roughly, it holds that marriage is a form of exchange and that cross-cousin exchanges are better for societies than other rules. They are better because they foster greater social integration and "organic solidarity." Anthropologists point out that such rules make families exchange wives among a larger number of different families in the society than rules that permit exchanges back and forth between the same pairs of families. More general exchange strengthens the bonds among all the families. And, indeed, the more frequent kind of cross-cousin marriage, boy's marrying maternal uncle's daughter, provides even more "organic solidarity" than the less frequent, boy's marrying paternal aunt's daughter.

The explanations for the persistence of preferential cross-cousin marriage are clearly functional. They are ones in which a property of the whole society is attained by the institution of cross-cousin marriage, a property that is advantageous for the society's survival and/or success. Though unabashed about offering such a functional explanation, anthropologists are reluctant to accept the kind of causal underpinning that such explanations call forth in biology. Some anthropologists do hold that greater reciprocal exchange has been selected for because societies blessed with it are fitter, through greater "organic solidarity." But these are a minority. More popular is a view, common among "structuralists," that some social structures, like cross-cousin marriage rules, exist because they are "good" for a society. At most, we may suppose that marriage rules, like other beneficial social facts, arose out of the unconscious processes of the human mind. This approach provides a connection between the discoveries of the cultural anthropologist and Freudian psychoanalysis, a connection that we cannot pause to explore but that reflects the way in which holism seeks deep meanings behind the marriage rules known to a society's members.

Social Facts and Rational Choices

Many social scientists have been unable to accept both the general approach of holism with functionalism and the specific explanations it offers. As we saw in Chapter 5, their criticisms of this approach have been in part methodological, but they have also been substantive. Opponents have attempted to provide individualist and nonfunctional explanations for the same social facts, thereby showing that we are not driven by the data to holism or functionalism. Such substantive arguments have always been more convincing among social scientists than "mere" philosophy. The trouble, as we shall see, is that these approaches bear their own burden of philosophical difficulties.

It would be an important vindication for methodological individualism, either of the rational choice variety or the sociobiological approach, if it could explain these two facts about cross-cousin-marriage rules. For such rules and these facts about them are at the core of holism's attraction.

Here is a simplified version of one such an individualist explanation that exploits rational choice assumptions. First, why is marriage with cousins on the mother's side preferred in patrilineal societies, in which descent is traced through the father, and marriage on the father's side preferred in matrilineal societies, where descent is traced through the mother? In matrilineal society the head of the clan, the family authority figure, is not the mother but the mother's brother or some other male in her family. It is never the father, who may not even live with the family in which the boy is raised. The father is thus a more indulgent figure, not responsible for discipline, education, and so forth, but a focus of friendship, informality, and fun. It is only natural for a boy to seek a wife on his father's side and for his father to encourage him to do so; hence matrilineal cross-cousin marriage tends to be "patrilateral"— to the father's side. When a society is based on patrilineages, the father is the locus of authority, discipline, and education, and the mother's brother the more pliant and informal agent. Thus, boys are likely to seek brides on this side. In other words, in patrilineages, cross-cousin marriage is likely to be matrilateral. In both cases it's the preferences and expectations of boys, and their uncles, that result in the regularity that gets ossified into expectations and eventually a marriage rule.

Second question: Why are three-quarters of all cross-cousin marriage systems matrilateral, and only one-quarter patrilateral? Not because the former is somehow better for the society, but because most tribal systems are patrilineal—the father and his family form the primary line of descent.

There remain questions to be answered here, like why patrilineal descent is more prevalent than matrilineal descent, and how practices that begin with preferences become molded into institutions like a marriage rule. But there are at least as many questions facing the holist view, and some of them are more pressing than these. The ability of a theory of individual tastes and beliefs to accommodate one of the most imposing of the cultural anthropologists' findings is a pretty compelling argument in favor of the general strategy individualists advocate—that of showing social institutions, rules, and other social facts to be the *unintended* outcomes of the aggregation of intended individual behavior guided by rational choice.

And such explanations are by no means limited to explaining social facts we might agree to be adaptive, beneficial, or advantageous for societies or the individuals who compose them. To see this, consider the following rational choice explanation of a pattern of racial segregation, an explanation that shows how segregtion might arise through rational choice, even on the reasonable assumption that none of the rational agents has any objection to racial integration. The explanation is due to Thomas Schelling and provides a perfect example of the powers of "economic modeling" and the way the invisible hand is exploited in economic theory. The fact that it explains an apparently sociological phenomenon, and not a narrowly economic one, enhances the attractiveness of this explanatory strategy.

Assume our city is like a checkerboard, so that except on the borders, each square is surrounded by eight other squares. Distribute members of two groups, say, blacks and whites, randomly over the board, leaving a large number of squares unoccupied. Assume that all prefer to live in integrated neighborhoods over segregated ones, but that each prefers that at least one-third of his neighbors be like himself, black or white. Each individual can have up to eight neighbors, one in each of the surrounding eight squares, so, if a person has one neighbor, he prefers him to be of the same color; two neighbors, one should be of the same color; four or five, at least two neighbors should be of the same color, and so on. Perfect alternation of white and black occupants of each of the squares on our checkerboard (except the four corners which are left empty) will result in an integrated distribution that satisfies everyone. No one will want to move. But most other distributions will lead to segregation, provided that there are empty spaces in which to move.

Suppose that in the "first round," each person who finds that less than one-third of his neighbors are of the same color moves to a square in which at least one-third are. The result is a snowballing segregation effect, even if just a small number of individuals of both colors are slightly dissatisfied. Because they live next to just one too few persons of their own kind, in this first round a handful of people move to vacant squares, thereby leaving a vacant square for someone else to move into and leaving behind a neighbor of the same kind now more likely to be discontented. For in that neighbor's eight adjacent squares the number of similar neighbors has been reduced by one. If this person was just barely satisfied with the proportion of similar neighbors, white or black, he is no longer satisfied, and moves as well. Where will these "second-round movers" go? Because some are black and some white, they can occupy spaces vacated by the first-round movers. And so on. With a finite amount of space to move to, the result is more and more self-segregation, which results in large patches of completely segregated areas or, in the extreme case, complete segregation in each half of the checkerboard. It is easy to simulate this scenario with coins of two different denominations randomly spread on the board or to simulate the process on a computer many times. One can also vary the strength of preferences we attribute: Instead of wanting one-third of neighbors to be of the same kind, we can examine the effects of one-quarter, or two-thirds, et cetera; we can expand the checkerboard to more than sixty-four squares, change the ratio of blacks to whites from 50:50 to other proportions, and examine the consequences of rational choice given these preferences and these constraints. What is interesting is that for any given set of proportions and any given set of preferences, no matter what the starting distribution, the results are almost always the same: In the case described above, it's almost always unintended segregation.

What Schelling has provided is a "model," an intentionally oversimplified set of assumptions that economists and others often employ to study a particular phenomenon. Often such models are "formal" in the sense that they are stated in mathematically expressed axioms, from which theorems are formally derived. Unlike theories, models have no pretensions of being true, yet this sort of model seems to cast a good deal of light on the social fact of segregation. Of course the model doesn't explain everything about it, and it is irrelevant to many cases of segregation. But it does show how segregation can be the unintended consequence of a large number of tolerant individuals all acting *rationally*, all maximizing their utilities. It is a sort of "perverse" example of Adam Smith's "invisible hand" explanation. His aim was to show how some social fact beneficial to each individual arises through the interaction of selfish agents, none of whom aim at this result, so that it arises as if through the operation of some hidden hand working through their actions. Here we have a socially undesirable result arising through the interactions of individuals, none of whom aimed at it.

If this model can explain the macrosocial phenomenon of segregation, it exemplifies the methodological individualist strategy for explaining social facts without recourse to other social facts and the functions these facts might reflect. The example is thus a paradigm of how rational choice explanation proceeds in economics, parts of political science, and elsewhere in social science where formal and informal modeling has taken hold.

But does it really explain anything at all? First of all, the approach seems to face the problems of intentional explanation examined in Chapter 2: the problem of improving such models into predictively powerful theories. Second, it faces the special problem broached in Chapter 3 of how unrealistic idealizations can have explanatory power. Beyond these two problems it faces a third one, a challenge that economists have devised, but that holists, and other opponents of a rational choice approach to human behavior, will certainly seize on to undercut its explanatory strategy: the problem of "public goods."

The first problem, how to protect formal models of rationality from objections to their intentional character, has given economists and political scientists little pause, as we saw in Chapter 3. The same can be said of the problem of how idealizations can have explanatory and predictive power. The boundary conditions on our model, that people are randomly distributed and can always move, are utterly false in the "real world."

The assumption that we all have the same relatively tolerant preference about our neighbors is equally baseless. As we noted in Chapter 3, these two problems really go together. For the second problem, how unrealistic assumptions explain, does not arise as a distinctive problem for social sciences. The natural sciences face it too. And there it is pretty easily solved: Unrealistic assumptions are good enough approximations and getting better, at that. The social scientists' problem is that their unrealistic assumptions are not getting any better. And the reason is that they are assumptions about intentionality, beliefs and desires, which we cannot improve.

But these problems give little pause to formal modelers. Should they? No, say the individualists. First of all, for all its defects, rational choice theory is the only game in town. There is certainly no better alternative account of individual human behavior to be had in a behaviorist approach or in any other. And as for the interpretative employment of rational choice theory to reveal intelligibility, this is not so much an alternative as the surrender of any attempt to provide improvable scientific explanation. Economic theorists and other methodological individualists have little patience with this approach.

It is certainly true that a scientific theory should not be surrendered, despite evident defects, unless and until a better theory is in the offing. Giving up a partially true theory for no theory at all is certainly an ill-advised scientific strategy. And perhaps this is enough justification to continue to explore economic modeling. But rational choice theorists often go on to embrace the instrumentalist treatment of their theory we examined in Chapter 3, according to which unrealistic and idealized assumptions are acceptable as long as their implications for observation are borne out, that is, as long as they meet with predictive success.

Independent of the objections to this defective defense discussed in Chapter 3 is the evident fact that a rational choice model like the one we sketched above for racial segregation does not seem to have much predictive content. Indeed, it is tempting to say we find it explanatory only because it makes racial segregation *intelligible* as an unintended consequence of the choices racially tolerant people might face. One important puzzle for economic modeling is this tension between the naturalistic aims of economic modelers and the nonnaturalistic character of their models' explanatory power. They hope to provide predictively useful models based on rational choice theory. But by and large their results are interesting and significant to the extent they render macrosocial facts intelligible, provide their meaning or significance.

Unrealistic economic models are sometimes said to have explanatory power because they are "robust." This means roughly that the social facts we can derive from them, like segregation in our example, will follow from a wide range of assumptions about the initial conditions to which the model is applied: the minimal proportion of neighbors of the same race each person wants; the number of turns in the game, and so on. Thus, we can produce segregation on our checkerboard by starting with other assumptions: Instead of assuming each individual wants to have at least one-third of his neighbors of the same race, we can assume any larger fraction and still get the same result in roughly the same number of moves. And if we assume each agent is willing to live with a lower proportion, say one-quarter, then if we increase the number of rounds in our simulation, we will still get segregation in the end. This shows that the model's "result"—unintended segregation—is robust under a wide variety of assumptions.

But robustness will be a desirable feature of an economic model only if it predicts something new or improves on the precision of a prior prediction. If a model predicts a phenomenon hitherto unnoticed or enables us to improve the quantitative precision of a prediction, then knowing that these predictions will be derivable from the model, even if our best estimates of its initial conditions of application are off the mark, is a strong point in its favor. However, when all a model does is show how something we already know to have actually happened *could* have happened, by deriving what happened from assumptions we have no independent reason to think to be true, it is tempting to treat the model as little more than an exercise in post hoc reasoning. And if the model is robust as well, one is inclined to call it empty or untestable post hoc reasoning. For a model that explains something we already know to have happened, instead of predicting something we don't yet know to have happened, robustness implies that the same event would have been explained by a wide variety of differing assumptions, in addition to the one we actually employed, and that there is no way to narrow this field down. This is precisely the state of affairs in our explanation of segregation.

We know that segregation occurs and that its occurrence follows from the false assumptions of our model. We also know that it follows from many other equally false assumptions—that is, our model is robust. So, if our model really does explain, its explanatory power remains mysterious. Economists won't accept the idea that it explains segregation by rendering it intelligible, and yet the very feature they cite to ground its explanatory power—robustness—deprives it of any alternative explanatory foundation.

Economists and other methodological individualists do not worry much about the ways in which their individualist explanations work. This is largely because they operate on the assumption that in the long run they will be able to trade in unrealistic, though robust, rational choice models for successively more realistic, though perhaps less robust, models with increasing predictive as well as explanatory content. If the arguments of Chapter 2 are right, however, this may be a vain hope. For such models will remain daunted by problems of intentionality.

But, as noted above, there is another problem that both social scientists and philosophers treat as far more immediate and pressing a threat to methodological individualism: the problem of public goods.

Public Goods and the Prisoner's Dilemma

Questions about the power of rational choice theory to explain social facts and about its claims to explain individual behavior come together in a famous puzzle known as the prisoner's dilemma. As we shall see, besides its attractions as a conundrum, the prisoner's dilemma has acquired a central place in the concerns of philosophers of social science and social scientists themselves.

The prisoner's dilemma is a problem in game theory, the study of how rational individuals choose strategies for maximizing their utilities in the face of other individuals with competing aims—hence the name "game" theory, because such competitive interactions resemble games we play against one another, like chess, monopoly, poker. The puzzle is produced as follows: Suppose you and I set out to rob a bank by night. However, we are caught with our safe-cracking tools even before we can break into the bank. In one another's presence we are read our constitutional rights as criminal suspects and then offered the following "deal." If neither of us confesses, we shall be charged with possession of safe-cracking tools and imprisoned for two years each. If we both confess to attempted bank robbery, a more serious crime, we will each receive a five-year sentence. If, however, only one confesses and the other remains silent, the confessor will receive a one-year sentence in return for his confession, and the other will receive a ten-year sentence for attempted bank robbery. Before we have any opportunity to communicate with one another, we are separated for further interrogation. The question each of us faces is whether to confess or not.

Let's go through my reasoning process. As a rational agent I want to minimize my time in jail. So, if I think you're going to confess, then to minimize my prison sentence, I had better confess too. Otherwise, I'll end up with ten years and you'll get just one. But come to think about it, if I confess and you don't, then I'll get the one-year sentence. Now it begins to dawn on me that *whatever* you do, I had better confess. If you keep quiet, I'll get the shortest jail sentence possible. If you confess, then I'd be crazy not to confess as well, because otherwise I'd

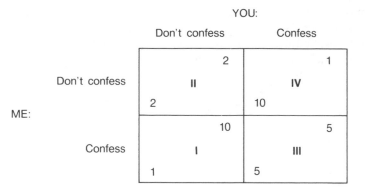

Figure 6.1 The prisoner's dilemma

get the worst possible outcome, ten years. So, I conclude that the only rational thing for me to do is to confess.

Now, how about your reasoning process? Well, it's exactly the same as mine. If I confess, you'd be a fool to do otherwise, and if I don't, you'd still be a fool to do otherwise.

The result is we both confess and both get five years in the slammer. Where's the dilemma? It's best seen in Figure 6.1, a diagram of the situation: The top of the box labels your choices, confess and don't confess. The left side labels mine, confess and don't confess. The numbers in the lower left of each square are the number of years I'd serve under each combination of choices, and the numbers in the upper right of each square are the numbers you would serve. Each square is labeled in roman numerals for reference. The rational strategy for you and the rational one for me lead us to square III, where both of us confess. These are called the "dominant" strategies in game theory because, as the reasoning shows, they are the most rational ones for each of us, no matter what the other person does. They dominate all other strategies. But now, step back and consider the preference order in which each of us would place the four alternatives. My order is I > II > III > IV; in each successive square I get more years in jail. Your order is IV > II > III > I, for the same reason. We end up in square III. But notice, if we compare our orderings, we both prefer square II to square III, that is we prefer both getting two years to both getting five years in jail. Yet rationality, maximizing our utility, led us to a "suboptimal" outcome, one less desirable than another that was "attainable." The dilemma is this: In the terms of the story, there is no way we can rationally get to square II, even though both of us rationally prefer it to square III. The reason is easy to see.

If, after being separated, we both take out a paper and pencil, draw up the box above and notice that square II is preferred to square III by the other guy and conclude that therefore our fellow bank robber *may* decide not to confess (in the hope that we won't either), in order to get to square II, then the rational thing for each of us to do is still to confess. For that way I'll stand a chance of getting to my most preferred square, I; and if I am wrong about you, not confessing will risk me getting my worst case alternative, square IV. The same goes for you. The problem gets worse when we see that both of us prefer square II to square III. For now we have even more reason both to confess, and thus there is a greater likelihood that we will end up in square III.

Is there any way for rational agents to get themselves into the more preferred square? Well, suppose before starting on the job we both swore oaths not to confess. If either of us believed that the other party would live up to the promise not to confess, this would make confession even more tempting, for it would increase the chances of getting the lightest sentence by confessing. Suppose we backed up the promise by hiring a hitman to shoot whoever confesses and gets out of jail first. Then of course the rational thing is to make a further secret payoff to the hitman not to carry out his job, and then to confess. In short, there seems no way for rational agents to secure a more preferred alternative. This then is the dilemma: By trying to maximize utility in this case, the agents are prevented from attaining a utility-maximizing alternative.

Now, the prisoner's dilemma is just a graphic way of posing a general problem for the explanation of social facts by rational choice models. To see this, consider a less fantasized example of the same dilemma: You and I are both concerned about street crime and would both be better off with a street light on the sidewalk between our houses, even though we would have to share the expense of putting one up. Of course, I would be even better off if you were to shoulder the whole expense. For then I would get the same benefit of street lighting that I'd get if I were to pay my fair share. So, if I think you are sufficiently afraid of street crime to pay the whole cost yourself, I have an incentive to hide my own preferences, deny any need for extra lighting, and make you pay the whole cost. Because there is no way you can provide yourself the security of extra street lighting without providing it to me, your neighbor, I am tempted to be a "free rider." However, you are in the same position. If you dissimulate your desires to have extra lighting, then maybe I'll provide it and you can be the free rider. The result is no extra lighting, though we'd both be better off with it even if we both had to divide the cost. Now in a case like this we can negotiate, and though we may hide our true preferences in order to improve our bargaining positions, making the one who wants the extra lighting the most pay more than the other, for example. Nevertheless, there is still a chance that we will end up with the extra lighting both of us want.

But what if the number of players in our game is too large for negotiation or for effective enforcement of any bargain struck? Suppose a million and one people vote to place air-pollution abatement devices on their cars. The benefit is cleaner air—a commodity that no one person can consume without others being able to consume it as well, and the cost is the price of purchase and maintenance of the air-pollution abatement devices, the loss in fuel economy, the decline in performance of our cars, et cetera. What should a rational person with such a device on his car do? Well, if everyone else is using one, he might as well disable his. For after all, if everyone else uses such a device, then pollution from his one car will not make any difference to air quality, and he will avoid the costs of using abatement equipment. And in contrast, if no one else uses such equipment, he would be a sucker to do so himself, for he would incur its costs without enjoying the benefit of clean air. After all, one car that doesn't pollute, among a million that do, will have no effect on air quality. The upshot, as in the prisoner's dilemma, is to disable your air-pollution abatement gear, no matter what anyone else does. Between being a free rider and not being a sucker, there is no third alternative for the rational agent. And if all the million and one people reason this way, the result is just like square III of the prisoner's dilemma, dirty air and no extra costs, an outcome less desirable than square II, in which all pay the costs and all share the benefits of clean air.

Clean air and street lighting are examples of what economists call public goods—commodities that cannot be consumed by one person without being consumed by others. One person can pay for a public good, but in providing it to himself, the buyer also willy-nilly provides it to others. So, all rational agents have an incentive to let the other guy pay for a public good, if they can. And no rational agent will ever pay the whole cost of a public good unless the benefit he derives from it himself is greater than the cost. But that means public goods would hardly ever be provided. For their cost is usually far greater than the benefit any one agent would derive from them. (It's worth noting that we cannot say that the total benefit to all agents is greater than the total cost, or the average benefit to each agent is greater than the per capita cost, unless we can make interpersonal comparisons of utility. See Chapter 3.)

Not all public goods problems are prisoner's dilemmas, but the prisoner's dilemma does reveal two problems of public goods: a normative one and a descriptive one. The normative problem is what the rational agent should do when faced with a choice to free ride or risk being a sucker. It can't be rational to choose an alternative that is less desirable, that fails to maximize utility; yet this seems to be the result of employing the rationally dominant strategy. The descriptive problem may be more serious. It's the problem of why most of us don't disable our air-pollution gear, don't run red lights, or cheat on our taxes. Most of the institutions that characterize society are public goods, and only a small number of us free ride on our obligations to pay for these institutions, where paying means incurring all the costs—money, inconvenience, annoyance—required to maintain them. It can't be that we do so out of fear that we will be caught and subjected to criminal or civil penalties or be made objects of social obloquy. For a society's enforcement and compliance mechanisms are far too inefficient to make free riding an irrational pursuit.

This is a potentially serious problem for the rational choice theory version of methodological individualism. Given the boundary conditions about inefficiencies in enforcement, the theory predicts that no public goods will be provided, out of the rational agent's fear of being a sucker and his hope to be a free rider. Yet here we are, faced with all these public goods.

Now there are some apparently easy ways to get around this problem. But they are too easy, for they threaten the theory with vacuity and trivialization. We can make some special assumptions about individuals' beliefs and/or desires. For example, if every agent's chief preference is to be altruistic or to be cooperative, or if each attaches enormous disutility to the chance of being caught free riding, no matter how low the risk, then the prisoner's dilemma disappears and so does the problem of explaining the rationality of public goods. Or suppose agents attach an irrationally large probability to being caught cheating. This will have the same effect as attaching an enormous disutility to being caught cheating. But there is no reason to believe these assumptions to be true. The fact that economic theory has no account for tastes (they are treated as "exogenous"—assumed and not explained within the theory) enables us to adopt any assumptions about tastes we like that are permitted by rational choice theory, in order to make the theory consistent with observations of actual choices. But because it can neither justify nor exclude such assumptions, the theory is threatened by vacuity whenever they are introduced. (See Chapter 3, "Behaviorism in the Theory of Rational Choice" for further discussion of this problem).

Another easy way to escape the problem is to deny that individual agents are rational in the economist's narrow sense. Perhaps they are rational in some broader sense that enables them to see the virtues of cooperation. If we hold the view that they act from other considerations besides maximizing utility, then making cooperative choices may turn out not to be surprising after all. If agents act on social norms or rules that overwhelm mere preferences in the determination of action, then we can appeal to a sense of morality, fair play, and justice, as explaining the preservation of social institutions. We may go further and hold that each of us is socialized to behave in cooperative ways, because only this would enable social institutions to maintain their functions. But notice, we now find ourselves on a slippery slope toward holism and functionalism, exactly what the rational choice theorist wishes to avoid.

Though functionalists and holists do not employ the notion of public goods to describe the institutions that they hold social science should account for, it is natural to view these institutions as such. In claiming that such institutions have a social function, fill a need of society, functionalists implicitly suggest that these institutions enable society to fulfill important individual needs and wants. If rational choice theorists cannot show how individual economic rationality maintains such institutions, then Adam Smith's invisible hand will not be powerful enough to provide an alternative to holistic social science. But let's consider whether Darwin's invisible hand might do better.

Egoism, Altruism, and Sociobiology

Though holism cum functionalism has craved the support of evolutionary theory almost since its inception, contemporary evolutionary biology is strongly "individualist." Current thinking about human and nonhuman evolution strongly endorses the notion that the kind of thing on which selection works is the individual organism—it is the "unit of selection." This means that although we can identify traits of the individual as having functions because they are selected for in order to maximize individual fitness, we cannot identify traits or features of society, or of groups of individuals, as fulfilling functions for those groups, as opposed to the individuals that make them up. The reason evolutionary theory gives for this conclusion is a variant of the public goods problem faced above, as we shall see.

But even if modern biological considerations militate against traditional functionalism, they still seem to some to hold out the prospect for a theory that can explain many significant social facts. This theoretical approach has acquired the name "sociobiology" and has become a controversial subject both within the philosophy of science and among social scientists. One of its attractions is that it enables the social sciences to help themselves to Darwinian explanatory strategies without facing the objections lodged against them by antifunctionalists and individualists, objections that were enumerated in Chapter 5.

Sociobiology begins with a problem much like the prisoner's dilemma. Recall that this problem is one of reconciling utility maximization with cooperation. The same problem, even more sharply posed, faces any attempt to apply evolutionary theory to social behavior. Darwin's theory held that evolution proceeds through the survival of the fittest. Very roughly, in any one generation of a species, the organisms that can secure more resources ensure their own survival, thus leave the most offspring and will pass their genes down to the largest number of members of the next generation. If the traits that enable individual organisms to do this are hereditary, then they will be carried by the genes. In the long run, selection for these adaptive traits and the genes that bear them will ensure that an increasing proportion of the whole species comes to bear them. Thus, like rational choice theory, Darwinian theory holds that individual organisms always "look out for number one," but the theory provides a stronger argument and a more modest interpretation for this claim.

The more modest interpretation is that organisms don't literally make fitness-maximizing calculations. It's just that in the long run the organisms that happened, by random variation, to develop behavior patterns that maximized fitness survived in competition with others, and those that failed to do so did not survive. Of course the theory does not require that surviving organisms be perfect fitness maximizers. It is only that the surviving organisms more closely approach fitness maximization, on average, most of the time, than their competitors for survival. Therefore, the genes of the fitter will be more heavily represented in the next generation's gene pool. In these ways the theory makes less stringent claims about its subjects than does rational choice theory, but this modesty may be an advantage.

However, the theory of natural selection is stronger than rational choice theory, at least in the sense that the former has amassed a far more impressive record of confirmation that the latter over the century since it first came into circulation. Unlike rational choice theory in social science, evolutionary theory is accepted in the natural sciences as the best account of biological adaptation and diversity available.

But evolutionary theory, with its commitment to individual fitness maximization, faces a problem when it reaches the point of explaining human behavior, as opposed to the behavior of animals. For it seems perfectly evident that our behavior is not fitness maximizing. We certainly do not act in ways that maximize our chances of leaving more of our genes in the next generation than other people. It's not just that we don't even think about reproductive success in making our choices. (Evolutionary theory doesn't require that we do that, any more than it requires simpler organisms to calculate the evolutionary fitness of their behaviors.) Our everyday behavior is rife with fitness-reducing actions, from using birth control, or helping our friends and family, to gratuitous kindness to strangers, and noble acts of self-sacrifice. The phenomenon of altruism seems to be an unbreakable bulwark against the tide of evolutionary thinking about human affairs. It seems to provide an even better argument against the pretensions of sociobiology than it does against the application of rational choice theory, and for the same reason. Both are maximizing theories—one focusing on utility, the other on reproductive fitness—and neither can explain the cooperative character of social life. Or so it was long thought. At worst, evolutionary theory is just refuted by human behavior. At best, it was long held, the constraints evolutionary biology sets on human behavior are so broad that though evolutionary biology is not refuted by altruism and cooperation, it can hardly be expected to explain them either.

At one time biologists, like functionalist social scientists, thought that they could provide evolutionary explanations of cooperative social institutions by treating the whole society or large groups of individuals as units of selection. The biologists reasoned that these groups faced evolutionary forces as a whole, and the environment selected groups that showed such cooperation, by contrast to groups that failed to do so. The trouble with this explanation is the free-rider phenomenon. For example, suppose that we set out to explain why some species of birds emit warning calls that draw attention to themselves in the face of a predator, so that the rest of the flock can escape. We may hypothesize that flocks whose birds evince this self-sacrificing behavior are fitter than flocks in which each individual bird selfishly dives for cover whenever it sees a predator.

Any individual member of such cooperating groups will maximize its reproductive fitness by not cooperating—by diving away instead of drawing the attention of the predator—when it can get away with doing so. And if the payoff to free riding is greater than the benefit of cooperating, as it is in this case, the selfish bird will out-reproduce cooperating members of the group. If it is genetically programmed to free ride because, for example, it is missing the "genes" for warning the flock about a predator, then in the long run, its offspring will increase in their proportion of the whole group, so that in the end, warning the flock may be extinguished. Thus, where group selection operates, it will usually be extinguished by free riding. Accordingly, biologists reject group selection as an explanation for the cooperative behavior they find in the animal realm. (Notice that rational choice theorists can avail themselves of a similar argument against functionalism to show that an institution with a benefit for the whole society should collapse under the effects of rational free riders. Their opponents will argue that the fact that our institutions haven't collapsed shows that individuals are not utility maximizers or that their behavior is constrained by non-individual factors.)

Sociobiologists, however, have hit upon a theoretically creative way around this problem. It involves the notions of "kin selection" and "inclusive fitness." Consider our flock of birds again. Suppose that all are full siblings, that is, each bird shares one-half of its genes in common with every other bird in the flock. Now suppose that when it sees a predator and calls attention to itself, thereby enabling its brothers and sisters to escape, it dies, thereby forgoing the chance to reproduce. But in sacrificing itself, it has enabled far more of its siblings to survive than would have if it had simply escaped and let the predator surprise the rest of the flock. If by sacrificing itself, it has saved at least three of its siblings, then the fitness payoff to its own reproductive success will be greater than if it had escaped alone without warning the rest of the flock. For three times one-half is more than one, and the selfless bird has enabled a larger number of its genes to survive into the next generation than it would have by saving itself alone. This is kin selection, behavior that maximizes the reproductive fitness, not of the individual, but of its genes and their copies in its kin. If we measure fitness, not in terms of individual reproduction, but in terms of inclusive fitness of all copies of the individual's genes, then for cooperative behavior toward family members, the evolutionary problem of cooperation is at least theoretically solved. Of course we need to document the existence of kin-selective altruistic behavior and eventually to locate the set of genes that program this behavior. But we now see how cooperation is at least compatible with an evolutionary theory that attributes fitness maximization to individuals.

The sociobiologist claims that we have a handle on cooperative behavior among humans as well. For now we can explain such basic social facts as the existence of family units, the sacrifice of parents for children, the cooperation of siblings, and the old adage that "blood is thicker than water." People are altruistic toward kin because evolution has programmed them to be fitness maximizers—inclusive fitness maximizers. Of course, the sociobiologist does not hold that individuals calculate inclusive fitness any more than he holds that individuals calculate individual fitness. Sociobiology is silent on the immediate proximate cause of cooperation and altruism; it may be the result of benevolent intentions, domestic socialization, behavioral conditioning, or deep psychological needs that only Freudian psychoanalysis could grasp. Which one is true is of no concern from an evolutionary perspective. The evolutionary perspective is that of ultimate causes: the interaction of environmental and hereditary factors that shaped, through blind variation and natural selection, dispositions to such behavior.

So, when I play the prisoner's dilemma with my siblings for stakes that mean survival or extinction, the optimal thing to do from the evolutionary perspective may be to cooperate, no matter what they do. And if they play with the same evolutionary objective, the result will be the most advantageous outcome (square II), from the point of view of individual as well as inclusive fitness. When organisms are faced with the choice to free ride or risk being a sucker, then, at least sometimes, maximizing fitness dictates the evolutionary "rationality" of taking the risk of being a sucker. And this results in cooperation all the way around. In this case, the invisible hand appears to be strong enough to resolve the dilemma. Though every individual organism behaves in ways that maximize its own inclusive fitness, the result maximizes the individual fitness of each organism as well. In nature, of course, we cannot describe this outcome as the *unintended* result of individual action, for most nonhuman organisms don't engage in action. But it is an unexpected result at any rate, and its optimizing effects on the individual organism certainly justify the employment of Adam Smith's idea of the invisible hand.

Sociobiologists have been eager to apply the notions of evolutionary fitness to the explanation of particular human institutions and social rules. The most obvious extension is the explanation of the incest taboo. In almost every society there is a rule against the marriage of siblings. Anthropologists have long sought an explanation for its universality in terms of its cultural meaning. The obvious sociobiological explanation is that such close inbreeding results in the expression of recessive genes. Such genes are usually maladaptive, which is why mental retardation seems so common in the offspring of incestuous reproduction. Now, neither primitive societies nor many advanced ones for that matter knew enough about the maladaptive results of inbreeding to ban it because of its genetically deleterious effects. But if close inbreeding has been selected against since sexual reproduction arose geological eons ago, then genes that program reluctance to inbreed with siblings will have been selected for long before the appearance of Homo sapiens. And in us, this genetic information may operate by producing a repugnance of incest that is consciously expressed in the incest taboo. Thus, the marriage rule of not marrying sisters or brothers is a social institution to be ultimately explained by considerations of fitness, even though the proximate explanations of how the rule gets expressed and how it is enforced will vary from society to society.

An even more powerful example is provided by the sociobiologist's explanation of preferential cross-cousin marriage. Recall the interesting anthropological phenomenon described at the beginning of this chapter: In widely separated tribal systems, the marriage of cross cousins, either patrilaterally or matrilaterally related, is encouraged. Anthropologists have identified such rules as paradigm cases of social facts not open to individual psychological explanation. We traced an individualist psychological explanation provided for the same phenomenon: In patrilineages, boys tend to like their maternal uncle and to find his daughters agreeable wives; in matrilineages, they will prefer the paternal aunt's daughters. Few anthropologists have accepted this explanation, in part because they want one that relates the asymmetries of cross-cousin marriage to other meaningful cultural patterns in the tribe, cultural patterns imposed on the psychology of its members, and not the result of their preferences and beliefs. This kind of explanation is available only in a holistic functional approach, they argue.

The sociobiologist has, however, an alternative explanation, one that is nonpsychological while still individualist in its character. It involves the notion of inclusive fitness and explains cross-cousin marriage as the result of an evolutionarily adaptive strategy, though not one individuals may recognize consciously as such. To begin with, cross-cousin marriage is a form of kin selection: Cousin marriage will increase the inclusive fitness of the dominant male in a lineage because his grandchildren will also be his nieces and nephews. They will have as much as three-eighths of his genes, instead of the one-quarter grandchildren normally share with a grandparent. One-eighth may not sound like a big difference, but when repeated generation after generation, it can mount up. So, when resources are marginal and survival of one's genes is a matter of keeping as much within the family as possible, inbreeding rules are likely to crop up for reasons of inclusive-fitness maximization. But too close inbreeding—incest—is maladaptive: It brings out recessive traits that tend to be unhealthy. So cousin marriage is probably as close as selection will tolerate.

But kin selection can go further. It purports to explain not just cousin marriage but cross-cousin marriage as well. To do so, we need to view kin relations from the point of view of the father of the bride, marrying her off to a nephew, instead of from the point of view of the groom, marrying a maternal cousin. And we must add in the crucial genetic fact that mothers can be more confident that the children they raise are genetically related to them than fathers can be, for sexual "cheating" is rife among humans and animals. Indeed, in non-Western tribal systems, it is often permitted among in-laws. The genetic relatedness of a child to its mother is a matter of observation: The child comes out of the mother's womb.

But the genetic relatedness of a child to its father is a function of whose sperm caused conception, a question difficult to establish even by scientific means. Therefore, in tribal societies, on average a man will be uncertain about whether his wife's children are really his or the result of extramarital relations. He will be even more uncertain about who is the real father his brother's children. But he can be much more confident about whether his sister's children are really hers. If there is a lot of extramarital sex, he may be more closely related genetically to his sister's children than to his brother's. So, not only will his inclusive fitness be enhanced by marrying his daughter to a nephew, but it will be enhanced even more, if it is a nephew on his sister's side. Going back to the nephew's point of view, this is, of course, matrilateral cross-cousin marriage. Thus inclusive fitness explains the existence of matrilateral cross-cousin marriage.

As for patrilateral marriage, recall that it is most prevalent in matrilineal societies, ones in which inheritance passes through females to their sons. In such societies, the same considerations of inclusive fitness will dictate marriage to father's sister's daughter—patrilateral cross-cousin marriage. They do so because in matrilineal societies, though descent is traced through mothers' families, the head of each family is almost always a male. The causes of male dominance are obscure, but this dominance means that the inclusive fitness of dominant males will be served by marrying their sons *within* their genetically related families, that is, to their sister's daughters. Hence patrilateral cross-cousin marriage obtains in the less common matrilineal societies. Thus, the lower frequency of patrilateral cross-cousin marriage is explained by the fact that evolutionary forces have made patrilineal descent, descent through the male line, not the female, a far more common system of descent than matrilineal descent. Why this is so is another, and a controversial, question.

If relatively small differences in inclusive fitness can be selected for, at the level of the individual, then the result is the marriage rules anthropologists have reported, and there is no need to invoke anything but natural selection operating on individual people as the ultimate explanation of these social facts. None of the people who participate in the social institution of lateralized cross-cousin marriage realize that it arose through the survival of the (inclusively) fittest individuals, and the proximate causes that inclusive fitness leads to may be varied and different in their details. Nevertheless, sociobiologists argue, it can be no accident that marriage rules coincide so nicely with what the invisible hand of evolutionary considerations would suggest.

Of course, without a good deal more confirmation and an account of how such behavior might be hereditarily coded, this exercise suggests at most a theoretical possibility. But it shows us how the same phenomenon can in principle be given three different types of explanations: a holistic one, an intentional one, and an evolutionary one. Presumably philosophy alone cannot chose among them.

Meanwhile, there is an obvious problem that sociobiology still has to face, along with rational choice theory. That is the problem of explaining cooperation among organisms that are *not* kin. For the fact is that the extent of cooperation vastly exceeds the limits of genetic relatedness. Inclusive fitness may explain some things of interest to the social scientist, but not enough. Some extremely interesting work has been done on this problem, especially by rational choice theorists working together with evolutionary biologists and, thereby, showing how much these two explanatory strategies have in common. A brief summary of it will enable us to raise some general questions about invisible hand explanations of both kinds.

Suppose that instead of having to play the prisoner's dilemma just once, each of us has to play it repeatedly against everyone else an indefinite number of times, in a "tournament": Each player faces each other player a certain number of times, and on each occasion both face an opportunity to cooperate or to refuse to do so, with payoffs, let us say, in dollars, given in accordance with the matrix above. This is a more realistic situation than the classical problem, for opportunities to cooperate or to free ride occur repeatedly in our lives, and against differing players, not just once against a fellow safecracker. Under the circumstances, which would be the best strategy to employ? One way to examine this problem is to simulate the situation on a computer. Suppose we match a dozen or so players, each employing a different strategy against one another, in a long series of prisoner's dilemma games. Each strategy is played by one player against all the others two hundred times. Among the strategies, we can include: always cooperate, never cooperate, cooperate whenever a flipped coin comes out heads, and other, more complex strategies.

One particularly interesting strategy is called "tit for tat": Cooperate in the first game with any player and, then in the next game with the same player, do whatever the opponent did last time. Tit for tat has some interesting features: It is "nice"—it always begins with cooperation; it is forgiving—if an opponent free rides on one game, tit for tat retaliates just once and goes back to cooperation the very game after the opponent starts cooperating again; and it is clear—after just a couple of rounds, the opponent can figure out what the strategy is. Other strategies are harder to figure out, more forgiving, or less nice. For example, a strategy may involve free riding first and switching to cooperation if the opponent cooperates. Or it might be a tit-for-two-tats strategy: Start out cooperating and only switch to noncooperation after two successive noncooperative moves by an opponent, then go back to cooperating.

When the dozen or so strategies are matched against each other a couple of hundred times, it turns out that tit for tat does best; it provides its players with the largest total payoff at the end of the tournament, even though it gets suckered a few times initially by noncooperating strategies. Other, nicer strategies, like tit for two tats don't do so well, and nasty strategies, like always try to free ride, do poorly.

Now add a wrinkle to the simulation. Run the tournament again, but this time eliminate the least successful strategies after each ten rounds or so, thereby simulating the effects of natural selection weeding out the least fit. The result is an even more decisive victory for tit for tat, and in general strategies that are nice, forgiving, and clear will do better than ones that are nasty, unforgiving, and hard for opponents to figure out. What this shows is that when public goods are the result of repeated interactions, cooperation may turn out to be the most rational behavior.

But if all the other players are "defecting," refusing to cooperate, then cooperation can never get started. In fact, tit for tat will lose a tournament against other players, all of whom defect all the time. For in its first game with each of the other players, it will be suckered, and the other players will never be suckered, so in the total score tit for tat will come out a loser, with all the defect-strategy players tied for first. In any selective process it will be weeded out. In other words, a group composed of players who always play to defect cannot be "invaded" by a tit-for-tat player. But contrarywise, a group of tit-for-tat players cannot be invaded by an always-defect player either. For the former will all cooperate with one another, and after the first contest with the always-defect player, the tit-for-tat players will defect in games against it. So it will be weeded out.

However, suppose a couple of tit-for-tat players are introduced into a group of always-defect "rational egoists." Then, the former stand a chance of invading the group successfully and in the long run displacing the noncooperators completely. All that is required for this to happen is that the "tit-for-tat'ers" get to play one another often enough to pile up more points than the defectors. If we simulate selection and reproductive fitness by increasing the number of players with the best strategy after, let us say, every tenth game and eliminating the players with the worst strategy, then if we play enough rounds, in the end, there will be nothing left but "tit-for-tat'ers." Their strategy will have invaded and overwhelmed the dominant strategy of always defecting.

So, once enough tit-for-tat players appear in a repeated prisoner's dilemma tournament, they can be expected ultimately to win out. Thus, cooperation can emerge even among fitness or utility maximizers, provided certain conditions are met. Or at any rate our simulation shows how cooperation is at least compatible with enlightened self-interest, "looking out for number one." But why should we expect enough tit-for-tat players ever to appear, so as to get the process going? Here, inclusive fitness, kin selection, and uncertainty of genetic relatedness can help. Among closely related organisms, as we have already seen, "always cooperate" may be the inclusively fittest strategy, even when one player is taken for a sucker by the free rider. If they share enough genes in common, the sucker's behavior is still adaptively optimal. But in some cases it is difficult to "determine" the degree of genetic relatedness: An opposing player may be a sibling, parent, or offspring, or may not be, and the players can't tell. If the chances of its being genetically related are high enough, then it will be worth some risk to play tit for tat, especially if repeated meetings are expected. Thus two unrelated players who "mistake" one another for relations may cooperate until one defects. If neither ever does, this is in effect playing tit for tat. As less adaptive strategies are weeded out, these strategies, though based initially on mutual risk taking about relatedness, become a larger and larger proportion of the strategies employed in the group, even when the issue of relatedness disappears altogether. Thus, cooperation, once given a start among related organisms, can evolve among unrelated ones.

Our simulation, by showing how fitness or utility maximizers can become cooperators and how a social institution based on cooperation might emerge through the invisible hand of nature, thus provides a theoretical solution to the repeated prisoner's dilemma.

Problems for Invisible Hands

But this sort of sociobiological reasoning has many of the same problems as the employment of theoretical models of rational choice. This should be no surprise because this reasoning differs from rational choice models only slightly. For the maximization of utility, it substitutes the maximization of fitness. For the intentionality of belief and desire, it substitutes the apparent teleology of random variation and natural selection over geological epochs. Though it avoids the explicit problems of intentionality, it carries the burdens of analogous problems of its own. Can we really expect that genetically encoded behavioral strategies like tit for tat might have appeared in nature quite randomly, and under conditions favorable enough to have been selected for over the time available for the evolution of Homo sapiens? And in light of the fact that we can never establish the conditions under which cooperation first emerged, is the development of these theoretical models any more than an interesting speculation about how *the actual* might after all have emerged?

It is true that sociobiology has the backing of biology's independently established theory of natural selection and that it does not bear the weight of a dubious theory of group selection that holistic views seem to require. Moreover, sociobiology seems to fulfill the teachings of methodological individualism while in theory avoiding some of its most glaring difficulties. But sociobiology faces an explanatory dilemma of its own, for it seems to teeter on the brink of either irrelevance or falsity. Sociobiologists are often accused of being "biological determinists," of holding that human behavior is genetically programmed, so that we have no choice about our behavior, given our genetic inheritance, and so that cultural and social forces play no role in the explanation of our behavior. This view seems evidently false, and if sociobiology is committed to it, the theory should be disregarded. Defenders of sociobiology will respond that it is not committed to any such a thesis: Evolution is the joint product of genetic inheritance and environmental conditions, including culture and social facts. It's just that natural selection for fitness maximization sets constraints on behavior and provides the mechanisms and dispositions that result in it. But if these constraints are very broad, then sociobiology has no power to explain what people actually do. For it will turn out that many possible types of behavior, many nonactual social institutions, are all equally adaptive from the evolutionary point of view, and the sociobiologist cannot explain why only some of them are actual. This threatens the theory with irrelevance, for we may accept the idea that human behavior has been subject to evolutionary constraints, just because evolutionary theory is as true of us as of the rest of the biological world. But it would not follow from this that any detail of human behavior could be explained by biology, any more than the fact that we are all bodies with mass gives Newton's laws any power to explain human action.

But if sociobiologists hold that the constraints of selection are narrow enough to provide real explanations of our behavior by showing that alternatives to our behavior are so maladaptive as to be extinguished by selection, then they will after all be guilty of biological determinism, guilty of denying that we are autonomous, responsible creatures, who choose our actions in the light of their meanings—personal, cultural, social. Some sociobiologists have been tempted to embrace such a view, for at least some human behavior. And they are not alone in doing so. Behaviorists like B. F. Skinner have openly held that the image of human agents as free and autonomous creatures is not only false but also dangerous to the efficient design of a truely livable society. We will return to this matter in Chapter 7.

But holding that a given type of human behavior, such as incest avoidance or cross-cousin marriage, or sex-role differences, can be explained by evolutionary considerations is threatened by untestability and triviality when it attempts to avoid irrelevance or falsity. For the theory of natural selection, which backs up these claims, is itself easy to render untestable.

This is a point we briefly touched on in Chapter 5, "Methodological Individualism Versus Functionalism." The theory of natural selection holds that the fittest traits survive, but fitness is usually measured in terms of survival. Thus it is tempting to label any trait that has survived as the fittest. If our only mark of fitness is the persistence of the trait, then the theory will not be subject to a real test. For it will, in effect, explain persistence and survival by fitness—that is, by persistence and survival. But providing a different measure of fitness is no easy matter. We know relatively little of the long-term selective forces operating in the biosphere. And features for which we have no evolutionary explanations may well be subtle adaptations to forces we have not yet recognized. So, among biologists at least, there is a strong temptation to hold that persistent traits are the products of adaptation, even though we do not yet know what they are adaptations for. And when a particular adaptational hypothesis is refuted, few will surrender adaptive explanations altogether. Consider, for example, the plates on the back of a stegosaurus dinosaur. Were they adaptations for protection from predators, or perhaps cooling devices, mate-attracting adornments, or something else? If one hypothesis fails, biologists are tempted to search for another function to explain persistence. But this threatens their theory with triviality, unless there is at least some conceivable evidence that would lead them to reject the hypothesis.

The problem in evolutionary biology is almost the same as the problem in intentional psychology. We have no general means of measuring the initial conditions to which we apply the theory of natural selection independent of the theory itself. The problem is almost the same, but not quite so serious, because in biology we have some restricted means of identifying fitness independent of the theory. But these means are so restricted that they cannot provide a measuring device in more than a couple of cases. We know, for example, that being white coated is an adaptation in the arctic, independent of measuring the reproductive rates of polar bears; and long necks are adaptations among giraffes. But we have no general way of identifying adaptations, and this threatens the theory with explanatory and predictive weakness. For when we explain a trait as an adaptation, we are usually unable to provide a detailed enough account of what exactly it is an adaptation for, to test the explanation.

In the case of sociobiology, the difficulty of identifying what a behavioral disposition is an adaptation for is particularly great. We can apply almost none of the experimental methods biologists might use because we cannot treat people as laboratory subjects, we cannot control the environment to see how traits are selected, and we cannot wait around the requisite number of generations to see which traits survive under varying conditions and which do not. Nor is the historical and prehistorical record much help either. We can of course examine the behavior of nonhuman animals and make inferences from them. And this is what many sociobiologists do.

But these inferences are fraught with danger as well, for animals lack culture and language, and most of all, human intelligence. To make direct inferences from what is adaptive for animals to what is adaptive for us is to set the causal force of culture, language, intelligence, et cetera, at zero. And this encourages from another direction the charge against sociobiology of biological determinism and sheer falsity.

Short of the kind of detailed data and theoretical development that characterize evolutionary theory in biology, sociobiology seems to face most of the methodological difficulties of rational choice theory. It can provide interesting models and simulations, which seem to shed light on significant social facts. But the question remains how idealized models and unrealistic assumptions can explain. As with rational choice theory, the answer cannot be that these idealizations are a good enough approximation to reality, that is, good enough because distinctive, observationally confirmable results are derivable from them, as from idealized theories in natural science. For neither sociobiology nor formal models in economics have any such strongly confirmed distinctive consequences. Nor, in the case of sociobiology, can the answer be that the model shows us how some social fact is *intelligible*, for meaning and significance have no place in biology. And moreover, sociobiologists will not accept intelligibility as a criterion of explanatory adequacy any more than rational choice theorists will.

For all its intellectual beauty, the invisible hand has not proved much of an improvement on the macrosocial theories of social facts. What is more, like the moral charges that individualism lodges against holism, it too is held to be an ethically dangerous strategy, both in its rational choice and in its sociobiological garb.

Even more than functionalism, sociobiology has been accused of being an ideological rationalization for the status quo and a bulwark against improvements in social justice. The theory explains varying social facts as determined in the long course of evolution, not of societies, but of individual genetic inheritance. Thus, it has been taken to suggest that these social facts can no more be eliminated than we can change the human genome. If xenophobia, sex-role differentiation, class structure, and other social phenomena that sociobiologists have tried to explain are really "in our genes," then there may be no hope of environmental changes eliminating them, not within a socially significant amount of time. Moreover, by holding that such human traits as altruism or cooperation are merely evolutionarily optimal responses to selective forces, instead of motivated by high ideals and moral responsibility, sociobiology stands accused of attempting to rob us of our autonomy and dignity.

Some intellectual historians trace the pedigree of contemporary sociobiology back through Darwin's theory of natural selection eventually to Adam Smith's explanatory strategy, and to the laissez-faire social policy it encourages. They go on to explain its acceptance along with the adoption of Smith's policy because of the interests of the capitalist system that it serves. Here the attack on sociobiology makes common cause with critical theory.

Smith's theory held that the self-seeking—preference maximization—of all individuals leads to unrestrained competition among them and that instead of producing anarchy and chaos, the result is efficient markets that benefit everyone individually. This unintended though happy outcome, produced as though through the operation of an invisible hand in the affairs of men, suggests an economic policy of laissez-faire, of leaving things alone and not interfering in the operation of the economy. As such it is a doctrine made to order for modern industrial capitalism's battle against governmental constraints, restrictions, regulations, and expropriations.

Darwin has often been accused of falling under Smith's influence in his view of nature as the competitive struggle for survival among organisms selected for their ability to be as self-seeking as a rational economic agent, that is, selected for their fitness to win the struggle for survival. It is no surprise that the modern mathematical development of the theory of evolution has taken over both the form and the theorems of mathematical microeconomics, for all that has been required is the replacement of maximization of utility by the maximization of fitness.

But if we view the animal realm as a fundamentally competitive one, then it is easy to so view human society, when we assimilate Homo sapiens to nature, thus reinforcing the picture of agents as rational egoists that Smith bequeathed to us. If, as with Smith, evolutionary competition leads to improvement of the species, to increased adaptation to the environment through selection, in short, to progress, then organic evolution has proceeded as if under the direction of the same beneficent but invisible hand.

Now, when sociobiology turns Darwin's thinking about evolution back to human society, it comes under exactly the same suspicions that Smith's laissez-faire economics does. Opponents attribute to it the blindly optimistic notion that those social institutions that have emerged from evolution are optimal from the point of view of nature. Opponents also attribute the profoundly pessimistic thesis that most institutions are probably unchangeable by human intervention anyway. They are optimal because they reflect an equilibrium between competitive forces in evolution the way that prices, for example, reflect an efficient equilibrium between supply and demand in an economy. They are unchangeable because they are written into our genetic inheritance and likely to overwhelm any short-term attempts to modify them by changing social arrangements.

So, along with the methodological infirmities, sociobiology and rational choice theory are held to share moral defects as well. It is of little use for the sociobiologists to reject these charges or to show how they rest on mistakes and misinterpretations of sociobiological findings, theories, and intentions. For, as with many scientific results, the ramifications of abstract theory beyond science itself are often beyond the control of its originators and developers. Regardless of whether sociobiology or economic theory really has these allegedly nefarious consequences, as long as persons in a position to influence policy think it does, its status as science may result in policies of which economists or sociobiologists would not approve. But it is far from clear that these are philosophical problems of social science. They are problems both of applied science and of intellectual honesty in general. The immediate philosophical problems associated with the moral dimension of social science is the topic of the next chapter.

In an important respect, the problems to be addressed in the next chapter are quite separate from those addressed hitherto. For up till now we have been wrestling with the same broad problems of method, explanatory strategies, and their broad philosophical presuppositions, in differing contexts, as they affect the different social sciences. We have faced the problems imposed on social science by intentionality and by attempts to circumvent the limitations of intentional explanation of individual action. We have seen that the focus on macrosocial science at most results in the substitution of other philosophical problems for the problems about explaining individual action that it hopes to avoid. Now we shall see that in addition to these issues, naturalism and interpretationalism are closely tied to theories, not about what is the case in human action, but about what *ought* to be the case.

Introduction to the Literature

R. Needham, *Structure and Sentiment*, together with G. Homans and D. Schneider, *Marriage, Authority and Final Causes*, provides a perfect example of the debate between holists and individualists as it affects their empirical research. Needham's aim is in part to vindicate the structuralist approach of C. Lévi-Strauss, though it is by no means clear that the latter is in fact a holist. See his *Structural Anthropology*. Needham's book is one of the most thoroughly antinaturalistic monographs ever written in social science.

The invisible hand strategy that Homans and Schneider exploit derives from A. Smith, *The Wealth of Nations*, certainly the most formative text for modern economics. For its influence in economic theory see M. Blaug, *Economic Theory in Retrospect*. An excellent introduction to the farthest reaches of formal modeling in economics and to its methodological background is T. Koopmans, *Three Essays on Economic Science*. The example of invisible-hand explanations discussed in the text is due to T. Schelling, *Micromotives and Macrobehavior*, which contains other equally illuminating examples.

The prisoner's dilemma is clearly explained and its significance traced in several of the papers in J. Elster (ed.), *Rational Choice*. R. D. Luce and H. Raiffa, *Games and Decisions*, is a well-known introduction to game theory and the background to the prisoner's dilemma. As an issue about public goods, the problem for explaining and justifying social organization it poses goes back to T. Hobbes, *Leviathan*. A modern discussion of the difficulty of securing public goods and explaining how we ever could have provided them is M. Olson, *The Logic of Collective Action*. A. Sen, "Rational Fools," in *Choice, Welfare and Measurement*, is a well-known attack on rational choice theory based on its inability to deal with the prisoner's dilemma.

The intimate connection of game theory and evolutionary biology is illustrated in J. Maynard-Smith, *Evolution and the Theory of Games*. R. Axelrod, *The Evolution of Cooperation*, discusses the prisoner's dilemma problem at length, within the context of both rational choice and sociobiological theory. The discussion of tit-for-tat strategies and their features in the text derives from his work, and that of biologist W. D. Hamilton.

The idea of group selection as an explanation of how group properties can have selective advantages for groups, as well as its displacement by individual selection, is traced in E. Sober, *The Nature of Selection*. The potential for explaining apparent group traits by the invisible hand of selection over individual behavior was a powerful impetus to sociobiology. See E. O. Wilson, *Sociobiology* and *On Human Nature*. The application of these ideas to deal with the data of cultural anthropology is reported in R. Alexander, *Darwinism and Human Affairs*. This work contains a sociobiological alternative to Needham's holist and Homans's individualist explanations of kinship rules. The most sustained and well informed methodological attack on sociobiology is P. Kitcher, *Vaulting Ambition*.

M. Harris, *Cultural Materialism*, argues for the combination of a naturalistic method and a biological approach that explains social facts in terms of individual behavior, without appeal to genetic evolution.

7

Shall We Commit a
Social Science?

IN A POEM entitled "Under Which Lyre," W. H. Auden once enjoined his readers thus: "Thou shalt not sit with statisticians nor commit a social science." It may not be clear exactly what Auden meant by this injunction. But leaving literary analysis aside, there is something morally troubling about social science; indeed, there are several things that are troubling about it. In this chapter we examine some of them.

Among these troubling subjects are the consequences of either attempting or succeeding in the development of a scientifically promising science of human behavior. For attempting to do so may involve treating people in morally unacceptable ways, and succeeding may enhance our powers to so treat them. Indeed, it may go farther and, as we have seen, encourage us no longer to view people as agents—responsible, autonomous subjects of moral concern. Social science, some hold, is fundamentally dehumanizing. Then there is the prospect, which others take seriously, of morally dangerous knowledge—of questions about humans that we should not take up at all, for answering them correctly can do no good and only harm individuals and groups, even if it does not dehumanize them.

Social science cannot escape from moral issues, in the way that many believe natural science can. For its subject is humankind. It provides the knowledge that guides human affairs, both individual and collective. If there is moral knowledge, then we should expect social science to help provide it. An atomic scientist might be excused from facing questions of what physics should be applied to—bombs or nuclear medicine—on the grounds that questions of application are not raised in physics. Can economists or political scientists avail themselves of the same neutrality?

Or are moral prescriptions, prohibitions, and permissions built into their aims, theories, and methods? And even if they are not built in, does the social scientist have a special responsibility to provide substantive moral guidance, a responsibility resulting from a specialist's knowledge of human affairs? Should we judge the acceptability of explanations and predictions in social science on moral standards and, if so, on which ones? These are questions that social scientists answer either explicitly or implicitly in their work. But they are pretty clearly philosophical questions, and on balance it would be best if the answers provided were both explicit and well informed.

Moral Problems of Controlled Research

Assume that the goal of social science is predictively improvable explanatory theories of human behavior and that the methods appropriate to attaining this goal are roughly those common in natural science: hypothesis formation, followed by the collection of observations and the construction of experiments we require in order to test and improve these hypotheses. This brings us face to face with a moral problem that the physical sciences do not face and that the biological sciences face only on certain controversial assumptions. This is the conflict between the methods of empirical science and the rights of individual agents. In the biological sciences, the problem exists in part on the controversial assumption that nonhuman animals have rights. There are many proponents of animal rights struggling to restrict experimentation on animals, no matter how great the benefits medicine, agriculture, or cosmetology may secure for humans from such experiments. But there are even more people who consider unreasonable the idea that animals have rights that enjoin us from raising them for food and from killing them, let alone experimenting on them. But nobody thinks that the idea that morally people cannot be treated the same way as animals is silly. And this makes for a large obstacle to empirical methods in social science. To see how large an obstacle, let's consider some real examples.

Perhaps the experiment that combines the most startling results with the most serious ethical violations in recent social science is the famous "Milgram experiment." Stanley Milgram, a social psychologist, wished to examine the degree to which people would obey authority, even when their actions in obedience to authority would lead to what they believed were painful and even fatal results for others. Subjects were asked to "help" in an experiment on the effects of painful stimuli on learning tasks. They were to control a device that was attached to the experimenter's confederate and that they were falsely told could administer electric shocks of varying strengths. The pretend subject would fail to accomplish the learning task, and the experimenter would order the real subject to administer a "shock." The pretend subject would emit an appropriate sound of discomfort. Successive failures would lead to instructions to increase the voltage and thus to louder and louder expressions of discomfort. Milgram found that most people were willing to administer shocks they thought to be near lethal, in spite of complaints, expressions of pain, and indeed feigned loss of consciousness by the pretend subjects. People would do so, provided they were encouraged, authorized, or ordered to do so by an experimenter willing to take responsibility.

After the experiment each of the subjects was "debriefed" in order to show that no harm had really come to the pretend subject. However, Milgram reported that some harm came to the real subjects as a result of this experiment. Some showed extreme nervous tension during the experiments and some subsequently suffered from acute mental disturbance, despite the debriefing. Two obvious questions are raised by this experiment: Was it worth it—do the benefits of knowing ordinary people can behave like this outweigh the costs to subjects? Is it permissible to deceive subjects in order to acquire such knowledge? Notice that without deception, the experiment would not have been possible at all.

The conditions required by more passive observations also lead to similar problems, such as those reflected by Laud Humphrey's 1970 study of homosexuality. In order to study homosexual behavior and its social correlates, Humphrey began by posing as a homosexual in public facilities used for sexual encounters. By recording the automobile license numbers of participants in these encounters, he obtained their addresses and subsequently interviewed them, posing as a public health survey taker. Humphrey's conclusions were that homosexuals in general led conventional lives, that a large number were married with children and posed no danger to the society as a whole. Indeed, he concluded that only ignorance of these facts and repression of such behavior posed a threat to individuals and society at large.

Now, the consequences of Humphrey's research are widely viewed as beneficial. But the methods he was forced to employ, both by the nature of the phenomena he studied and by the need to ensure reliable observation, pose several serious moral questions. In addition to the several deceptions he had to practice and his violation of the subjects' privacy, the risks to his subjects could have been very great. Had Humphrey's data, including names and addresses, fallen into the hands of the unscrupulous, great harm could have been done to his subjects. Do the benefits of enlightening research like this outweigh its potential risks? Humphrey, of course, knew the potential damage his data could do and acted to minimize such risks. But can we sanction such research even when the risks are quite low? And, if so, is our social science reliable enough in its predictions to enable us to estimate these risks in order to learn whether they are low enough?

Sometimes observation and experiment have morally questionable effects beyond their immediate subjects. In the 1950s, social scientists secretly recorded the deliberations of six different juries in Wichita, Kansas, in order to provide empirical data to test certain assumptions about the U.S. legal system. Though their aim was to improve the system of justice by providing information that might help people to understand it better, these social scientists may have put it at risk. For when the study became known, the confidentiality of jury trials everywhere was undermined and with it a fundamental provision of the Bill of Rights of the U.S. Constitution. Moreover, though no harm came to jurors or defendants as a result of the study, their rights were certainly violated.

In order to explore the moral problems these cases raise, we need some tools, principles that reflect our moral convictions, and theories that explain and justify these principles, and enable us to apply them. Similar problems in biomedicine have led to the identification of certain moral principles to guide research. It may be convenient to consider them and their application to the social sciences.

One principle illustrated by our cases is that individuals have some rights that cannot be abridged and that individuals must be allowed to make their own decisions *autonomously*. Autonomy can be reduced by failure to inform persons of the circumstances in which they act and to secure their well-informed consent to research in which they will be subjects. Being well informed is not enough, however. Autonomy is reduced when informed consent is secured under circumstances of implied or expressed coercion. Thus, it is sometimes held that even telling a prison inmate about all the possible effects of an experiment he may volunteer for cannot respect his autonomy. For, as a convict faced with the inducement of a reduced sentence for "good behavior," his consent may not be fully autonomous.

In medicine this principle seems less restrictive than in social science, though it certainly reduces the supply of experimental subjects. For, except in the case of placebo experiments, deception does not seem essential to an experiment's success, once a subject's agreement to the experiment is secured. But because of the reflexive nature of social science, that is, because a subject's behavior is likely to be influenced by learning what hypotheses the investigators are studying and what methods they are employing, a blanket prohibition against deception on grounds that it violates autonomy would severely restrict social science. This means that if we employ deception, and we need to violate subjects' rights to autonomy, we also require a moral justification for overriding this right.

A further principle important in medicine is the injunction not to inflict harm on subjects and to benefit them to the fullest extent possible. The first part of this principle, nonmaleficence—doing no harm—takes precedence over the second, beneficence—making positive improvements. In medicine this principle certainly restricts the scope of experiments greatly. It requires empirical studies to proceed slowly and with the greatest caution. Before examining whether a new drug can help anyone, it must be ascertained that the drug will do no positive harm. And in medicine, when a procedure provides both harms and benefits, there is a presumption against it because of the priority of nonmaleficence over beneficence. Even where benefits are held to outweigh harms, the greatest difficulty surrounds how we measure them in order to make comparisons. In the social sciences, applying this principle to the treatment of experimental subjects, who presumably have given informed consent, is even more difficult.

For the social sciences, employing this principle is not only more difficult but also exposes them to a frustratingly vicious circle. In order to expand knowledge in the social sciences, we may have to undertake experiments. For these experiments to be morally permissible on the present principle, we need to know what harms and benefits we can expect our experiments to produce, and perhaps also to weigh them against each other. But determining harms and benefits requires the very sort of social scientific knowledge that the experiments are designed to produce. What is more, if our theory tells us that harms and benefits cannot be given cardinal weightings, or cannot be summed among different people, because of the difficulties of cardinal or interpersonal comparisons, applying this principle will be impossible on substantive theoretical grounds as well as on logical and methodological grounds.

There is another moral principle generally more relevant to research in social science than to biomedical contexts. It is a principle of fairness, equality, and justice. It requires equal treatment of individuals, equality of opportunity and equal access to potential benefits and advantages. For example, large-scale studies of the effects of social policies, like a negative income tax, or free day-care centers, involve randomly selecting some individuals to receive the benefit, and others not to, followed by comparison of the effects of this differential treatment. But subjects relegated to the control group and thus deprived of the experimental group's benefit may complain that they have been treated unfairly, their right to equal treatment having been violated.

As with other ethical problems, there are ways around this issue, but they involve forgoing experimental designs, in favor of "quasi-experiments," like the imaginative use of data already available, collected by government agencies often for other purposes. Intelligent observation of phenomena that social scientists have not themselves arranged shifts the burden of injustice or unfairness to whoever is responsible for the unequal treatment to be studied. Moreover, such unobtrusive measures also avoid some problems of autonomy, like informed consent and the nonmalef- icence/beneficence calculation, for the subjects studied at any rate. But such measures do not circumvent all of the moral problems of social science research. There remain threats to privacy and confidentiality and the balancing of harms and risks to social institutions and public confidence in them. But clearly, such nonexperimental alternatives are a second-best solution, in a domain where even the best approach often provides little insight itself.

Social Science and Moral Theory

These moral principles that restrict inquiry in social science raise a broad philosophical question: What justification can we provide for these principles? Why should we obey them? The justifications that have traditionally been offered for them by philosophers have significant connections to the methodological issues dwelled on in this book, as we shall see.

For many, these moral principles are sufficiently well justified by the fact that they are widely recognized, historically venerable principles to which almost everyone gives assent; they lie at the foundations of civilized society and therefore are beyond the need of justification. Others find the grounds for adherence to these principles of conduct in the teachings of various religions. Philosophers are rarely satisfied with either of these answers to the question of how moral principles are justified. The first answer is undermined by the fact that in many societies some of these principles are not accepted, and even where they are, mere acceptance, even when universal, is no sure mark of truth or justifiability.

The second answer, that these principles are God's command, has little force for the scientist. More important, the question of whether, for instance, respecting autonomy is morally right because it is enjoined by the Lord, or whether it is enjoined by the Lord because it is morally right, is left open. Presumably it is the latter, but then we need to ask what it is about this principle that recommends itself to the Lord as the morally right one. And that is our original question all over again: What justifies these principles as the morally right ones?

One answer we must exclude is that we should obey these principles because they are written into the statutes and common law of our legal systems. Like others, social scientists are legally responsible for their actions and may be held liable by individuals or by public prosecutors for wrongs they knowingly or even unwittingly inflict on subjects and nonsubjects. And governments have adopted laws inhibiting certain methods and subjects of research because of their morally disturbing ramifications. The Wichita jury study, for instance, led to legislation that explicitly prohibits the recording of federal jury deliberations. And in recent years, the U.S. government's chief sponsor of social scientific research (the Department of Health and Human Services), to govern inquiry that it supports, has promulgated regulations that reflect most of the principles described above and require review boards to supervise research on human subjects in order to prevent ethical abuses.

But this does not answer our question of what the moral justification of such principles might be. At most it provides a justification for them in terms of our self-interest: We want to avoid punishment. Social scientists who fail to abide by them may be at risk of criminal or civil prosecution. In fact, governmental regulation raises the same moral problem all over again. For we need to examine whether and why governments have the moral justification to enforce these principles in the conduct of research.

The second problem these principles raise is how to adjudicate conflicts between them. Sometimes, both within and beyond experimentation and observation, the principles pull us in different directions: Preserving autonomy may prevent us from providing "benefits" to those unwilling to accept them, mistakenly or not. Sometimes, we must forgo potentially great benefits to society, if we are to preserve individual rights. Sometimes we must violate those rights to secure such general benefits or to avoid great harm to large numbers of people. How do we decide these cases of moral conflict?

Both of these problems call for a general moral theory, one that will justify some or all of these principles and will establish a priority among them when they come into conflict. The trouble is that there seems little agreement on such a theory, and the leading candidates simply embody the conflicting dictates of the moral principles we have summarized. Moreover, the leading candidates among moral theories reflect the two divergent trends in methodology of social science that we have examined in the past six chapters. Therefore, taking sides on questions of scientific method may commit us to taking sides in fundamental matters of moral philosophy.

The two leading accounts of the foundations of moral judgment and the grounding of moral principles are utilitarianism, of which the British empiricist philosopher and economist John Stuart Mill was the founder, and a theory of duties and rights developed by the German philosopher Immanuel Kant. This latter sort of theory is often called a "deontological" theory, from the Greek for "theory or knowledge of what is binding or obligatory."

Utilitarianism holds broadly that actions are to be assessed as morally acceptable or not on the basis of their consequences for the happiness, satisfaction, welfare, or "utility" of those affected by them. Thus, any moral principle must be considered in terms of the consequences of adopting it for all affected parties. In order to decide whether we ought to respect the autonomy of any one individual, or treat this person strictly on the basis of nonmaleficence and beneficence, we need to calculate the effects on all individuals of such treatment of this person. If the costs to everyone of such treatment outweigh the benefits to everyone, then, at least sometimes, we must forgo these principles and violate rights in order to attain a more generally desirable outcome.

It often seems that some violation of individual rights will result in a greater benefit for a larger number of people. More often, the reverse seems true. Either way, utilitarianism seems to give us a means of resolving conflicts between moral principles pulling in different directions. Moreover, some utilitarian philosophers have tried to show that violating rights *never* really results in greater benefits, so that there is no conflict between these principles when properly employed.

Utilitarianism is pretty clearly a bedfellow of the naturalistic approach to social sciences, and its weaknesses reflect problems in the development of a predictively improvable science of human behavior. Utilitarians initially advanced their doctrine on the assumption that welfare or satisfaction could be measured cardinally and compared between people and that people are utility maximizers—rational economic agents. Thus, the principle could be stated more explicitly as requiring that we adopt those actions, institutions, and practices that maximize average utility, or total utility, or the utility of the least advantaged in a society.

With the eclipse of cardinal and interpersonal utility, the principle must be considerably weakened. In welfare economics, utilitarian prescriptions that we maximize the greatest happiness become the requirement that we adopt a policy if it can be shown to increase at least one agent's utility without decreasing the utility of any other agent (called the Pareto principle, after its first expositor, Vilfredo Pareto). This means of course that we cannot deprive a millionaire of $1000 in order to increase the utility of a pauper because we cannot be sure that the loss in utility to the former will be smaller than the gain to the latter (see Chapter 3, "Behaviorism in the Theory of Rational Choice"). Nor will we be able to gauge accurately the costs of violating someone's privacy or deceiving someone in a social experiment against the benefits of the knowledge produced for all affected individuals.

As we have seen, this restriction has led to serious charges leveled against modern welfare economics by critical theorists, among others (see Chapter 4). Even if their charges are unwarranted, the prospects for a utilitarian theory's solving our problem of adjudicating moral conflicts seem slim.

But the core of utilitarianism seems right to many people because it focuses moral decisions on consequences for all affected parties. Though we cannot measure welfare very well, we all believe that there is such a thing as individual welfare, and it seems right that policies should be judged in the light of how they affect everyone's welfare to whatever extent we can measure it. Thus many who will not accept utilitarianism are nevertheless "consequentialists." They ground their moral decisions on the consequences of policies for affected parties. But consequentialism makes very strong demands on social science.

In order to determine the consequences of a policy, we need to know, with considerable accuracy, its effects. We need to know how the policy will interact with other social and natural processes as they influence people's welfare. Even if all we need is knowledge of whether more people will be benefited by a policy than harmed by it, the demands on social scientific knowledge will be very great. And the demands are predictive ones. They can be met only by uncovering laws and generalizations that will enable us to derive projections about the future when combined with descriptions of the policies we adopt. So, consequentialism requires a predictively improvable science of human behavior and its aggregation. This will be true for consequentialism about whether we should undertake experiments to further social science, and for consequentialism as a basis for public and private policy of many different kinds. Conversely, limitations on our ability to provide such predictive knowledge will severely limit a consequentialist approach to many vexing social problems. For without confidence about the effects of a policy, consequentialism provides no recommendation at all. If prediction beyond the powers of folk psychology is impossible, then consequentialist justification for many governmental policies is a dead letter.

Consequentialism is so closely tied to this approach to social science that it may turn out to undermine seriously some of the moral principles described above. For, suppose that the unsuitability of notions like belief and desire, and especially action, to a predictively powerful science leads us to surrender these notions as accurate descriptions of human behavior and its consequences. Behaviorists following Skinner certainly endorsed this view. But, they claimed, surrendering these concepts as unscientific also requires us to surrender other concepts built up out of them, concepts like autonomy, freedom, dignity, responsibility, informed consent, privacy. "Autonomy," for instance, means doing what you really would *want* to do, if you had all the facts—that is, the relevant true *beliefs*. If these concepts turn out to have no explanatory function with respect to human behavior and its causes, then a consequentialist approach to social policy can safely neglect them. Indeed it should. For, Skinner has argued, our system of criminal justice, educational institutions, and political processes are inefficient in meeting our goals because they are based on theories of human behavior that embody these baseless notions.

In effect, Skinner held that these notions will ultimately suffer the same fate as, say, the concept of witchcraft or demonic possession. In the fifteenth and sixteenth centuries, the behavior of the mentally disturbed was explained by appeal to such notions, and the treatment meted out to such persons reflected the theory that their behavior was caused by the devil. Doubtless, contemporary treatment of the mentally ill is far more humane, and this in part reflects our decision to forgo explanations that appeal to the concept of witchcraft. One way that we put forth this point is by saying there are no such things as witches. Similarly, Skinner holds, it may turn out that our treatment of criminals, for example, would be more humane and more effective in rehabilitation if we stop treating them as autonomous agents, "responsible for their crimes," and start viewing them as having been exposed to schedules of reinforcement that must be changed in order to elicit socially more beneficial behavior.

If the social sciences must abjure such notions in order to provide the kind of theory consequentialism needs, then they can hardly be expected to justify principles embodying these notions. In fact, many moral conflicts will turn out to rest on our false beliefs about the causes of human behavior, so that the advance of science will dissolve the conflicts without recourse to fundamental moral theory.

The most widely endorsed objection to consequentialism leads us directly to a deontological moral philosophy, one that is as closely related to nonnaturalistic approaches to human behavior as consequentialism is connected to naturalistic ones. Suppose someone offered you the opportunity to enrich the lives of a hundred, or a thousand, or a million persons, in return for the opportunity to kill by the most painless means possible a randomly chosen child. Though many of us might accept such an offer, most people would agree that doing so would be morally wrong. Why? Because we would be violating the rights of this entirely innocent person. It seems a very deep-seated conviction that at least some rights cannot be trampled on, no matter the beneficial consequences. Indeed, our moral conscience holds that some rights cannot even be given away or sold willingly by their bearer. Recall the U.S. Declaration of Independence: "All men are endowed with certain inalienable rights, . . . life, liberty and the pursuit of happiness." And these are not mere words. They reflect a moral theory fundamentally opposed to consequentialism: the theory that human beings have certain special rights and that these rights always take precedence over other less fundamental rights, and over policies that would trade these rights for something else.

Where do these rights come from? According to Kant, they emerge from pure reason, untainted by experience. Reflection alone leads us to see the truth of certain a priori moral principles, that is, principles that we can know for certain, without experience. Because they are necessary truths, all possible experience must be compatible with them, so no particular experience can justify them. Kant called the principle that he identified the "categorial imperative," which enjoins all rational agents to endorse for themselves only principles that could be endorsed by all moral agents. The only such principles are ones that require that moral agents always be treated as *ends* and never as *means* to some purportedly greater end. Followers of Kant hold that treating people as "ends in themselves" means not allowing the consequences for some to influence the treatment of others. It means that people have certain rights and that we have certain duties to respect those rights, come what may. This is what is involved in individual autonomy and what grounds the moral prohibition against deception, the violation of privacy, unequal treatment. It subordinates to autonomy the principle of nonmaleficence and beneficence, and thus resolves the conflict between them in the opposite direction from many utilitarian conclusions.

What is more, the focus on autonomy makes few demands on improvable scientific knowledge of human behavior because such knowledge cannot influence our moral judgments about what is permissible and what is not. Indeed, this view positively prohibits steps to increase that knowledge to the extent that such steps require violations of human rights. In fact, it may encourage the conception of human behavior that makes such inquiry unnecessary and misguided. It does so in two ways.

First of all, the conception of rights and duties that deontological moral theories require makes the notions of belief, desire, and action fundamental to our conception of ourselves. Without them, morality has no foundation, on this view. For rights are rights to perform actions and duties are duties to do so as well, and actions are necessarily the outcome of beliefs and desires.

According to Kant, one of the features of an ethics that makes rights and duties paramount and subordinates consequences is that moral assessment must focus on *motives* for actions, instead of their consequences. A beneficial act, done for the wrong motives, will have no moral value, whereas a harmful act, done with the best of intentions and the right motives, may be morally praiseworthy. The essence of moral rightness for Kant was action motived by a desire to do one's duties and carry out one's obligations. And according to Kant, the relations among our beliefs about our duties, or desires to fulfill them, and the actions they explain, could not be understood causally without robbing human action of its moral dimension altogether. The reason, Kant held, was that causality implies determinism and the absence of free will, which is a prerequisite for moral responsibility. It is pretty clear how much this moral theory leans on a social science that takes human action and intentionality seriously.

Secondly, Kant's claim that we can have a priori knowledge—that is, perfect certainty about the truth of some statements without recourse to experience—fosters the conviction that we might acquire further knowledge simply by pure reason, by observationally unaided reflection. In particular, pure reason may also be the source of the conception of intelligibility that animates noncausal approaches to the explanation of human behavior. Kant defended the categorical imperative on the grounds of its intelligibility to pure reason and rejected consequentialist theories in part because their truth could not be warranted by intelligibility alone. This same criterion, intelligibility, might be enough to certify the explanatory power of a principle like [L] or some more profound insight into human action, just because it makes behavior intelligible.

It should be noted that Kant identified a moral principle—the categorical imperative—as justified because it was the only one that could recommend itself to pure reason. He did not suppose that particular moral decisions could be made by pure reason. Such decisions must be made by applying a priori moral principles to details about particular cases that only experience could provide. Similarly, an explanatory principle is itself justified a priori, not as a causal law, but as a principle that determines what counts as action. But it can only be applied to particular circumstances by adding facts available through experience. The point is not that social science is a priori but that the power of its explanatory strategy is based, not on experience, but on pure reason.

Much of Kant's complex argumentation for a deontological approach to morality has been unacceptable to philosophers, and other foundations have been sought for principles that give autonomy priority over consequences in deciding moral conflicts. One tradition that stretches back well before Kant accords individuals *natural rights* and, concomitantly, natural duties to respect those rights. A natural right is one that each individual has just in virtue of being human; it is part of what makes one a person, in contrast to a merely very complicated system composed of organic material. But any serious theory of natural rights must explain exactly what rights we have essentially and what it is about people that confers upon them such natural rights. Presumably it will have something to do with the fact that we are sapient and sentient creatures, that we have thoughts and feelings, intentional states, minds that other creatures lack. (Notice that those who accord such states to animals will find it more reasonable to also attribute rights to them.)

Like Kant's moral theory, a natural rights view seems to rest on a nonnaturalistic conception of human beings, one that exempts them from a thoroughgoing scientific treatment. Despite the confusing similarity of terminology, a naturalistic theory of human thought and behavior has no room for distinctive natural rights, for it assimilates humans to the rest of nature. It denies their distinctiveness. It aims at a causal account of their behavior and their minds, which shows humans to be no different in kind from other, simpler systems to which we do not accord rights.

There is yet a third approach to deontological theory that is sometimes combined with natural rights: social contract theory. This approach to morality attempts to derive and justify moral principles by showing that rational agents, endowed with certain natural rights, would agree among themselves to certain moral principles, as part of a contract for the organization of society. Social contract theories were advanced by many of the forefathers of modern social science, philosophers like Hobbes, Locke, Rousseau, and others. Their object was to ground the moral principles we recognize by showing that any rational individual *would* agree to them rather than live in a condition of anarchy, without the advantages of moral rules.

If, as rational choice theory claims, all individuals seek their own advantage, moral principles will be endorsed and obeyed by all individuals just in case the benefits of these principles to each individual outweigh their costs to each. Social contract theorists of the seventeenth and eighteenth centuries disagreed among themselves about which particular moral principles rational individuals would endorse. In the nineteenth century this approach to ethics fell out of favor. But the general strategy of justifying and identifying moral principles that social contract theory envisions began to exercise a renewed fascination, as rational choice theory developed in the twentieth century.

Reasons for this renewed interest are the difficulties of utilitarianism and the limitations economists imposed on the theory of rational choice that utilitarianism spawned. If interpersonal comparisons are impossible, utilitarianism cannot choose among many different moral rules or social institutions, all of which pass the Pareto test. What is more, it cannot provide moral decisions in the absence of information that we have no way of providing about consequences. Some economists and philosophers have hoped that social institutions and moral rules could be derived from the examination of rational strategies or hypothetical bargaining problems faced by perfectly rational economic agents.

The chief trouble that these theories face is that obeying moral rules is like providing public goods (see Chapter 6). Moral rules encourage free riding and the rational desire to avoid being made a sucker. In the context of the prisoner's dilemma, the "moral" thing to do is not to confess and especially not to break one's word, if a promise or a contract has been entered into not to confess. But confession, as we have seen, is just what rationality enjoins. Work in this area continues among economists and philosophers hoping to provide a contractarian justification for moral principles. Once it is found, they will have to face the problems of relating the unrealistic and idealized assumptions their approach shares with economic modeling to the decision procedure of real people.

Consequentialist moral theories and deontological ones are advanced both to underwrite moral principles and to order or prioritize their application, not just to experimentation in social science and elsewhere, but to all areas of social and individual life. But two such irreconcilable theories with differing ethical implications leave us with larger problems than we hoped they would solve. For now instead of justifying and ordering relatively concrete moral principles, we are faced with settling fundamental disputes in moral philosophy about the correct abstract, general ethical theory. Moreover, it appears that the two views about the nature of social science that we have examined in this book are closely associated with these divergent moral theories, so that in choosing between different methods in social science, we may also be making moral choices. We may, but perhaps we need not. For, despite the sympathy that each of our philosophies of social science may have for a different moral commitment, we have not shown that either entails an ethical theory. At most we have seen that consequentialism's relevance to real moral decisions requires a predictively improvable social science, and that deontology's commitment to rights and right motives for action presupposes the explanatory powers of intentional states, no matter what their predictive weakness.

Facts and Values

But according to some philosophers, the connection between ethics and social science is even closer than this, so that in social science we always take sides on moral questions. If this is so, it may be a crucial difference between natural and social science that we must examine. In fact, some hold it to be the source of what has been described as the difference between natural science's relative progress and the alleged lack of it in social science.

To understand this issue we need to understand the differences between facts and evaluations, or description and prescriptions. Our task is complicated by the fact that many who argue that social science always takes sides on moral questions do so by denying this distinction. Thus, whatever one says to introduce it is bound to be unacceptable to some parties to the debate.

A factual claim describes the way things are, while remaining neutral on the question of how they ought to be or whether they are good or bad or could be improved or worsened. It is "value-free." A normative or evaluative or "value-laden" statement expresses values or evaluations of facts based on those values, or it may both describe and evaluate. That is, it can express approval or disapproval, praise or blame, for the fact it also describes; it can reflect the conviction that that fact *ought* not to be the case or ought to be. A simple example is the contrast between saying that Lincoln was killed and saying that he was murdered. The former states the facts but is neutral on whether his killing was a *wrongful* death. The latter reports the same fact but takes a stand on whether it *ought* to have happened. It therefore presupposes some moral theory about what ought to be the case and what ought not to be the case, about whether some killings are morally permissible or not. Such statements reflect the ethical *norms*, often unexpressed, of the speaker.

Now one traditional view about science is that it is value-free or morally neutral. And indeed the theories, laws, experimental descriptions, explanations, and predictions of physics or chemistry seem quite independent of any ethical teaching. Of course, natural scientists make value judgments, and some of these judgments will often be informed by the scientists' specialized knowledge. But in doing so, they do not express views that follow from their scientific beliefs but from their scientific beliefs combined with their independent moral beliefs. For example, a physicist's opposition to a new weapons system may derive from his belief that it is unworkable or too expensive. In each case, his opposition to the system will only follow from these beliefs if we add in evaluative premises, such as his belief that money should not be spent on physically unworkable systems or spent on systems that are not cost effective. Though such principles may be obvious, they in turn rely on other, more basic, moral claims: It is morally wrong to waste scarce resources, et cetera.

Some philosophers have held that moral claims cannot be part of science because they do not constitute knowledge at all but rather expressions of emotion, taste, or subjective preference. One argument in favor of this view is the fact that people who seem to agree on a very wide range of factual questions may yet disagree about the most fundamental moral ones. Thus two physicians may agree on all the "facts" about a particular prospective abortion, including all the physical, psychological, and social consequences for mother and fetus of having the abortion or not; and yet they may still disagree about whether the abortion is morally permissible. A second consideration given in favor of this skeptical view of moral knowledge is the fact that moral principles differ widely among cultures, subcultures, and ethnic groups. Because it seems ethnocentric to insist that some of these are "false," it has been concluded that none are true. There is no such thing as true and false when it comes to values, and so knowledge of them is impossible.

It follows from this view that if social science is to be knowledge, it ought to emulate the value freedom of natural science. Social scientists ought to be careful about how they express their findings and theories, in order to ensure that value-laden descriptions don't contaminate them, and should be scrupulous to label any evaluative claims as such. Thus, like the physicist, a political scientist can oppose a weapons system as politically destabilizing. Here the political scientist's specialized knowledge of the effects of such a system on international relations is crucial, but his opposition follows only from this knowledge *plus* a normative claim that destabilizing policies ought not be pursued.

Even if we do hold that moral knowledge is possible, the persistent disagreements about it, even among those who share many other beliefs in common, suggest that acquiring such knowledge is difficult. Indeed, the tolerance that characterizes most Western societies in part reflects this belief that moral questions are difficult to answer with much unanimity and that moral certainty breeds paternalism, if not totalitarianism. This is another reason to favor "value neutrality" as a methodological principle for social science, even among those who do not demand that it emulate the features of natural science.

The conviction that social science should, like natural science, be value-free was first championed by Max Weber, and since his time has become widespread among experimental psychologists, economists, and the more quantitative of social scientists. Economists especially have insisted on advancing what they call a "positive," as opposed to a "normative," science. They have held that their discipline cannot make substantive policy recommendations because such conclusions are normative. It can only trace out the consequences of various policies, actual and possible, leaving it to the politician to decide which should be implemented. In fact the self-imposed restriction of their theory to ordinal utility and revealed preference (Chapter 3, "Behaviorism in Rational Choice Theory"), and of their welfare criterion to Pareto optimality, is most often justified by this commitment to a purely positive science.

Many exponents of positive social science provide a moral or, at any rate, an argument from self-interest in favor of value freedom. They hold that it is important to avoid a normative bias in social science, for it can destroy the *objectivity* crucial for informing social policy. Evidence slanted by personal values, conclusions shaded to advance individual interests, or theories that reflect implicit commitments, even high moral conceptions, all may destroy both the public confidence in social science's objectivity and factual reliability. They may frustrate the very social aims social science is called upon to guide. Sometimes it may be difficult to attain the sort of moral neutrality required, but the social scientist has an obligation at least to be explicit about the values held, again because they may color judgments and impair objectivity. When this happens, the information a social scientist offers to inform policy will reflect biases and impede the attainment of social goals chosen by the society through democratic procedures. Just as few would wish to have someone else's values imposed on them, so the social scientist has no right to impose moral standards on society.

But remaining value-free is, according to many, far more difficult for social science than for natural science. And according to others it is flatly impossible, whereas still others hold it to be undesirable. The argument that moral neutrality is impossible for social science often goes together with the claim that such neutrality would be itself morally undesirable. What the argument and the claim work together to show is that the steps we would have to take to free social science from value commitments would result in something no one would recognize as a science of human action, which explains events by uncovering their significance. At best, it would result in something like the kind of behaviorism Skinner advocated; at worst it would just be an empty exercise in "physics envy." Both of these outcomes are held to be morally repugnant because they threaten our view of people as morally responsible agents and objects of ethical concern, and because they would distract us from what some hold to be the social scientist's duty to make the world a better place, through the improvement of our moral consciousness of the social setting. This is a position on value neutrality that characterizes the critical theorists, among others (see Chapter 4).

Some proponents of the unavoidability of moral commitments in social science argue that there is no such thing as "objectivity" to begin with, either in natural science or social science. They hold the very notion of objectivity has been undermined fatally by advances in epistemology or the sociology of science, or its postmodern deconstruction. For "objectivity" means reporting the facts unvarnished by our opinions. But if the language in which we make these reports is already unavoidably laden with opinions—implicit theories or unnoticed interpretations and moral biases—then such reporting is impossible. Opponents of the very possibility of objectivity devote great effort to showing our descriptive vocabulary is really like this. Their arguments connect the issue of values in science with the agenda of the theory of knowledge: What sorts of facts can we have knowledge of? Are there facts we can know independent of interpretations, descriptions, and evaluations? Are there moral facts? Do they differ from other kinds? How can we tell them apart? Either side we take on the question of value freedom in social science commits us to sides on these fundamental epistemological issues.

If we cannot propound a good account of the difference between statements of fact and expressions of moral evaluation, then the debate over whether a discipline should be value-free or not is moot. The most popular argument against the distinction is based on the alleged impossibility of providing pure descriptions, without the implicit importation of evaluations or prescriptions.

It is certainly true that the vocabulary of ordinary language and of the social sciences is replete with "value-laden" terms. For example, to describe a tribal system as "primitive," or a political system as a "regime," or an economic system as "capitalist," or behavior as "intelligent" seems to combine description and evaluation. And even when social scientists give explicitly stipulative definitions of such terms, bereft of their ordinary connotations, the terms retain their "halo" of moral approval or disapproval. Thus, modern economic theory's definition of *rationality* as "utility maximizing" can be claimed to be neutral on the moral desirability of utility maximizing. But since the ordinary term *rational* is a term of approval, this caveat carries little weight. It is for this reason, among others, that social scientists who endorse the notion of value-free social science have often had recourse to neologisms and have been accused of producing jargon that merely rephrases common sense in undecipherable circumlocutions. Their aim, of course, has been to avoid ordinary connotations. But the results in scientific advance have never seemed to justify the effort.

The reason, argue proponents of value-laden social science, is that the moral dimension is an ineliminable part of the explanatory strategy that seeks to render human affairs intelligible. As Max Weber first noted and others have seen, the way in which a social scientist selects the problems on which to work, the factors he cites to explain behavior, and the evidence he seeks to substantiate these explanations all reflect the significance and meaning the social scientist attaches to them. To focus on a particular problem is to evaluate it as more important than others, and importance is based on evaluation in the light of human values. Moreover, the terms in which events, institutions, and behavior are to be described must be meaningful to the participants in these events, institutions, and activities. But again, meaningfulness is a reflection of rules, including moral principles. A social fact cannot be identified and described in terms of the "mere" behavior of the human bodies that participate in it. It must be described from within their points of view, and perhaps from the basis of the deeper meanings of these institutions.

A social science that sought to efface the moral dimension from its descriptions and explanations would simply serve the interests of a moral conception foreign to those that animate our conception of ourselves. If such a social science were successful in providing a predictively powerful theory of human behavior, it would serve the interest of those powerful enough and willing enough to disregard human rights and individual autonomy, by enabling them to override meaningful action and manipulate behavior. But more likely, such a social discipline would simply be a pseudoscience serving the interests of the powerful as an empty rationalization for their socially harmful goals. Thus, at any rate, the opponent of value-free social science will argue.

One line of reply to this argument grants that social science does have some or all of these ineliminable moral dimensions. However, the reply goes on to identify the same or similar features in natural science. The scientist's interests also determine what phenomenon will be singled out for study, in what terms the "facts" will be described, how the evidence will be assessed, et cetera. This is what makes science a fallible enterprise: Scientists are human, and what they do is as value charged as any other human activity. But, this means either that value-ladenness is no obstacle to scientific knowledge or that it is at least possible to reduce the obstructive effects of value-ladenness enough to make scientific progress. This indeed is how Max Weber viewed the matter.

This may well be the beginnings of a good argument against those who say that social science is impossible because we cannot be objective— value-free—in our account of our own activities. But it is no argument against the claim that social science is essentially a "nonobjective" enterprise, one in which progress is not measured by the standards in force among the natural sciences. Such an argument makes social inquiry of a piece with moral inquiry; thus the admonition to minimize its value-laden character is a profound mistake, for it would simply prevent us from pursuing our "science" of human action altogether.

It is clear that a full "positive" reply to this sort of "normative" argument involves little less than an entire philosophy of social science, one that successfully naturalizes the concepts we employ to explain human action. Short of this, the defender of value-free social science may still extol the importance of social scientists' being "up front" with their evaluative commitments, at least so that others can make appropriate adjustments in their own interpretations of social claims.

But if moral commitment is a central feature of social science, then perhaps it will provide us with both an explanation of why it is so different in its results from natural science and a justification for this difference as well. For few philosophers, even the most empiricist, have ever expected any sort of scientific "progress" in moral philosophy. This is indeed a discipline in which progress is never a matter of successive improvements in predictive success but rather a matter of deepening intelligibility and coherence. If social science is really a branch of moral philosophy, perhaps the opponents of naturalism are right after all.

Dangerous Questions, Moral Obligations, and Predictive Knowledge

Controversial subjects are the social scientist's stock-in-trade. We put a particular premium on social science that provides revisionist, debunking, or otherwise startling conclusions at variance with either common beliefs about the past or hopeful expectations about the future. But some social scientists, and even more nonsocial scientists, hold that some questions of potential interest to social scientists ought not be pursued, for the answers to them are morally dangerous and can serve no good purpose in the guidance of social policy. Accordingly, social science should exercise a sort of self-denial, steering away from these topics.

Examples of such morally dangerous topics come readily to mind. Perhaps the most famous are studies that employ IQ tests to measure intelligence and compare average IQs for sex, varying socioeconomic, ethnic, and racial groups. Some researchers have concluded that differences in average IQ among such groups can best be explained by genetic as opposed to environmental factors. It is pretty obvious why such a conclusion might be "dangerous." Regardless of what the social scientists who conduct such studies think that their policy ramifications should be, there are others with more power over the adoption and implementation of policy who might use such findings to discourage steps to equalize the educational opportunity of all people. Though such a policy does not follow from these findings, they are easy to misunderstand and even easier to abuse in order to clothe racist or sexist practices in the mantle of scientific respectability. The same consequences are said to follow from sociobiological speculations about the origins and character of social institutions. If sex-role differences, or fear of strangers, or caste and class systems are somehow "written" in our genetic programs, then it is widely supposed there is little we can do by altering the environment to eliminate these morally undesirable features of society. These studies thus seem a recipe for the status quo, if not for retrograde social policies.

Such studies provoke two sorts of reactions: first, examination of the scientific methods, theories, and findings, which seeks to show that these theories are in themselves inadequate, defective, or fundamentally confused solely on scientific grounds. Philosophers have taken an especially prominent role in this enterprise and have applied the tools of the logician and philosopher of science to the assessment of particular theories, like the IQ theory of general intelligence, sociobiology, and, for that matter, Marxian social and economic theories, which are said to have inimical effects on prospects for human freedom and economic progress.

But the moral repugnance of some potential answers to questions in social science provokes a second reaction: the suggestion that these questions not be studied at all. Some inquiries, it is held, can have no morally useful function and can only have bad consequences. Though constitutional guarantees of freedom of inquiry rule out no subject as illegal, nevertheless, it is held that social scientists should deny themselves certain topics because what they uncover may be dangerous, even if it is true. There is an obvious parallel here to moral injunctions that some have sought to impose on natural scientists, originally nuclear physicists working on topics with a payoff in weapons production, and more recently molecular biologists whose work may result in manipulation of human and animal genomes. Those who make this claim often qualify it. They insist that scientists have a responsibility to terminate certain studies if they have reason to believe that the results will be misused in the interests of injustice. There is, on this view, no blanket prohibition against certain lines of research, only a conditional one. But, they hold, the conditions that would morally require such self-censorship certainly operate in most societies today.

This moral injunction is evidently based on a consequentialist moral theory, one that enjoins certain acts if their costs for the whole society outweigh their benefits for it. One way social scientists have opposed the injunction is by pleading a deontologically based right to free inquiry. There is of course a tension between embracing such principles and the naturalistic methods these social scientists employ. Without debating this claim, let us consider how much social scientific knowledge is required of the social scientist in order to obey a ban on certain kinds of research. To know whether a certain research program is morally permissible, the social scientist, and the natural scientist for that matter, need to be able to predict with some reliability the long-term consequences of their research results and their dissemination. To do this scientists need a substantial amount of theory about human activities and institutions and about how both respond to scientific innovations and discoveries. Scientists need to be able to establish the initial conditions about the social contexts to which these theories are applied, and they need to be able to calculate the net costs or benefits for society of their discoveries.

In the absence of such knowledge, it may be argued, scientists should exercise caution, for it is better to err on the side of too much self-censorship, rather than too little. If there is just a chance of some scientific findings having a very bad net effect, then this should outweigh an equal or even a greater chance of a very good effect. But this cautious policy still requires a vast amount of social scientific knowledge. Moreover, because we can at this point predict with accuracy almost none of the effects of scientific discoveries and their dissemination, such a cautious principle would foreclose almost every line of research, pure, applied, natural, or social, as almost any discovery could, for the little we know, have costs that vastly outweigh its benefits.

In fact, studies aimed at acquiring the kind of social theory we would need to determine the impact of new ideas on society are themselves socially dangerous. Although they would enable us to decide on whether to pursue certain issues, they would also enable those in power to manipulate social changes in directions that they might prefer in spite of their great costs to society as a whole. So, perhaps the very theory we require in order to decide whether some questions should not be examined is itself such a prohibited area of inquiry.

The obverse of prohibited topics for social science is required ones. Critical theory, for example, tells us that the aim of social science should be *emancipation* of humans from bonds that restrict their freedom. The social scientist is responsible for uncovering the real meanings of social processes, institutions, events, and ideologies. This may, however, mean violating the "rights" of individuals to privacy and confidentiality in their pursuit of nonemancipatory goals. Thus, whereas ordinary moral scruple will prohibit "bugging" a jury room, critical theory may sanction or even require it, if it will provide understanding that demythologizes this coercive social institution and thus emancipates us from the system of justice characteristic of "late capitalism."

Like the prohibition against certain lines of inquiry, the prescription of some topics because of their emancipatory potential requires a great deal of social scientific knowledge. For to identify topics of inquiry as potentially emancipatory requires the same knowledge of the impact of new discoveries and their dissemination on society.

Otherwise, how can we tell if uncovering hidden meanings will emancipate or not, or whether the uncovered meanings will be greeted with indifference. In fact, providing such a predictively successful theory of the influence of new discoveries on society as a whole is probably the first priority for a philosophy of social science that makes human emancipation the central goal of social science. Because of the allegedly reflexive character of social science, however, such a theory may itself be impossible. Once it comes into general circulation, its influence on human actions may lead to its own falsification. What is more serious is the notion that a philosophy like critical theory, which rejects positivism as a method in social science, may require a theory that meets positivist standards of predictive success in order to underwrite the moral obligations it places upon social scientists.

Introduction to the Literature

T. Beauchamp, R. Faden, J. Wallace, and L. Walters (eds.), *Ethical Issues in Social Science Research*, is an excellent introduction to the issues, and contains many important papers. S. Milgram, *Obedience to Authority*, and L. Humphrey, *Tearoom Trade*, report examples of research that raise serious moral questions.

An excellent introduction to ethics and moral theories is W. K. Frankena, *Ethics*. A very different view is advanced in G. Harman, *The Nature of Morality*. J. S. Mill, *Utilitarianism*, and I. Kant, *Foundations of the Metaphysics of Morals*, present the two moral theories treated in this chapter. Kant's work is extremely difficult for the student to understand. The notion of natural rights stems from the thought of John Locke and is firmly entrenched in modern legal and political doctrine. A radical development of it is to be found in R. Nozick, *Anarchy, State and Utopia*. More influential but less easy to classify is J. Rawls, *A Theory of Justice*.

A. Buchanan, *Ethics, Efficiency and the Market*, traces the connection between moral theory, especially utilitarianism, and economics. B. F. Skinner's claims about the consequences for moral philosophy of behaviorism are advanced in his *Beyond Freedom and Dignity*. A general treatment of ethical issues surrounding behaviorism is E. Erwin, *Behavior Therapy: Scientific, Philosophical and Moral Foundations*.

N. Block and J. Dworkin (eds.), *The IQ Controversy*, treats the interaction of methodological and normative factors that bear on whether a potentially explosive line of research should be pursued at all.

The distinction between factual and normative, or evaluative, descriptions goes back to David Hume, *Treatise of Human Nature*, and more recently, G. E. Moore, *Principia Ethica*. E. Nagel, *The Structure of Science*, Chapter 13, introduces the problem well and provides a strong plea for value freedom. Before him M. Weber, *The Methodology of the Social Sciences*, argued strongly for value freedom among social scientists. A very different view is defended in G. Myrdal, *Objectivity in Social Science*.

The anthologies by L. I. Krimerman and M. Brodbeck both contain influential articles about the question of whether social sciences can or should be value-free or not. A. Ryan's anthology (*The Philosophy of Social Explanation*) includes an important article by Charles Taylor, "Neutrality in Political Science."

8

Social Science and the Enduring Questions of Philosophy

THE PROBLEMS of the philosophy of social science are problems both for philosophy and for social science. They are problems of philosophy because their ultimate resolution turns on the response to philosophical challenges that have been with us since Plato. They are problems of social science because social scientists must take sides on them, whether they realize it or not. Moreover, social scientists have defended competing and irreconcilable approaches to their own disciplines by appeal to philosophical theories.

Even the claim that philosophical reflection is irrelevant to advancing knowledge in social science is itself a philosophical claim. The social scientist indifferent to philosophy can embrace this view. But unless the social scientist argues for it, the view must appear to others to be sheer prejudice. Nevertheless, an argument for it is philosophy, whether we call it that or not.

It should not really be surprising that the social sciences and philosophy bear a profound and indissoluble link to one another. Like the natural sciences, each of the social sciences is a discipline that was once part and parcel of philosophy. Indeed, while the natural sciences separated themselves from philosophy in the 2,200 years from Euclid to Darwin, the social sciences have become independent only in the twentieth century. In separating itself from philosophy, each of the natural sciences left, for the continued reflection of philosophy, questions that the natural science could not answer. It has been easy for natural scientists to leave these questions to philosophy, for they have been busy, especially in the centuries since Galileo, providing more and more detailed knowledge about the objects in their domains. As Thomas Kuhn has noted, it has only been at periods of crisis in the elaboration of, for example, physics or chemistry, that natural scientists have turned to philosophy and taken seriously questions about the foundations of their discipline. And more often than not, the crises have been surmounted by a new piece of technology or a new nonphilosophical breakthrough. Indeed, since Newton, advances in physical theory have had a more profound impact on our view of philosophical problems than advances in philosophy have shaped the natural sciences. Natural science has forced philosophy to come to terms with materialism, mechanism, determinism and then indeterminism, relativity, natural selection, and so forth. Each revolution in the natural sciences has generated new problems for philosophy.

But this is certainly not the case in the relationship between philosophy and social science. There has of course been much new and original in each of the social sciences. But some of these novelties have not met with the uniform acceptance of social scientists that would force philosophy to take them seriously. And the rest have not forced philosophy to address any new problem in the way natural science has. The direction of influence between philosophy and social science still seems to be from philosophy instead of toward it. We can trace the leading ideas of almost all the social sciences back to the work of philosophers who wrote in the seventeenth and eighteenth centuries. This is not just a point about intellectual history. It shows how much more contemporary social science is bound up with the philosophical tradition than is contemporary natural science.

More than ever today, social scientists seem to be interested in philosophy, and especially the philosophy of science. If Kuhn was right, this is a symptom of intellectual crisis. In the heyday of behaviorism, methodological reflection was out of favor among psychologists, economists, and other social scientists inspired by their optimism. The philosophy of science was treated as the last refuge of a social scientist incapable of making a "real" contribution to the discipline. It is a matter of some irony that this confidence about the prospects for scientific progress was based on almost nothing but a philosophical theory, logical positivism, the latest version of empiricism. This is a doctrine that goes back certainly to the Enlightenment, and probably to Plato's contemporaries.

Pessimism about a thoroughly behavioral approach to human action returned many social scientists to a concern with philosophy. And they found in the philosophy of science a number of theories ready to explain both why behaviorism failed in social science, and why empiricism was inadequate as a philosophy of science altogether. But this is what another tradition in philosophy, and social science, had been preaching steadily for just as long as the empiricists.

This preoccupation with philosophy of science seems to be another reason to identify the distinctive problem of the philosophy of social science as that surrounding the issue of *progress,* and the allegedly invidious comparisons to natural science. But the practical concerns of the individual disciplines also make salient fundamental issues in epistemology, metaphysics, ethics, and logic.

The Unavoidability of Epistemology

The dispute about whether the goal of social science should be predictive improvement or increasing intelligibility is fundamentally a disagreement about the nature, extent, and justification of claims to knowledge. Of course, we'd rather not have to choose between seeking improvement in prediction and making human action more intelligible. Yet insofar as what we seek in social science is knowledge, this choice is forced upon us. The demands of predictive improvement rest on a conception of knowledge as justified by its consistency with experience, and not just past experience, for it is too easy to tailor a theory to be consistent with data that is already in. A theory that can tell us about the actual world must be composed of contingent claims that the actual world could show to be false. For a body of statements that actual events could not disconfirm would be consistent with whatever happens and thus explain nothing.

If increasing our understanding of the meaning of human actions improves our predictive powers, then of course there is no conflict. The kind of knowledge that the search for meanings provides will be the same as that which predictively confirmed claims provide. But as we have seen, there are serious obstacles in the way of providing such predictive improvements in theories that take the search for meanings seriously. We have to decide whether these obstacles are surmountable. If we decide they are not, we must face a forced choice between intelligibility and prediction. If we choose intelligibility, we are committed to a fundamentally different epistemology, one that does not require the same sort of justification for knowledge that prediction provides. Instead, the mark of knowledge this different epistemology demands is some sort of certainty or necessity of connections that the mind can grasp.

Well, why not simply hold that the house of knowledge has many mansions, that there are many different sorts of knowledge? Social scientists must choose among them, but all are equally legitimate ways of expanding our understanding. Some social scientists are interested in knowledge that can be applied to informing social and individual policy, that can be used to predict the consequences of planning or its absence. For them, prediction is crucial, and improvements in knowledge are measured by improvements in prediction. Other social scientists have other interests, to which improvements in prediction are irrelevant. For them knowledge accumulates in increasing our detailed understanding of a culture or subculture from the inside. Both are equally valid "ways" of knowing, which need not compete with one another.

This view, which sounds like an open-minded attitude of tolerance, is just a way of refusing to take seriously the problems social science faces. If there are really many different forms of knowledge, all equally "valid," the question must arise: What do they share in common that makes them all knowledge? After all, the term "knowledge" has to stand for something; it can't just be an arbitrary label for a heterogeneous collection of intellectual activities that share nothing in common. To suggest that religious knowledge, for instance, rests on revelation and that moral knowledge is justified by intuitions, while scientific knowledge is empirical, that our knowledge of human action is introspectively certain, and that they are all equally legitimate shows not so much tolerance as indifference. For it is the attitude that anything goes, that knowledge is whatever anyone cares to assert. If a social scientist chooses to seek one of these different kinds of knowledge, there must be a reason given for this choice. Surely, it cannot be merely a matter of taste whether improvable generalizations or empathetic insight into intelligibility is the aim of a social scientist's research program. What the social scientist will count as good evidence for a theory or explanation advanced in the pursuit of inquiry cannot be merely a matter of taste. And when a social scientist chooses one goal, but allows that all other epistemic goals (including incompatible ones) are equally correct, he deprives his own choice of a rational foundation.

This does not mean that once we have made a choice, we should not accept or tolerate other choices and other methods as possible alternatives. For our best views of what constitutes knowledge are fallible. Having made our epistemic choice, we could be wrong. But the fallibility of our choice does not entail either that it is the wrong choice or that there is no more evidence for it than for its competitors.

Having chosen to seek predictive improvement or intelligibility of our theories as the mark of knowledge, we must allow others to identify other goals, because for all we know we might be wrong about what constitutes knowledge. But if we don't have reasons to support our choice and perhaps also to oppose theirs, then our choice is not rationally justified.

This is what makes epistemology unavoidable for those who hold that the aim of social science is to provide knowledge. Indifference to issues of epistemology is sometimes in fact a cover for contempt. Some natural scientists, secure in their conviction about what the right methods for attaining scientific knowledge are, express great tolerance about the appropriate methods in social science and often decline to endorse their own methods as appropriate for the study of human action and social institutions. On their view, "anything goes" in social science. But without a good reason to show that human behavior and its consequences are so different from natural phenomena that scientific methods are inappropriate for its study, this attitude is a contemptuous one. It simply disguises the view that the "soft" sciences don't provide knowledge at all, just the free play of competing speculations, which succeed each other on grounds of fashionableness instead of justification. If social science is to provide knowledge, it cannot be indifferent to what constitutes knowledge. Nor can it accept a permanent agnosticism about the claims of incompatible theories of knowledge.

Science and Metaphysics

I have argued that the epistemic choice of predictive improvement as a mark of increasing knowledge must make us dissatisfied with intentional approaches to the explanation of human behavior. Similarly, an unswerving commitment to such strategies of explanation will seriously weaken the claims of prediction as an epistemic goal for social science.

Either of these alternatives raises fundamental questions about us human beings and our place in nature, questions that have always been the special province of metaphysics. And taking sides on them seems just as unavoidable for the social scientist as it does about matters of epistemology. The interpretative philosophy of social science that exempts the study of humankind from the methods appropriate in the study of the rest of nature owes us an explanation of this exemption. And the naturalistic philosophy that absorbs social science into this paradigm must explain away an equally recalcitrant fact about mankind.

Interpretative philosophy of social science teaches that the goals of natural science are inappropriate in the study of human behavior, and another set of aims not recognized in the natural sciences must be substituted for them. We may be able to show that this is so by an analysis of the way social science actually proceeds and by showing that it cannot proceed in any other way. But the question is left open of why this is so. It must be because of some fact about us, and in particular about our minds, thoughts, consciousness, and because of the facts of intentionality on which interpretation trades.

If, as Descartes held, the mind is a substance quite different from the rest of nature, operating in accordance with different principles, then we have the beginnings of an explanation of why its study, psychology, and the study of the consequences of human thoughts and actions, the rest of social science, cannot proceed in the way the study of matter does. Metaphysical differences dictate scientific differences. Descartes argued that the mind was distinct from the body on the grounds that the former has properties no chunk of matter could possibly have. His most famous argument was that our minds have the property of our not being able to doubt their existence, whereas no part of our bodies, including our brains, have this feature. I can well imagine what it would be like to wake up discovering I was missing a limb or even that my skull was empty. But I cannot imagine discovering that I have no mind, for "who" would make this discovery if I had none?

This dualism has the gravest difficulty with the evident fact that our mental states have both physical causes and physical effects. It is hard to see how something nonphysical can have such relations. For causation is preeminently a physical relation, one that involves pushes and pulls and the transfer of a kinetic energy, which is a function of mass and velocity. But the interpretationalist can turn this mystery to advantage. For the impossibility of causal relations between mind and matter provides an explanation of why a predictive science of human behavior, modeled on natural science, is quite impossible.

Of course, some will find that such an argument proves too much, because it seems to them beyond doubt that our desires and beliefs have environmental causes and behavioral effects. They may adapt Descartes's argument to a less controversial but still sufficiently strong argument against naturalism. We may grant that mental states have causes and effects, but the sort of causation involved is not physical and does not consist in generalizations that we may improve in the direction of laws. Indeed, the causal relations between mind and matter are singular and irregular; but they reflect logical or conceptual relations between the intentional content of the mind, the statements describing what we believe and want, and descriptions of behavior. It is these conceptual relations that force on us a study of meanings as the only way to come to grips with the mind and action.

Of course the explanatory power of such a doctrine rests in large measure on its initial metaphysical assumption that the mind is distinct from the body, and not a part of the physical world. Unless the interpretationalist is content to leave unexplained the distinctiveness of social scientific method, he must face the challenge of substantiating this metaphysical view.

The naturalist has the same problem in reverse, for naturalism purports to absorb the mind to nature and so to explain the appropriateness of methods drawn from the natural sciences to its study. And, as we saw in Chapter 2, this is no easy matter. We have as yet no plausible explanation for the most basic fact naturalism rests on: how physical matter can have intentional content, how one arrangement of matter— the brain—can represent other arrangements of physical matter. Yet if the mind is the brain, this is what our beliefs and desires will be: My belief that Paris is the capital of France must be an arrangement of neurotransmitters at the synapses of particular parts of my cerebrum. Without invoking someone or something (a little man in the head) to interpret this physical arrangement, it seems impossible to explain how it could represent some state of affairs obtaining thousands of miles from my brain, involving large areas of space and complex legal facts about them. This mystery is just as great as the dualist's mystery of how nonphysical events in the mind can have physical causes and effects. Merely announcing that the mind is the brain will not make it so. And even if the mind is the brain, we need to understand exactly how this can be if we are to employ this bit of metaphysics in the explanation of why some methods will be more appropriate than others in the study of the mind and its effects.

It would be understandable if impatience with these matters leads some to say that how the brain represents is a matter of science, and not metaphysics, and is therefore a matter left to scientists and not philosophers. But, first, this response simply fails to recognize that science is in fact continuous with metaphysics. Our fundamental conception of the nature of reality and our substantive study of it are on a continuum, and they heavily influence each other. Consider the impact of Newtonian mechanics on metaphysics—on issues of determinism, materialism, corpuscularism. Consider the way in which commitment to such metaphysical views led to the expansion of the domain of Newtonian science in the absence of factual evidence of determinism, materialism, corpuscularism. The explanation of the nature of reality that Newtonian metaphysics provided underwrote Newtonian mechanics' scientific strategy long before the evidence for the predictive powers of Newtonian physics became overwhelming. And finally, reflect on the fact that the overthrow of Newtonian physics had equally strong ramifications for metaphysics and indeed for epistemology.

The situation is the same in social science. Indeed, the role of metaphysics may be more critical here, for if the social sciences have little at present to show in the way of predictive success, then we need an explanation of why that is the case, and perhaps why they cannot have predictive success, or we need an explanation of why they will ultimately have it. Either sort of explanation so far transcends narrow factual matters that it must be metaphysical.

Solving the problem of how the brain actually represents requires first a solution to the puzzle of how it could possibly represent. For without a solution to the conceptual problems of intentionality, we have no hint of where to begin in searching for a solution to the factual problem of connecting psychology and neuroscience. What is more, naturalism needs to solve this metaphysical problem if it is to take our intentional explanations seriously here and now, not in some happy future time when neuroscience has established itself. For in the absence of such solutions, naturalism defaults to interpretative social science as the approach most suited to the study of intentional creatures like us.

Of course, one can always opt for the view of Skinner and other materialists who just refuse to take intentional states seriously at all. Among philosophers this view has had some currency. Though they hold no brief for the explanatory variables Skinner adopted, they agree that intentional states have no role in adequate scientific explanations and will in the long run suffer the fate of notions like "phlogiston" or "demonic possession." They will simply disappear from the best explanations of behavior. Such "eliminative" materialists have their own metaphysical problems, distinct from those of naturalists hoping to accommodate intentional phenomena to, instead of eliminating them from, the natural sciences. Perhaps most serious of these problems is the sheer implausibility of saying our actions are not caused by our desires and beliefs and that we don't have sensations or thoughts. This view is so implausible that its denial is often viewed as close to a priori true and as the most basic premise of interpretative social science (see Chapter 4, "Impasse and Epistemology," and Chapter 7, "Social Science and Moral Theory"). In fact, eliminative materialists have tried hard to render consistent their view that such concepts will disappear from scientific explanations with our first-person convictions that we do have such intentional states. The details need not concern us here. But the argument is as much a piece of fundamental philosophy as that required to justify naturalism or interpretationalism as a method in social science.

So, all sides of the dispute about the social sciences, their goals and methods, have a metaphysical mystery to deal with. Naturally, social scientists cannot be expected to cease their work and turn to the philosophy of mind, even though they have taken sides on these questions by choosing methods that answers to these questions underwrite. But neither can they pretend that the issues do not concern them and will not in the long run have an impact on the direction of research in the social disciplines.

Macrosocial Science, Instrumentalism, and Reduction

Those who hope to skirt these issues by fixing the agenda of the social sciences to macrosocial facts free from psychology and its metaphysical involvement must face equally fundamental questions addressed initially in the philosophy of science and eventually in metaphysics and epistemology. Reductionists and methodological individualists face the problem that at least some large-scale social phenomena, their descriptions and explanations, seem resistant to explanation and description in terms of the components that make up the phenomena. This fact is hard to reconcile with the reductionism characteristic of the physical sciences. Moreover, the obvious explanation, that such phenomena somehow reflect supraindividual agencies, is difficult to accept or even make sense of if society is composed of individuals and nothing else. Thus, individualists must search for another explanation. One strategy is to seek an analysis of the holistic language employed to describe a phenomenon, an analysis that reveals the phenomenon to be definable in terms of claims about individuals. This approach has certainly not met with any success. Another tactic is to explain away reference to irreducible wholes as a mistake. This is, however, unconvincing to those not already wedded to individualism. Still a third is to treat macrosocial theories, not as true or false claims about the world, but as useful instruments, tools for systematizing data, which should not be taken literally. But this approach raises questions that instrumentalism has always faced in philosophy: If these instruments are so good, what is the explanation for their usefulness? And more important, why can we not produce theories that are both good as instruments and true? Are there some computational or cognitive limitations on us that prevent us from producing theories in social science that, like theories in natural sciences, seem to be more than just good instruments? Or are all theories, natural and social, just tools for systematizing observations? Whichever move the individualist makes leads straight into the philosophy of science and thence into epistemology and metaphysics.

The holist is no better off, for holism may justify its extravagant ontology by the instrumental success of holistic theories, but it cannot rest with such justification. It too must explain how social facts, made up of the behavior of individuals, can nevertheless be distinct from individuals. Such explanations are plainly a part of metaphysics. And it must explain how we can have knowledge of such facts when all that ever meets our eyes is the behavior of individuals. Unless holism takes such questions seriously, its position collapses to the individualist's instrumentalism and faces the same questions that it does.

Philosophy and the Moral Sciences

Probably little needs to be said to convince us that moral philosophy has a profound bearing on the social sciences and vice versa. The latter were, in fact, at one time known as the moral sciences, and they remain the disciplines that help us decide matters of policy, private and public. The twentieth-century trend, evinced in economics and other disciplines, to divest the social sciences of a moral voice has never met with general agreement, and through the vicissitudes of the century, the plea for value neutrality has sometimes been reduced to the opinion of a small minority. The majority view is faced pretty directly with the question of what moral and social prescriptions ought to be offered.

In recent years moral philosophy has been as much a "consumer" or importer of theories and findings from social science as it has been a producer of and exporter to the social sciences of moral theories about what is right, good, required, prohibited, or permitted. This tendency has reflected the same doubts about a distinction between facts and values that has animated the opponents of value-free social science. There now seems little difference between the language of arguments in political philosophy and of those in welfare economics, for instance. But the philosopher seems less constrained by economic orthodoxy. Political philosophers are prepared to consider the possibility of inter-personal comparisons and perhaps even cardinal utility, notions that have no place among modern mathematical economists. For these theories to gain acceptance, however, the arguments economics has mounted against them must be disposed of. This is certainly a task to be faced by social scientists as well as philosophers who reject the constraints of Pareto optimality (see Chapter 3, "Instrumentalism in Economics," and Chapter 6, "Egoism, Altruism, and Sociobiology").

So here the situation is reversed. Social scientists need to concern themselves with moral philosophy both because they cannot avoid ethical issues and because the social scientist may have more to say about them than we might otherwise expect. In fact, the social scientist may be able to provide the kind of information philosophy needs in order to advance and improve its own moral theories. It is accordingly an intellectual duty to provide this kind of help. It is a duty that comes with the claim that social science provides, inseparably, normative as well as factual knowledge.

In a way the moral responsibilities of a normatively committed social science make the classical problems of epistemology and metaphysics even more compelling. As we have seen, choosing between competing methods of pursuing social science heavily tilts our choices about moral theories. Naturalism makes a consequential theory more inviting. Antinaturalism is more sympathetic to a theory of rights and duties, instead of general welfare. So, choosing among these moral points of view makes the epistemological and metaphysical problems behind these competing methods even more pressing than their purely intellectual or academic fascination might make them.

But even those who hold that social science is at its best free from value judgments and subjective impurities must face moral problems distinctive of social science. These problems are the constraints that ethics places upon our research methods, the steps we take to communicate them, and their impact on others, as well as the very questions we decide to pursue as social scientists. The moral neutrality of our theories, methods, and epistemic goals, if they are neutral, does not extend to us, the social scientists who pursue them. We make choices, either self-consciously or by default. These choices seem better made as a result of serious reflection than made by sheer oversight. And such reflection takes the form of moral philosophy and applied ethics.

The first thing one learns about moral philosophy is that, like the other divisions of the subject, it too is wracked with controversy and disagreements, both fundamental and derivative. Yet unlike other areas of philosophy, we cannot remain long agnostic about these disagreements. For they have an immediate bearing on our conduct and its effects on others and ourselves.

Conclusion

My purpose in introducing the philosophical problems of social science reflects my belief that current controversies in the philosophy of social science are almost always new versions of traditional debates. Sometimes it is difficult to recognize this fact because the jargon has changed and the participants themselves mistakenly think they have discovered a new issue. Today's argument between interpretational social science and naturalistic social science reflects the same issues that were debated among Weber and Durkheim, Dilthey and Comte, Mill and Marx, Hegel and Hobbes. This does not mean that current disputes are condemned to perpetual gridlock. Rather, it means that traditional insights bear a continuing relevance.

My second object in writing this book is to demonstrate the relevance of philosophy by showing that social scientists take sides on these disputes, whether they realize it or not. And sometimes they inadvertently take both sides, an intolerable result when the sides are mutually incompatible. For example, a naturalist cannot offer functional explanations while holding that there is no underlying causal mechanism to underwrite the explanation. An interpretationalist cannot advocate a particular policy that reflects our empathetic understanding of action while denying that prediction of the policy's effects is relevant to assessing the policy.

The third purpose of making the social scientist see the seriousness and the relevance of questions that daunted Plato, Descartes, Hume, Kant, and their discipline, reflects the conviction that the search for knowledge is all of one piece. But this conviction is also the basis of another end, one that could animate an introduction to the philosophy of social science—to encourage philosophers to recognize the bearing of work in the social sciences to their traditional concerns. For if social scientists take sides on philosophical issues in their work, then the findings, theories, and methods of these disciplines must test, and eventually inform, the thinking of philosophers.

Bibliography

THE FOLLOWING LIST contains all the books mentioned in the introductions to the literature that follow the chapters. It is not a complete bibliography of the subject. Guidance to further work in the literature can be found in the bibliographies of the principal anthologies of the field. Additionally, there are several journals that publish papers in the philosophy of social science regularly. Among them, the most prominent are *Philosophy of Science, Philosophy of Social Science,* the *British Journal for the Philosophy of Science, Economics and Philosophy,* and *Behaviorism.*

Alexander, R. *Darwinism and Human Affairs.* Seattle: Washington University Press, 1979.

Axelrod, R. *The Evolution of Cooperation.* New York: Basic Books, 1984.

Beauchamp, T., Faden, R., Wallace, J., and Walters, L., eds. *Ethical Issues in Social Science Research.* Baltimore: Johns Hopkins University Press, 1982.

Becker, G. *The Economic Approach to Human Behavior.* Chicago: University of Chicago Press, 1976.

Berger, P., and Luckman, T. *The Social Construction of Reality.* New York: Doubleday, 1966.

Blaug, M. *Economic Theory in Retrospect.* Cambridge: Cambridge University Press, 1978.

_____ . *The Methodology of Economics.* Cambridge: Cambridge University Press, 1980.

Block, N. *Readings in the Philosophy of Psychology,* vol. 1. Cambridge, Mass.: Harvard University Press, 1980.

Block, N., and Dworkin, J., eds. *The I.Q. Controversy.* New York: Random House, 1976.

Braybrooke, D., ed. *Philosophical Problems of the Social Sciences.* New York: Macmillan, 1965.

_____ . *Philosophy of Social Science.* Englewood Cliffs, N.J.: Prentice-Hall, 1987.

Brodbeck, M., ed. *Readings in the Philosophy of Social Sciences.* New York: Macmillan, 1968.

Brown, R. *The Nature of Social Laws.* Cambridge: Cambridge University Press, 1984.

Buchanan, A. *Ethics, Efficiency and the Market.* Totowa, N.J.: Rowman and Allanheld, 1985.

Burgess, R., and Bushell, D. *Behavioral Sociology.* New York: Columbia, 1969.

Charlesworth, J. C. *The Limits of Behavioralism in Political Science.* Philadelphia: American Academy of Political and Social Science, 1962.

Chomsky, N. "Review of B. F. Skinner, *Verbal Behavior.*" *Language* 35 (1959): 26–58. Reprinted in N. Block, *Readings in the Philosophy of Psychology.*

Churchland, P. "Eliminative Materialism and the Propositional Attitudes." *Journal of Philosophy* 78 (1981): 67–90.

————. "The Logical Character of Action Explanations." *Philosophical Review* 79 (1970): 214–236.

————. *Matter and Consciousness.* Cambridge, Mass.: MIT Press, 1984.

————. *Scientific Realism and the Plasticity of Mind.* Cambridge: Cambridge University Press, 1979.

Collingwood, R. G. *The Idea of History.* Oxford: Oxford University Press, 1946.

Cummins, Robert. "Functional Analysis." *Journal of Philosophy* 72 (1975): 741–764.

Davidson, D. *Essays on Actions and Events.* Oxford: Oxford University Press, 1980.

Dennett, D. C. *Brainstorms.* Cambridge, Mass.: MIT Press, 1978.

————. *Content and Consciousness.* London: Routledge and Kegan Paul, 1969.

Dray, W. *Law and Explanation in History.* Oxford: Oxford University Press, 1957.

————. *The Philosophy of History.* Englewood Cliffs, N.J.: Prentice-Hall, 1964.

Durkheim, E. *The Rules of the Sociological Method.* New York: Free Press, 1965.

————. *Suicide.* New York: Free Press, 1951.

Easton, D. "The Meaning of Behavioralism in Political Science." In J. C. Charlesworth. *The Limits of Behavioralism in Political Science.* Philadelphia: American Academy of Political and Social Science, 1962.

Elster, J., ed. *Rational Choice.* New York: New York University Press, 1986.

Erwin, E. *Behavior Therapy: Scientific, Philosophical and Moral Foundations.* Cambridge: Cambridge University Press, 1978.

Fiske, D. W., and Shweder, R. *Metatheory in Social Science.* Chicago: University of Chicago Press, 1986.

Fodor, J. *The Language of Thought.* Cambridge, Mass.: Harvard University Press, 1979.

————. *Representations.* Cambridge, Mass.: MIT Press, 1981.

Frankena, W. K. *Ethics.* 2d Ed. Englewood Cliffs, N.J.: Prentice-Hall, 1973.

Freud, S. *New Introductory Lectures on Psychoanalysis.* New York: Norton, 1933.

Friedman, M. "Methodology of Positive Economics." In *Essays in Positive Economics.* Chicago: University of Chicago Press, 1953. Reprinted in D. Hausman, *The Philosophy of Economics.*

Garfinkel, H. *Studies in Ethnomethodology.* Englewood Cliffs, N.J.: Prentice-Hall, 1967.

Geertz, C. *The Interpretation of Cultures.* New York: Basic Books, 1973.

Geuss, R. *The Idea of Critical Theory.* Cambridge: Cambridge University Press, 1981.

Giddens, A. *Sociology: A Brief but Critical Introduction.* New York: Harcourt, Brace, Jovanovich, 1982.

Giere, R. *Understanding Scientific Reasoning.* New York: Holt, Rinehart and Winston, 1979.

Grunbaum, A. *The Foundations of Psychoanalysis.* Berkeley: University of California Press, 1985.

Gutting, G., ed. *Paradigms and Revolutions.* Notre Dame: University of Notre Dame Press, 1980.

Habermas, J. *Knowledge and Human Interests.* Boston: Beacon Press, 1971.

Hampshire, S. *Thought and Action.* New York: Viking Press, 1959.

Harman, G. *The Nature of Morality.* Oxford: Oxford University Press, 1977.

Harré, R., and Secord, P. *The Explanation of Social Behavior.* Oxford: Blackwell's, 1972.

Harris, M. *Cultural Materialism.* New York: Random House, 1979.

Hausman, D., ed. *The Philosophy of Economics.* Cambridge: Cambridge University Press, 1984.

Hempel, C. *Aspects of Scientific Explanation.* New York: Free Press, 1965.

_____. *Philosophy of Natural Science.* Englewood Cliffs, N.J.: Prentice-Hall, 1966.

_____. "Rational Action." *Proceedings of the American Philosophical Association,* 1962.

Hobbes, T. *Leviathan.* Indianapolis: Bobbs-Merrill, 1958.

Homans, G. *The Human Group.* Cambridge, Mass.: Harvard University Press, 1951.

Homans, G., and Schneider, D. *Marriage, Authority and Final Causes.* New York: Free Press, 1955.

Hume, David. *Enquiry Concerning Human Understanding.* Oxford: Oxford University Press, 1975.

_____. *Treatise of Human Nature.* Oxford: Oxford University Press, 1888.

Humphrey, L. *Tearoom Trade.* Chicago: Aldine, 1975.

Kant, I. *Foundations of the Metaphysics of Morals.* Indianapolis: Bobbs-Merrill, 1959.

Kitcher, Philip. *Vaulting Ambition.* Cambridge, Mass.: MIT Press, 1986.

Knorr-Certina, K. *The Manufacture of Knowledge: An Essay on the Constructivist and Contextual Nature of Science.* Oxford: Pergamon Press, 1981.

Koopmans, T. *Three Essays on Economic Science.* New York: McGraw Hill, 1957.

Krimerman, L. I., ed. *The Nature and Scope of Social Science.* New York: Appleton-Century-Crofts, 1969.

Kripke, S. *Wittgenstein on Rules and Private Language.* Cambridge, Mass.: Harvard University Press, 1984.

Kuhn, T. S. *Structure of Scientific Revolutions.* Chicago: University of Chicago Press, 1962.

Latour, B., and Woolgar, S. *Laboratory Life: The Social Construction of Scientific Facts.* Beverly Hills, Calif.: Sage, 1979.

Lévi-Strauss, C. *Structural Anthropology.* New York: Harper, 1968.

Luce, R. D., and Raiffa, H. *Games and Decisions.* New York: Wiley, 1957.

McCarthy, T. *The Critical Theory of Jurgen Habermas.* Cambridge, Mass.: MIT Press, 1978.

Malinowsky, B. *A Scientific Theory of Culture.* Chapel Hill, N.C.: University of North Carolina Press, 1944.

Maynard-Smith, J. *Evolution and the Theory of Games.* Cambridge: Cambridge University Press, 1982.

Melden, A. *Free Action.* London: Routledge and Kegan Paul, 1961.

Merton, R. *Social Theory and Social Structure.* New York: Free Press, 1957.

Milgram, S. *Obedience to Authority.* New York: Harper, 1974.

Mill, J. S. *A System of Logic.* London: Macmillan, 1866, and subsequent editions.

————. *Utilitarianism.* Indianapolis: Hackett, 1974.

Moore, G. E. *Principia Ethica.* Cambridge: Cambridge University Press, 1907.

Myrdal, G. *Objectivity in Social Science.* London: Duckworth, 1970.

Nagel, E. *The Structure of Science.* Indianapolis: Hackett, 1979.

Nagel, T. *The View from Nowhere.* Oxford: Oxford University Press, 1986.

Natanson, M., ed. *Philosophy of Social Science: A Reader.* New York: Random House, 1953.

Needham, R. *Structure and Sentiment.* Chicago: University of Chicago Press, 1959.

Nozick, R. *Anarchy, State and Utopia.* New York: Basic Books, 1974.

Olson, M. *The Logic of Collective Action.* Cambridge, Mass.: Harvard University Press, 1965.

Papineau, D. *For Science in the Social Sciences.* New York: St. Martin's, 1978.

Parsons, T. *The Social System.* Glencoe, Ill.: The Free Press, 1951.

Peters, R. S. *Concept of Motivation.* London: Routledge and Kegan Paul, 1958.

Plato. *Phaedo.* Translated by D. Gallop. Oxford: Oxford University Press, 1975.

Popper, K. *The Open Society and Its Enemies,* vols. 1 and 2. London: Routledge and Kegan Paul, 1962.

————. *The Poverty of Historicism.* London: Routledge and Kegan Paul, 1957.

Putnam, H. *Meaning and the Moral Sciences.* London: Methuen, 1978.

Rachlin, H. *Introduction to Modern Behaviorism.* San Francisco: Freeman, 1970.

————. "Maximization Theory in Behavioral Psychology." *Behavioral and Brain Sciences* 4 (1981): 371–418.

Radcliffe-Brown, A. R. *Methodology in Social Anthropology.* Chicago: University of Chicago Press, 1958.

Rawls, J. *A Theory of Justice.* Cambridge, Mass.: Harvard University Press, 1971.

Riker, W., and Ordeshook, P. *Introduction to Positive Political Theory.* Englewood Cliffs, N.J.: Prentice-Hall, 1973.

Rosenberg, A. *Microeconomic Laws: A Philosophical Analysis.* Pittsburgh: University of Pittsburgh Press, 1976.

————. *Sociobiology and the Preemption of Social Science.* Baltimore: Johns Hopkins University Press, 1981.

————. *Structure of Biological Science.* Cambridge: Cambridge University Press, 1985.

Rudner, R. *Philosophy of Social Science*. Englewood Cliffs, N.J.: Prentice-Hall, 1966.

Ryan, A. *The Philosophy of Social Science*. London: Macmillan, 1970.

Ryan, A., ed. *The Philosophy of Social Explanation*. Oxford: Oxford University Press, 1973.

Sahlins, M. *Culture and Practical Reason*. Chicago: University of Chicago Press, 1976.

Schelling, T. *Micromotives and Macrobehavior*. New York: Norton, 1978.

Schmitt, R. *Introduction to Marx and Engels*. Boulder, Colo.: Westview Press, 1987.

Searle, J. *Intentionality*. Cambridge: Cambridge University Press, 1983.

Sen, A. *Choice, Welfare and Measurement*. Cambridge, Mass.: MIT Press, 1982.

Shweder, R., and Levine, R., eds. *Culture Theory: Essays on Mind, Self and Emotions*. Cambridge: Cambridge University Press, 1984.

Skinner, B. F. *Beyond Freedom and Dignity*. New York: Bantam, 1971.

————. *Science and Human Behavior*. New York: Macmillan, 1953.

Skyrms, B. *Choice and Chance*. Belmont, Calif.: Dickenson, 1966.

Smelser, N., and Warner, S. *Sociological Theory*. Morristown, N.J.: General Learning Press, 1976.

Smith, A. *The Wealth of Nations*. London: Penguin, 1970.

Sober, E. *The Nature of Selection*. Cambridge, Mass.: MIT Press, 1984.

————, ed. *Conceptual Issues in Evolutionary Biology*. Cambridge, Mass.: MIT Press, 1983.

Stich, S. *From Folk Psychology to Cognitive Science*. Cambridge: Mass.: MIT Press, 1983.

Taylor, C. *Explanation of Behavior*. London: Routledge and Kegan Paul, 1964.

Taylor, R. *Action and Purpose*. Englewood Cliffs, N.J.: Prentice-Hall, 1966.

Weber, M. *The Methodology of the Social Sciences*. Glencoe, Ill.: Free Press, 1949.

Wilson, E. O. *On Human Nature*. Cambridge, Mass.: Harvard University Press, 1978.

————. *Sociobiology*. Cambridge, Mass.: Harvard University Press, 1975.

Winch, P. *The Idea of a Social Science*. London: Routledge and Kegan Paul, 1958.

Wittgenstein, L. *Philosophical Investigations*. Oxford: Blackwell's, 1953.

Wright, L. *Teleological Explanations*. Berkeley: University of California Press, 1976.

Index